New Deal Politics in the Correspondence of H. P. Lovecraft

Tyler L. Wolanin

Introduction

H. P. Lovecraft underwent a considerable political transformation over the course of his life. For most of his life he was an utter reactionary, favoring a feudal or aristocratic control of the United States and unrestrained capitalism. However, after the stock market crash of 1929 and with the ensuing Great Depression, Lovecraft's political views would come to change as he experienced increasingly dire economic circumstances. Lovecraft came to view capitalism as untenable as a result of increasing mechanization, which he thought would leave an ever-increasing percentage of the population permanently unemployed. He also looked unfavorably upon the Marxist revolution in Russia, which completely transformed that country's society; and he saw socialism as a comfortable middle ground that would correct the flaws of capitalism without completely destroying the culture that was important to him. In fact, Lovecraft thought that socialism would be good for Western culture; he recognized that leisure time was important to artistic expression, and that socialism would (theoretically) provide an increase in leisure time. As he put it, "I am as set as ever against any *cultural* upheaval—and believe that nothing of the kind is necessary in order to achieve a new and feasible *economic* equilibrium. The best of culture has always been non-economic. Hitherto it has grown out of the *secure, non-struggling* life of the aristocrat. In future it may be expected to grow out of the secure and not-so-struggling life of whatever citizens are personally able to develop it" (*SL* 5.63).

However, Lovecraft's political transformation is beyond the subject of this essay.[1] This essay is intended only to catalogue and comment upon the extended mentions of New Deal–era contemporary politics in Lovecraft's correspondence, both by Lovecraft and by those he wrote to. Lovecraft would touch on the subject of politics many times over the course of his extremely extensive correspondence, and in his left-wing period it would become a very important subject to him, and he would bring it up frequently. Many would hear of his new political views in this era, and he would hold long-running discussions with his friends and most frequent correspondents of the elections and contemporary political developments of the time. He spent much time talking about the 1934 midterm elections with Robert E. Howard and Clark Ashton Smith, and he expounded on the 1936 Presidential election at length with C. L. Moore and R. H. Barlow. These correspondents would offer their own political observations in return, often leading Lovecraft into arguments about both specific political occurrences (such as elections) and broad political issues. Understanding Lovecraft's views on contemporary politics (as well as the views of those he corresponded with) is an important part of understanding his overall political philosophy, as well as providing a rich and engaging catalogue of politics in the mid-1930s.

Lovecraft and Howard

The correspondence between H. P. Lovecraft and Robert E. Howard is defined by their long-running debate on the merits of civilization versus those of barbarism. A detailed exploration of this debate can be found in the essay "Barbarism Versus Civilization" by S. T. Joshi. However, outside of the realm of the philosophical and purely speculative, Lovecraft and Howard also engaged in a discussion of contemporary politics that would encompass the election and first term of President Franklin Delano Roosevelt. Additionally, Howard's comments on the politics of his home state of Texas would illuminate Lovecraft as to the state of governance in the Southwest, and Lovecraft would always be sure to

---

1. For an excellent summary of this transformation by HPL himself, see his letter to J. K. Plaiser (8 July 1936), quoted in Appendix A.

THE LOVECRAFT ANNUAL

Edited by S. T. Joshi   No. 7 (2013)

Contents

Abbreviations used in the text and notes:

AT   *The Ancient Track* (Hippocampus Press, 2013)
CE   *Collected Essays* (Hippocampus Press, 2004–06; 5 vols.)
D   *Dagon and Other Macabre Tales* (Arkham House, 1986)
DH   *The Dunwich Horror and Others* (Arkham House, 1984)
HM   *The Horror in the Museum and Other Revisions* (Arkham House, 1989)
LL   *Lovecraft's Library: A Catalogue*, 3rd rev. ed. (Hippocampus Press, 2012)
MM   *At the Mountains of Madness and Other Novels* (Arkham House, 1985)
MW   *Miscellaneous Writings* (Arkham House, 1995)
SL   *Selected Letters* (Arkham House, 1965–76; 5 vols.)

Copyright © 2013 by Hippocampus Press

Published by Hippocampus Press, P.O. Box 641, New York, NY 10156
http://www.hippocampuspress.com

Cover illustration by Allen Koszowski. Hippocampus Press logo designed by Anastasia Damianakos. Cover design by Barbara Briggs Silbert.

Lovecraft Annual is published once a year, in Fall. Articles and letters should be sent to the editor, S. T. Joshi, c/o Hippocampus Press, and must be accompanied by a self-addressed stamped envelope if return is desired. All reviews are assigned. Literary rights for articles and reviews will reside with *Lovecraft Annual* for one year after publication, whereupon they will revert to their respective authors. Payment is in contributor's copies.

ISSN 1935-6102
ISBN 978-1-61498-073-5

follow the election returns from that region in his own newspapers so that he could keep pace with Howard. Howard himself would hear of the ethnic voting blocs in Rhode Island, and the record of some of Rhode Island's elected officials. Both Howard and Lovecraft approached their economic leftism and support of Franklin Roosevelt from different angles: Howard as a populist and Lovecraft as a socialist and an aristocracy-enthusiast. Lovecraft's correspondence with Howard would come at the beginning of his leftist period; his views expressed in later letters would express markedly different attitudes and opinions, possibly influenced by those of Howard. Howard himself had political views fitting in with his own character, displaying a common-man populism and an us-versus-them mentality pitting native Texans against outside interests, often on racial and ethnic lines. Both men were very aware of the contemporary politics of their time.

The correspondence between Howard and Lovecraft started with a discussion of race (the Celtic race, specifically), and the first mention of contemporary politics was in the context of race as well. While providing a general overview of his home state of Rhode Island and the various ethnic enclaves in the city of Providence, Lovecraft said of the Italians that "The better-grade Italians here have a great deal of public spirit, and have served really notably in the Providence city government" (*MF* 235). Lovecraft was most comfortable with ethnic minorities when they assimilated into the dominant Angle-Saxon culture. He lamented that "The Poles and French Canadians, however, act only in blocs for the furtherance of their own racial interests. That is, the bulk of them do—although individual high-grade French-Canadians have held with honour the highest positions in the state. Our present junior U.S. Senator—Felix Hebert—is one of the latter, and is always eager to discourage the anti-assimilational activities of his narrower kinsfolk" (*MF* 235). A Republican, Senator Hebert would be voted out of office in 1934.

Despite this initial foray into the politics of Rhode Island, most of the discussion of politics between the two centered on either presidential politics or on Howard's home state of Texas. The two overlapped in July 1932 when Franklin D. Roosevelt selected Texas senator John Nance Garner to be his running mate. Howard was "pleased" to see Garner nominated, saying, "John deserved it, because it was his votes that swung the nomination of President for Roosevelt [at the convention]." Howard liked Garner for personal, political, and geographic reasons, saying: "Its well said John is for the people; I lived three years in Red River County where he was born, and anyone born there is bound to be of the people. No bloated capitalists there, not in those days, anyhow" (MF 317–18). He recounted an anecdote from a woman who frequently saw Senator Garner working in his own fields. However, he notes that his preferred nominee for president would have been Oklahoma governor Bill Murray, but he "knew he didn't have a chance from the start" (MF 318). Howard appeared to identify with the populist, agrarian governor of the state bordering his own, saying: "Murray has more solid timber in him than any other man in American politics, a certain news-paper man spoke rather condescendingly of him, over the air. Let no man be deceived by the fact that Bill scorns the dapper dress and airy ways so much thought of by some people. Bill Murray has more real education than any other man in politics today" (MF 318). Howard appears to have held up Governor Murray as an ideal frontier man, against the soft elites on behalf of whom Lovecraft argued. Murray was the underdog, and Howard always liked to back an underdog.

William Murray, known in his time as "Alfalfa Bill" Murray, was the governor of Oklahoma from 1931 to 1935. Born in Toadsuck, Texas, he moved to Oklahoma to work at law and become involved in populist politics. He was president of the Oklahoma statehood convention in 1906, where he inserted segregationist and white supremacist clauses into the new state constitution. President Theodore Roosevelt forced the removal of these before he would admit Oklahoma as a state. Elected governor in 1930 by running against "The Three C's: Corporations, Carpetbaggers, and Coons," he governed by martial law, calling out the National Guard thirty-four times while in office, including to shut down three thousand oil wells in 1931 when the price of oil dropped too low (Egan 108–9). After his promise to deliver "bread, butter, bacon, and beans" to every American failed to gain him the presidential nomination in 1932, Murray would become an enemy of the New Deal, but would not win any subsequent elections (Egan 120–21, 160).

Robert E. Howard thought that Bill Murray resembled Andrew Jackson more than any man in American politics, and was proud to have been born in the same county as him (*MF* 318). When it came to the 1932 convention, despite Murray's loss, he was very pleased with the showing of his home state in helping to nominate Franklin D. Roosevelt (according to Howard at least) and in having John Nance Garner nominated as vice president.

Lovecraft was less impressed with the convention. In his response to Howard, he wrote: "I have heard some of the Dem. Convention speeches over the radio while in Brooklyn, but did not find them much different from the usual irrelevant campaign hokum" (*MF* 333). He lambastes the "blindness of conservatives" and states that "of Hoover and Roosevelt, I think the latter is preferable by at least a small margin; though he has his weaknesses" (*MF* 333). However, he does not seem to have much confidence in either party, saying that "all parties are really irrelevant so far as the needs of the future are concerned" and that "it probably matters very little what set of candidates gets in the White House next year—but one may hope that the winners will be to some extent disposed to view realities and give archaic slogans a rest" (*MF* 333).

His fire doused to some extent, Howard replies: "You are right, of course, about the relative merits of both political parties. I got a big kick out of the Democratic Convention, but then, I'm so constituted that I get momentarily enthusiastic about nearly everything I encounter" (*MF* 338). He draws a clear line in the sand between the two candidates, though, saying: "Roosevelt no doubt has his faults—as who hasn't?—but I'd cut my throat before I'd vote for Hoover" (*MF* 338). Roosevelt would take 88% of the vote in Texas that year (Egan 131).

Though a strong supporter of Roosevelt on the national level, Howard saved his real passion for Texas politics. In the same letter stating his support of Roosevelt (2 August 1932), he mentioned his preferences in several state races, often basing his support on which candidate was more populist and more opposed to outside and corporate interests. He said: "We're going to elect Mrs. Ferguson governor again, or I miss my guess. Of course, [former governor] Jim [Ferguson] will be the real governor; he'd run himself, only he can't, because he's been impeached. The last elections seemed to show that the Fergusons were very unpopular in Texas; but it's not [incumbent governor Ross] Sterling against Ferguson, the issue is deeper. It's the common people, mainly the country people, against the corporations and the richer classes" (*MF* 355). He goes on to describe the geographic separation of state politics, with his allegiance the same as that in the poorer and less-settled areas. "The governors are always men from the East or South. We Western Texans can't elect a governor—yet. But you wait a few years, till the West is completely settled up. Sterling is strong in the Southeast, but he lost the vote of the common people in East Texas proper, by imposing military rule in the oil fields" (*MF* 355). (Howard does not mention Governor Murray doing the same in Oklahoma when noting his support of the latter.) Howard's voting patterns on the federal and state level appear to have been mainly class-based, with geographic overtones.

Howard's opposition to corporate interests was again noted in that year's race for attorney general in Texas. "Allred, candidate for attorney general, as opposed to a man who was avowedly in favor of Wall Street, was not even allowed to speak over the radio, or to get his speeches published in the big papers, I understand. He had to go over in Louisiana, and talk from Old Man Henderson's station in Shreveport—and we elected him about four to one" (*MF* 355). Howard also showed his knowledge of smaller-scale local politics, saying, "as an evidence of our democracy, it looks like this district is going to elect a full-blooded Syrian to the legislature. He runs a small dry-goods store in this town" (*MF* 355–56). This was Cecil Lotief, a man Howard appears to have known personally. A leading citizen of Cross Plains, Lotief did indeed go on to serve in the Texas State Legislature (Sasser).

The election Howard was looking forward to at this point was the primary runoff, where the top two winners from the primary face off, so that the eventual nominee has received the support of a majority of the party electorate. In 1932, this meant former governor Miriam "Ma" Ferguson, wife of former governor Jim Ferguson, was pitted against incumbent governor Ross Sterling. Howard told Lovecraft of the result in late September: "Well, the election is over. No fights anywhere. That alone shows how utterly cowed the people are. Sterling was elected by a narrow margin. I'm disappointed but after all, not too surprized [*sic*]" (*MF* 392). However, Howard would later learn that these were not the final election results: "When I wrote the above about the election, I made a mistake. Sterling had a lead and I thought all the returns were in. Later returns have the Fergusons nearly four thousand lead. These returns are being questioned, and the Sterling gang is yelling about illegal voting, and the like, and demanding an investigation. Feeling is running pretty high in Texas, as shown by the fact that people have quit discussing the election on the street" (*MF* 395). Earlier, Howard had discussed his reasons for supporting Ferguson:

> Not that I'm a rabid Ferguson man. I looked on it merely as a choice of two evils. I was for Tom Hunter of Wichita Falls [in the primary], but we can't elect a West Texas man, and he was defeated in the primaries. . . . But I agree with Jim [Ferguson] about the forty million dollars resulting from the gasoline tax. Sterling and his mob intend to put it all on the highways, and, I hear, build some kind of elaborate state building. Jim wanted to put a third on the highways, utilize another third for general purposes, and use the other third to pay the poor damn teachers of the state, hundreds of whom haven't received a cursed cent in months and months. I like good highways as well as the next scut, but I'd a sight rather see the teachers get their money than see a lot of expensive highways built. (*MF* 392)

This support for the teachers may have been due to the influence of Howard's sometime girlfriend, Novalyne Price, a schoolteacher.

Lovecraft dashed out a quick response during a trip: "Was pleased to read in the press some time ago of the triumph of your candidate—'Ma' Sterling" (*MF* 400), mixing up the names of the candidates. Despite this error, Lovecraft did make an effort to follow Texas politics through newspaper reports. Howard's response showed his cynicism about the political process:

> Thanks for the congratulations regarding the election. It remains now to see whether Jim will double-cross us when he gets in office, like so many other candidates have done. Anyway, he'll never get in if the Sterling mob can keep him out. They took the fight

to the state convention; the convention affirmed Mrs. Ferguson's nomination, and now they've dragged it into court. It looks like a deliberate plot to take the voting power away from the people. . . . The common people nominated Mrs. Ferguson; the big interests are fighting teeth and nail to keep her out of the chair. Some claim if Jim gets in, he'll sell us out to the railroads; better railroads than Wall Street owned oil companies. . . . It looks like the courts, the laws, the government, all wealth and authority are combined to crush the last vestige of freedom out of the common people. (*MF* 432)

Howard does not appear to have been in a positive mood at the time of this letter, as he admits at the end. However, in early November, shortly before the general election, he seems to be more upbeat about the status of the race. He tells Lovecraft:

your comment about individuals having no right to expect favor from the opposition (which is quite true) could be well applied to the defeated party in Texas right now, the anti-Fergusonians. For the first time in more years than I like to remember, the old Texans have won an election. We won it fair. Not a shot was fired, not a voter slugged. And you ought to hear the mob howl! After all who represents society? Is it the millions of people, who, if they are poor and not individually important, still compose the great bulk of the population?—Or is it the handful of special privileged businessmen, absentee owners, and politicians who have grabbed the reins of the state? Primitive backgrounds should not, as you remark, be allowed to hinder the march of progress. But what if the progress is used as a camoflage [*sic*] for wholesale exploitation? . . . I repeat—*which group represents society?*—the great common majority, or the wealthy and powerful minority? (*MF* 451)

In the next section of the letter, Howard took great pride in the victory of his social class and what he considers to be his race, and it is worth quoting at length:

Jim Ferguson's wide was nominated in the teeth of such obstacles as have seldom been confronted by any candidate. She was opposed by big business; wealth, power; by the bulk of the so-called intellectual class; by thousands of white-collar workers who might have found themselves without a job had they ventured to vote against their bosses; as well as by thousands of honest people, who sincerely considered it to be their best interests to vote for the exploiters. Add to that, the fact that most of the Republicans in Texas seem to have cast their votes for Ross Sterling. It was the common people who nominated Jim Ferguson's wife—the common folks, the poor people, the ignorant, the down-trodden, the oppressed—the scum of the earth, as it is the fashion to designate them. Jim Ferguson, with his ragged followers, whipped Sterling to a standstill: in the primaries; in the run-off; at the state convention; in the courts. Now from the Sterling mob goes up an awful yell, and scores of them are preparing to bolt the party and vote for the Republican candidate; including a number of college professors who formed an organization to promote "good government" and primly set to work to defeat Jim and his uncultured tatterdemalions. They would hand their state over to a tribe of Vandals, if the Vandals wore good cloths [sic] and had a civilized air, rather than to side with their own race which is considered backward and out of style. . . . I don't give a damn about the Fergusons. But I do give a damn about the people, the common, the low-down, the ignorant people whom the great call the scum of the earth. This has been their victory. They came down from the hills, out of the forks of the creeks, from the mesquite flats, the post-oak ridges, the rover-bottoms, the tenement-districts, the oil field shacks: with their hickory breeches sagging their suspenders, their shoe-soles worn through, their shoulders slumping and their calloused hanging from years of bitter toil. Their victory won't help them much materially, perhaps; it matters little to the poor who is in power. But I rejoice in that victory. It is the last stand of the old Texan race. They'll never win another triumph. They are fading into oblivion, following the red-men. And I am ready to go with them; for with all its faults, follies, and cruelties, it's my breed and my race, and I am alien to all others. (*MF* 451–52)

This passage is an eloquent rebuttal to Lovecraft's own elitist views, as well as a reinforcement of Howard's own race-based view of the world, considering "his people" to be Texans of Anglo-Saxon descent.

In Lovecraft's response, written on election day, he sympathized with the idea that freedom from corporate influence is more important than a lack of machine-style corruption:

> Even if, as some suggest, the Ferguson following is not of the type to give the most stable sort of government, it is probably better to try them than to allow outside corporations to dominate the state against the interests of the native agriculturalists. When ideal weapons are lacking, one must use whatever one has—and if a lesser evil can dispose of a greater one, there is every reason to be thankful. The first job of the Texan is clearly to crush outside plutocratic control. Then will come a time to look inward and see what can be done toward orderly and effective government. (*MF* 472)

Writing the next day, Lovecraft learned of Ma Ferguson's victory: "I see 'Ma' got in! Congratulations—and let's hope for some tangible progress in the liberation of Texas from industrial and financial carpetbaggers." He switched to national politics.

> Whether the nation at large will accomplish any real political evolution under the new administration remains to be seen. At least, the Democrats are less openly enslaved by the plutocratic fetish than the Republicans were. The trend of the age ... is toward government oversight or control of large production enterprises, planned economy with minimisation of the profit motive, and automatic and mandatory relief of the unemployed and unemployable. This kind of thing is bound to come somehow, and it remains to be seen how far we get toward a transition in the next four years. (*MF* 477)

Lovecraft also suggested that Howard, with his writing skill, get involved in politics by writing a pamphlet about the corruption in his area (*MF* 476). Howard shot this idea down in his response in December, saying, "I'm afraid a written statement of affairs wouldn't do much good, unless signed by some one in authority; even if I dared to publish such a paper. So much stuff is circulated in campaigns and the like—charges, refutations and counter-charges. . . . If the Gladewater Journal doesn't have any effect, I'm afraid nothing I could write would, except to make dangerous enemies" (*MF* 506). Thus began and ended the political career of Robert E. Howard.

Over the course of Governor Ma Ferguson's term (1933–35), Howard would occasionally remark to Lovecraft that the condition of the Texas state government and the police force were improving from the state they were in during Governor Sterling's term. In June 1933 he writes:

> Conditions were never as bad in Texas as they were during the Sterling regime, an administration openly under the complete domination of interests in the East. Since the Ferguson election there has been a complete shake-up of the police force in Fort Worth, and some changes in other parts; the whole Ranger company which worked in the East Texas fields was dropped from the force – the work of the Gladewater Journal, or I miss my guess. I'm not trying to say that everything is hotsy-totsy and all abuses by and corruptions of authority have been wiped out. But there seems to be a start in the right direction, at least; and such reforms as have been made, have been the work of native Texans, or men who have become Texans by settlement and honest desire to work for the good of their adopted state. (MF 603)

Howard seems to have been invested less in the 1934 gubernatorial election than he had been in the previous one, stating in December of that year:

> The recent elections were certainly a triumph for Roosevelt, in most of the cases; I wish I could be as equally well satisfied with our Texas elections. One thing gratifies me; the man who was elected governor had to pretend that he was opposed to the big interests before he could get elected. Most of the folks who voted for him did so because of an illusion that he was fighting these interests. The time is past in Texas when a man can come out openly and declare himself for alien corporations. From now on a candidate's task will lie in fooling the people into believing that he's opposed to the systematic looters. And when the people finally learn to distinguish lies from the truth, we'll begin to get somewhere in our state government. (MF 820)

This pessimism is surprising, because the man elected governor in 1934 was Attorney General James Allred, the man Howard told Lovecraft about in August 1932, who had been banned from the

Texas airways, but elected anyway. In November 1932 he repeated the story, saying: "Our candidate for Attorney General had
to go into Louisiana in order to broadcast his speeches; and we
elected him by a terrific majority." He added that "now he's sink-
ing the gaffs into the looters" (*MF* 452). Howard appears to have
lost confidence in Allred between his election as attorney general
in 1932 and his election as governor in 1934.

Howard also kept an eye on elections in other states, saying
that "I notice the big boys are singing jubilation because of Sinclair's defeat in California. Well, I didn't believe he'd be elected
because I didn't believe the campaigns against him, or the elections, would be run on the level" (*MF* 820–21). Howard went on
to say that this was the defeat of the last chance to free wrongly
imprisoned labor agitator Tom Mooney, a *cause célèbre* of the era
whom Sinclair had promised to pardon. Mooney would later be
pardoned by California's next governor, Culbert Olson.

1934 was the last election year that Robert E. Howard would
see. Though his philosophical stances toward civilization and barbarism are well known, a person's practical views on the politics
of their day will often necessarily differ from his ideal philosophy.
Howard and Lovecraft both thought that it was acceptable to
compromise in their political views, and that sometimes you had
to vote for the lesser of two evils. Lovecraft showed this when he
backed Roosevelt, despite his preference for Norman Thomas and
a radical change toward "fascistic socialism" in the American political system. Howard, an economic leftist like Lovecraft despite
their other differences, was willing to vote for a candidate like
Ferguson, who was not his first choice, but better than the alternative; he would also have contradictory views, such as disliking
Governor Sterling's declaration of martial law in the oil fields, but
extolling Bill Murray as a presidential candidate when he had done
the same. Howard and Lovecraft followed contemporary politics
very closely and painted excellent pictures of Texas, New England, and the nation as a whole during the Great Depression and
the New Deal through their correspondence.

EPIC Fantasy: Lovecraft, Smith, and the 1934 California Governor's Race

Although it was less prominent than his debates with Robert E. Howard, Lovecraft engaged in another political debate with Clark Ashton Smith in 1934 over the candidacy of novelist Upton Sinclair in that year's race for governor of California. Sinclair's quasi-socialistic End Poverty in California (EPIC) program and resulting victory in the Democratic primary in August of that year garnered national media attention and received the support of Lovecraft, who at this point supported socialism, regarding it as the economic model that would allow Western culture's preservation.

Clark Ashton Smith, a California native, appears to have thought differently. Though his exact letters to Lovecraft on the subject do not appear to survive, he tells his friend Lester Anderson in July 1934 that he has "read Sinclair's EPIC plan and am much inclined to doubt its workability. I fear it would break down in operation through the inevitable conflict between public and private enterprise. Sinclair too obviously intends it as an entering wedge for socialization; and he will have all the forces of the present system against him. Personally, I do not believe that socialism will ever work in the US; and I shouldn't be surprised if it were to fail even in Russia. The human interests of aggrandization are against it" (*Selected Letters* 191). He states in another letter that he "simply can't see the collectivist idea as anything but a new and particularly odious form of tyranny" (*Selected Letters* 192).

Smith must have expressed these views to Lovecraft, because September 1934 found him writing to Smith about his belief that laissez-faire capitalism is no longer a viable economic model due to the march of mechanization, and that socialism is necessary to preserve national order and the culture that Lovecraft belonged to (*SL* 5.38–39). He states his opinion that "Upton Sinclair is out for much the same thing" (*SL* 5.40). He states that any of Sinclair's bad ideas are no worse than the bad ideas of the business world opposing him. He endorses Sinclair, saying: "I believe I'd vote for Sinclair (diametrically as I disagree with his theories of aesthetics, and little as I think of his novels) if I were a Californian" (*SL* 5.41). Despite his professed dislike of Sinclair's writing, Lovecraft did take cultural comfort in Sinclair's heritage, calling him a "100% Anglo-Saxon descendant of Virginia gentlemen" (*SL* 5.41).

This endorsement did not appear to sway Smith, who apparently sent Lovecraft some clippings on the subject. Shortly before the election, in late October 1934, Lovecraft wrote again that "[Sinclair] has his weak spots and extravagancies, yet his general orientation is in the direction toward which all Western civilization is inevitably moving" (*SL* 5.56). He dismissed the idea that political programs must not change existing institutions, and believed that "reactionaries base their plea" on "dead material—words—attitudes—opinions—prejudices" (*SL* 5.57). This was quite a change for the normally antiquarian Lovecraft and comes very close to self-awareness of his own reactionary attitudes on race. He further defended Sinclair by saying that any attempt at change is better than none, and that it is improper to reject ideas merely due to a link with Soviet Russia. He did admit his armchair-observer status in his conclusion, saying: "Of course I can see how alarming the whole thing looks to anyone on the spot—but the fact is that all change must begin somewhere some time . . . and the need of legal change, if we are to avert a revolution, is pretty manifest today!" (*SL* 5.59). Lovecraft's radicalism is perhaps surprising, in light of his prior conservatism. He frequently criticized the New Deal as being too incremental and said that if it did not go fast enough, then he might expect people to turn to more radical options such as Sinclair or Huey Long. It is debatable whether Lovecraft views this as a warning against a bad option or satisfaction toward the advancement of a good option. His relatively positive endorsement of Sinclair would seem to point to the latter. In any case, he expressed a much more positive opinion of contemporary leftist politicians than he had a few years earlier, when talking to Howard prior to Franklin D. Roosevelt's election in 1932. Lovecraft continues this letter to Smith by noting his political transformation since the Depression began, from Republican to eventual socialist. He hopes that Smith would come to embrace socialism as well and makes an artistic argument, saying that art requires leisure time, which he (Lovecraft) had previously thought was only the reserve of aristocrats, but that he now realized that socialism would lead to leisure time as well (*SL* 5.63). He also spoke at length of the economic necessity of socialism, and how mechanized capitalism would not lead to a fully employed workforce. He continues to reject Marxism while praising Sinclair, saying that "Sinclair is far enough from the alien New York communists who long for another Moscow!" (*SL* 5.59). In this and in lamenting the movement of migrants toward Sinclair's California, there was still a racial element, sometimes overt and sometimes not, to Lovecraft's politics.

It is unclear how Clark Ashton Smith voted, but Upton Sinclair would lose the 1934 governor's race in California. Lovecraft expresses frustration with this in a letter to Woodburn Harris in May 1935, saying that "the real job is to educate the herd to accept some system other than unsupervised capitalism. They won't accept it now—look what happened to Sinclair! They've got to see one halfway measure after another fail, until they get it through their thick heads" (*SL* 5.162). He and Howard also commiserated over the institutional opposition to Sinclair's campaign, as seen previously. Lovecraft did not see his candidate win in California and may not have swayed Clark Ashton Smith to his side in this battle, but he would have other political debates, and come to see his opinions validated electorally in the remaining elections of his lifetime.

Contemporary Politics in the Correspondence of Lovecraft and Barlow

Politics was not a frequent subject of discussion in the seven-year correspondence of H. P. Lovecraft and Robert H. Barlow. Philosophically, it is made up of a couple of asides summarizing Lovecraft's political positions at the time, and several other brief allusions to Lovecraft's antiquarianism and moderate socialism, as contrasted to the radicalism of Lovecraft's friends such as Frank Belknap Long and, increasingly, Barlow himself. As Barlow corresponded with Marxist members of the Lovecraft circle, such as Long and Kenneth Sterling, Lovecraft remarked to him that "[Long] speaks of your growing seditiousness with approval. He had a call from [Sterling] the other day, & he says that infant has become an utterly incredible compendium of Soviet & Marxian history. Damme, but are all you kids going Bolshevik on Grandpa?" (*OFF* 386–87). Lovecraft would poke fun at Barlow's evolving radicalism throughout their correspondence.

When it comes to contemporary electoral politics, the only mention is in a few letters bracketing the 1936 presidential election. Only Lovecraft's half of the correspondence from this time period survives, so statements that Barlow makes must be extrapolated from Lovecraft's responses to them. The three sections in question, from three consecutive letters, are as follows:

At the end of September ("Sept. the Last") 1936, Lovecraft wrote:

> Commiserations on the rock-ribb'd reactionary milieu! Yeh—it's provocations like that which drive a guy into Sonny Belknap's [radical leftist] position! I have a milder version of the same experience, since all our family friends without exception are blind & febrile past-dwellers howling for Let-'Em-Starve Landon & closing their minds to the common-sense articles in *Harpers* & the obvious indications of history & sociology. The other day an old dame who called during my absence left two Landon sunflower buttons—one for me aunt & one for *me!* Hawk, p'tew! Gawd, ef I'd a ben home! And my aunt is too much on the fence to give 'em hell as they'd orta be gave. However—that ain't so bad as living in the same house with a prominent & active Republican party worker. For explosion-breeding predicaments, I hand it to you! (*OFF* 362)

Several weeks after the election, on 30 November, Lovecraft wrote:

> Welcome back from the realms of suspended animation! I didn't know but that the savage Republicans of Sunflower-Land had tortured you to death or cast you into a dungeon or something of the sort. Well—they've got something to think about now, & a couple more similar treatments may jolt them half-awake! It surely was quite a victory! On Oct. 20 I had my first sight of Pres. Roosevelt, who was in town in the morning & who spoke from the terrace of our marble state-house. . . . The subsequent election was satisfactory enough! Whilst of course the general result was apparent long in advance, the *extent* of the landslide surely was a pleasant surprise. The feeble arguments, obvious hokum, absurd accusations, & occasionally underhanded tactics of the enemy reacted against them, while some obscure instinct of common sense

seemed to keep the extreme radicals from wasting their votes on obviously hopeless tickets. It amuses me to see the woebegone state of the staid reactionary reliques with whom I am surrounded. Around election-time I came damn near having a family feud on my hands! Poor old ostriches. Trembling for the republic's safety, they actually thought their beloved Lemke or Langston or Langham (or whatever his name was) had a chance! However, the alert university element was not so blind—indeed, one of the professors said just before the election that his idea of a bum sport was a man who would actually *take* one of the pro-Lansdowne (or whatever his name was) bets offered by the white-moustached constitution-savers of the Hope Club easy-chairs. Well—even the most stubborn must some day learn that the tide of social evolution can't be checked for ever. . . . John L. Lewis might not make a bad candidate in 1940—we'll see how he stands, & how the situation stands, when the time comes! (OFF 368–69)

Finally, on 11 December, Lovecraft wrote:

Glad to observe that you are still unlynched! Yes—I know how many genuinely brilliant persons are to be found in the enemy's ranks. Look at Ernie Edkins! I haven't a doubt but that your uncle is a delightful person, whose influence in social & civic affairs is all on the right side except where certain underlying principles are concerned. It is like the case of the many profound scholars & distinguished thinkers who retain odd fragments of religion & other superstitions—vestigia of youthful indoctrination—in the back of their consciousness. We have lots of such right around here! (OFF 378–79)

Lovecraft's side of the correspondence reveals several anecdotes of the election season that year, and the allegiance of most of his (often older) relatives. Lovecraft viewed Republican presidential nominee Alf Landon, governor of Kansas, as such a minor figure that one of his many running jokes was that he would pretend to forget his name, or confuse him with other public figures, such as another presidential candidate, William Lemke. Apparently, much of the country shared Lovecraft's opinion, as Roosevelt would win 60% of the vote in 1936 and 46 of the then-48 states.

From Lovecraft's statements, we can extrapolate that Barlow's uncle, a Republican operative, was living in the Barlow household at the time. Even as Barlow notes this, he must have defended the character of this uncle, because Lovecraft backs off the criticism and jokes about the uncle in his December letter. Florida, part of the Solid South, went 76% for Roosevelt in the 1936 election, so it is perhaps surprising to find any Republicans in the area at all. Of course, not knowing of Roosevelt's third term won in 1940, Barlow speculates that labor leader John L. Lewis could be the next presidential candidate. Lewis was a charismatic and well-known figure of the time, leading the United Mine Workers of America.

Lovecraft and Barlow had their political interest sated by the 1936 campaign season, and their subsequent correspondence would focus more on their writing, friends, and philosophy. Lovecraft and the members of his circle would have a profound effect on the political opinions of Barlow at the time, as noted previously.

Nice Bankers: Lovecraft and Moore

For someone whose only exposure to H. P. Lovecraft's correspondence is what is reprinted in Arkham House's *Selected Letters*, it would appear that his letters to Catherine Lucille Moore, fellow *Weird Tales* writer and pioneering science fiction writer, were heavy in political content. This is based on four of Lovecraft's letters that appear in Volume 5 of *Selected Letters*,[2] wherein Lovecraft embarks on an exhaustive explanation of his political views and support of the New Deal. These letters appear to have been picked for this purpose by Arkham House and give a misleading picture of the correspondence between Lovecraft and Moore. They are the only ones in this long correspondence with any political content and represent a long exposition by Lovecraft after Moore made a remark that he disagreed with. This political content appears to be largely one-sided, as Moore appears to have been largely apolitical, and for the most part only repeats the conventional wisdom of conservatives about Roosevelt and the 1936 elections. Lovecraft, on the other hand, takes the opportunity to do battle for his chosen causes, and this exposition shows Lovecraft at his most progressive. Due to the length of these letters,

2. Letters 856, 869, 884, and 920.

only the content most relevant to the elections at the time has been included, and it is suggested that they be read in full for the complete catalogue of Lovecraft's political views.

When she began her correspondence with Lovecraft (introduced to him by Robert H. Barlow), C. L. Moore was in her mid-twenties and was writing science fiction and fantasy stories while working as a secretary in an Indianapolis bank. At some point, in the middle of long discussions of writing, architecture, and everyday life, Lovecraft told Moore in a letter from June 1936 that the civilizations of Europe evolve independently toward a socialistic system, at separate paces and with individual quirks (AHT 9.6). Lovecraft disparages Marxism, saying that he awaits a time when Russia is free of it; he says that the Marxists are approaching the same socialistic ideal from the left as the rest of the world approaches it from the right. He lays out his main objections to Marxism: that it invents links between fields that do not exist (namely culture and economics), and that it "violates profound psychological principles . . . on which basic happiness . . . depends" (*SL* 5. 269–70). After his opinion of orthodox Marxism, Lovecraft goes on to discuss the situation as it applies to the United States:

> If the socialist party of Thomas . . . had a chance of winning, I'd advocate efforts toward its election to power. Since it *hasn't* such a chance, I advocate throwing all progressive votes to whatever potentially successful party may have made (under popular pressure, to retain the votes which the smaller parties & the sporadic mass movements like Coughlinism, Towsendism, & Huey-Longism would otherwise capture) the most concessions in the direction of a planned economy, a guaranteed social security, & a public ownership of large resources & processes. This year I'm for the New Deal. If the La Follette party were national in scope I'd probably be for that. . . . With patience & judgment, a rational order can be secured (barring destructive wards, or revolutions precipitated by such wards or by capitalistic reaction) in the United States in from fifty to one hundred years—& without any of the blows & setbacks to general culture which Russian has experienced. (*SL* 5.270)

Moore responded in late July, in a small section buried in the middle of a long letter. She said, "Your views on the probable future of the various nations were extremely interesting. You don't think, then, that Roosevelt is rushing Utopia at the expense of the taxpayers? What did you think of Landon's speech of acceptance the other evening?"[3] She then goes on to admit that "My knowledge of the political situation scarcely deserves to be dignified by the use of the word." Moore was disagreeing with Lovecraft in a very non-confrontational way, not even stating her disagreement, but merely questioning his statement. Lovecraft senses this disagreement, however, and takes up the argument.

In his next letter, after lamenting that "torpor and ignorance" prevent the Socialist Party from having a chance of winning elections, he said:

> Therefore I turn to the only reasonably sane & more or less contemporaneously conscious political mechanism in sight which does have a chance to get adopted & play its part in the needed social & economic evolution—the New Deal. Yuggoth knows it has its faults & inefficiencies—but what else is there for an historically literate adult to favour? "Rushing Utopia at the expense of the taxpayers"? Mehercule! I hardly call it rushing to begin that series of desperately necessary revisory steps which every civilised European nation has already been through, & which make England & the Scandinavian nations relatively well-balanced today while the U.S. still wallows in indecision & archaic delusion & sentimental memories of town-meeting & pioneering days! (AHT 9.7)

This is a dramatic shift for Lovecraft, the staunch antiquarian. He continues, "What do the taxpayers expect—a stable nation while millions starve & move toward justified revolt because of an obsolete governmental policy favouring individual accumulation by the few people lucky enough to get any of the decreasing number of jobs? If such taxpayers aren't willing to let their net incomes be lowered for the sake of greater national stability I hope to gawd some new government will withdraw the protection whereby their artificial ideas of what they 'ought' to earn were formed" (SL 5.292). Lovecraft continues what must be termed a rant for several

---

3. All letters by C. L. Moore to HPL are quoted from manuscripts at the John Hay Library, Brown University.

pages: dismissing criticism of taxes; lamenting that candidates must promise the impossible to voters to win; stating that the socialist state must be established secretly, in the same manner that the Roman Empire supplanted the Republic; praising the aristocratic tendencies of FDR to look out for the public good instead of for his own profit (*SL* 5.292–93). He comes to FDR's non-Republican opponents: "The Lemke-Coughlin-Townsend move is wildcat stuff—a hopeless jumble of incompatible & unfulfillable promises, spiced with leftovers of the most nauseous, Republican sentimentalities & misleading catchwords . . .—yet it will unfortunately draw votes from the New Deal & create an actual danger of a Republican victory" (AHT 9.7). He describes the supporters of the movement as people who know that there must be change, yet who are limited in their conception of it. He goes on to describe Roosevelt's main opponents:

> As for the Republicans—how can one regard seriously a frightened, greedy, nostalgic huddle of tradesmen & lucky idlers who shut their eyes to history & science, steel their emotions against decent human sympathy, cling to sordid & provincial ideals exalting sheer acquisitiveness & condoning artificial hardship for the non-materially-shrewd, dwell smugly & sentimentally in a distorted dream-cosmos of outmoded phrases & principles & attitudes based on the bygone agricultural-handicraft world, & revel in (consciously or unconsciously) mendacious assumptions (such as the notion that *real liberty* is synonymous with the single detail of *unrestricted economic license*, or that a rational planning of resource-distribution would contravene some vague & mystical "American heritage") utterly contrary to fact & without the slightest foundation in human experience? Intellectually, the Republican idea deserves the tolerance & respect one gives to the dead. With the physically surviving corpse—now & then a menace as it appeals to greed, timidity, inertia, ignorance, & dissatisfaction—one must take such steps as one usually takes against social obstacles. (*SL* 5.293–94)

Lovecraft continues by talking about his theory that increased mechanization means that millions will be unemployed under a free-market system; that Republican administrations will not provide relief in future depressions; that economic control is not the same as social control; that Republicans talk about being enslaved by the government but don't care about being enslaved by corporations; and that Republicanism is the decadent ideology of the post–Civil War Gilded Age. He then came to speak specifically about Governor Alf Landon, Republican nominee, and his acceptance speech that Moore had referenced:

> But how about the ambiguous & benevolent platitudes of this well-meaning ex-New Dealer Mr. Landon? Well—we here have a sample of the real sources of whatever progressivism the Grab Our Profits party ever acquires. Mr. Landon's acceptance & other speeches, besides parroting some of the stock gags about "freedom", "individualism", & "business", show a quite unprecedented solicitude for social security. So does the Cleveland party platform adopted over the graves of the old guard. Unlike Mr. Hoover, Mr. Landon does not wish people to starve. He promises to put everybody to work through magic (for only magic could enable mechanised laissez-faire industry to reabsorb more than half of the present unemployed), but also promises a dole (a highly efficient & economical dole consistent with the budget-balancing sought by Business) to the trifling few whom the magic might overlook. And—his intelligence having reached the early 1900's in its survey of history—he would like to break up the big trusts & restore free competition. A sort of Bull Mooser—& somewhat suggestive of his rival Mr. Lemke in lack of logic regarding the incompatibility of small business on the one hand & intensive mechanisation & nation-wide commercial organisation (secret or open) on the other hand. . . . Even the Republicans know that the nation would sooner have a revolution than a Hoover-like regime. . . . But since the New Deal has not—amidst its harassment by reactionaries—brought the millennium in four years, vast masses of ignorant sufferers are dissatisfied. They are ready—though they wouldn't swallow Hooverism—to veer to any set of cheap catchwords opposite to the New Deal's provided they keep on getting the dole which the New Deal won for them. . . . It is plain to see that anything really civilised in Landon of the platform was plagiarised from the New Deal. (AHT 9.7)

Turning to prediction, Lovecraft stated that

> [T]he wise man will vote for Roosevelt & the real thing rather

than for Landon & the fake article. I doubt if the danger of a Republican victory is extreme, even though Lemke will cut into the Democratic vote. Even if Landon did win, there would be no immediate catastrophe. He would have a Congress on his hands, & when business tried to put the screws on him there would be a healthy reaction. The pressure of the New Deal would continue to exist & mould Republican policy against the latter's will—& after a miserable four-year struggle a New Deal landslide in 1940 would be almost a certainty. (AHT 9.7)

Lovecraft closes out the letter by lamenting the occasional timidness of Roosevelt and the New Deal, but reiterating that they are the only game in town. These many pages of writing all came as a reaction to Moore's insinuation that Roosevelt was "rushing Utopia at the expense of the taxpayer."

In her response from 6 October, Moore continues her evasion defense by saying that "Your outline of the political situation is horribly convincing, though it left me only with the conviction that the panorama is far too broad for any one person to grasp completely." Essentially, Moore does not want to engage Lovecraft on any specific points, but does not agree with his conclusions.

After noting her realization that political parties exist for the purpose of continuing institutional change for longer than a single administration, Moore moved on to her reasons for disagreeing with Lovecraft, though she does not explicitly phrase it this way. She says,

> Government control of business seems in theory, as you so convincingly argue, the only solution to many apparently unanswerable social problems. But in practice I can only judge from my own only contact with government officials—the banks examiners, federal and state, for whom I have worked from time to time, and I have come nearer to homicide during those periods than in any other hours of my life. Clothed in their little brief authority, the lamentably large majority of them are so arrogant, so puffed up with self-importance, and the knowledge that their social and financial superiors, the bank officers, must do as they recommend, that by the time they've gone the typists who worked for them are verging on hysterics and the officers are in a state of polite insanity.

She says that not all these government workers are bad, but a consistent portion are. She goes on to say that "If this is an example of the sort of people into whose hands authority would fall were the government to take over business, heaven preserve all capitalists."

This is the crux of Moore's argument, as she herself stated: "Everything you say is so clear and convincing that the only possible flaw I can see in it is the inevitable personal element, the people who will administer that centralized authority over industry." She states that the nature of politicians would have to be changed for them to be an improvement over businessmen: "Men in business for themselves are, generally speaking, fair and considerate in their relations with employees, because in the long run it pays, but politicians care only to make a big showing for the short term of their office."

As a counter-example to this flawed political system, Moore states that a dictatorship would be a better system, using her own bank as an example. She states that she has worked for almost every man in the bank, and though there is much in the way of nastiness, rivalries, and petty tyranny at the bottom, "The three men at the head of the bank are so darn nice and considerate and wise that, since keeping one's job hinges on conforming to their own standards, everyone else has to assume tolerance and generosity whether it's his nature or not." She downplays Lovecraft's notions, saying, "Of course there's much room for improvement, but the majority of the employees are well aware of their luck in working for these bloated capitalists in whose hands the bank is so well managed." She tells of how the owners contribute voluntarily to a disaster fund for workers, and that they have had very few job losses in the Depression, while a neighboring bank was taken over by the government and suffered because of it. However, she seems to acknowledge the anecdotal nature of her line of argument by closing with, "All of which doesn't necessarily prove anything, but it's worth considering."

This argument brings forth another long Lovecraft diatribe, expanding on many of the same topics as the previous letter. Lovecraft opens right away by mocking Moore's argument, saying, "Despite the niceness of big business-men to others in the same business, the system behind the existence of such (great) businesses as a whole is slowly & relentlessly dispossessing so many individuals in walks of life invisible to 'nice business people'—small farmers, miners, factory workers, clothing makers, mechanics, utility operators, &c.—that a continuance of it will not be tolerated by a majority of the population" (*SL* 5.319–20).

Having thus dispensed with Moore's anecdotal argument, Lovecraft continues on his political exposition, which again will be summarized instead of being quoted in full. He talks of the limited number of jobs regardless of an applicant's merit; how feudalism (such as Al Capone's rule of Chicago) is better for the masses at this point than capitalism; how the elitist Republicans are just as susceptible to emotions as the masses they deplore; how his love for aristocracy was really just a love for the characteristics of aristocracy, which can also be achieved through socialism; how those useful to society (such as scientists and philosophers) do not necessarily make money through the present capitalist system; how he does not "worship weakness" through his rejection of capitalism, but does in fact want to improve "backward" populations through education and eugenics; how the sensible Republicans don't see the light and still wish to save the old order; and how he supports Norman Thomas and hopes the New Deal is strong enough to have a lasting effect.

A note of how his older relatives are Republicans leads to a discussion of the political gap between generations; "All of our old family friends are hysterical Landonites, who regard me as a sort of wild maniac or reprehensible anomaly" (*SL* 5.324). He praises members of the older generation who have seen the light and embraced the values of the younger generation. When Lovecraft says, "All honour to Norman Thomas, FDR, Gov. Green[4] of Rhode Island, & other 19th century products who have broken through the meshes of tradition-clogged education & savage class bias & have headed toward the light regardless of the past, of environmental prejudice, or of material consequences to themselves!" (*SL* 5.325), it is easy to see him congratulating himself as well, having often identified with the older age group despite his comparative youth. Unable completely to disregard his antiquarianism, he compares this to the

---

4. This is one of HPL's surprisingly infrequent references to Rhode Island politics.

Enlightenment of the eighteenth century; hopes the "plutocrats" do not establish a Nazi-like regime with enough compromise to keep the people pacified; again lists the lack of profit for a list of noteworthy thinkers; and concludes by saying to his critics, implicitly including Moore, "We'll let history work out the problem in its own way. But as for anything *just* or *beneficent* in capitalism— Pfooey! Equine plumage!" (*SL* 5.327). Throughout this letter are sprinkled references dismissing the importance of "nice bankers."

After this letter, Moore seems to have accepted defeat, or at least realized that there was no point in arguing. In her tardy response, coming in December 1936 (thus after Roosevelt's reelection), she does make brief note of a pamphlet she read stating that the Works Progress Administration and Civilian Conservation Corps were "straightening" streams and thus botching conservation efforts, but otherwise seems willing to accept Lovecraft's political arguments. "The sort of world which would result from a projection of Utopia of the New Deal sounds pretty marvelous. I can understand now what had not occurred to me before, that gentlemen are the product of leisure and assured social position, however that security and leisure may have been achieved and through whatever social system may at the time be in power." This acceptance is rendered hollow by her parting shot, saying, "I am afraid, however, that I shall not live to see the new order of gentlemanly socialists—it will take a few generations after the new order is well established to produce them – and shall have to go on regarding such men as my much admired bankers as the highest social type of my time. The year of transition, when such petty government tyrants as the bank examiners I've warred with are in the high places, is going to be very nasty indeed and I hope I do not live to see it." Moore obviously does not wish to continue the argument.

However, despite (or perhaps because of) Moore's snub, Lovecraft was determined to have the last word. Early in 1937 he responded, thanking Moore for the return of his political arguments, and taking delight in the smashing election victory and the supposed permanent Republican defeat. He says that plutocracy is finished unless the "Hoovers & Mellons & polite bankers" start a revolt (*SL* 5.402), and that the political future will be battles between moderate socialists and Marxist radicals. He hoped that the socialists would win, the cultural sector would remain unmolested, and that there was no violence in the United States as there was in Spain at that point. In this conflict, Lovecraft referred to himself as a conservative, meaning here that he was a socialist as opposed to a Marxist.

He made a few more points against Moore (there may be a letter prior to this one which is now lost), saying: "The attitude which you outline—of a blind clinging to whatever immediate conditions give one the most luxuries & the most congenial social contacts in business hours, irrespective of the consequences to the bulk of the population—is indeed a very typical one, but I don't think it is of much ultimate significance because the immediate needs of *most people* (not merely most *nice* people or most *smart* people) are not on the side of reaction, but are on the side of rational change" (*SL* 5.404). Lovecraft says that not only are all the common people on the side of socialism, but some of the forward-thinking capitalists are as well. He rejects Moore's statement that it is the capitalistic system sustaining her livelihood, saying that her skills as a receptionist could be of equal use in a government-controlled system. He says that capitalism did not need socialism to destroy it, but was coming apart on its own. He finishes off the section, and thus the surviving Lovecraft-Moore correspondence, by telling of his delight with Roosevelt's victory, and how he watched the returns in a film house, and how they were never ambiguous as they were in the narrow 1916 election. He closes with some of the same Election Day anecdotes he had told to R. H. Barlow.

The political content of the letters between H. P. Lovecraft and C. L. Moore is somewhat different from that between Lovecraft and his other correspondents. Unlike in his correspondence with Robert E. Howard, here Lovecraft dominates the conversation with long expositions that are only replied to with brief asides. Unlike the correspondence with Howard or Clark Ashton Smith, here Lovecraft's correspondent does not engage in arguments on specific points or rebut any of Lovecraft's claims. Though she never explicitly says so, it is clear Moore is a supporter of the Republicans. It is equally clear that Moore is what would be termed a low-information voter. She does not follow politics closely enough to be able to rebut any of Lovecraft's claims, and instead bases her allegiance on her personal experience in the politicized environment of bankers and government regulators. Most of her arguments are anecdotal in form (though in fairness she does cite a pamphlet she read about alleged botched conservationism by New Deal agencies), and after her first mention of politics, when she asks Lovecraft what he thought of Landon's speech, she says that "Ideas seem to struggle up through my oatmeal brain with all the reluctance of bubbles busting 'plop-plop' in a pan of the cereal cooking, and my knowledge of the political situation scarcely deserves to be dignified by the use of the word." Moore's Republicanism was likely a simple result of her environment, both working alongside middle- and upper-class financiers and living in Indiana, which only narrowly went for FDR in 1932 and 1936, and went against him in 1940 and 1944. Perhaps sensing this environmental cause, Lovecraft sticks to criticizing generic Republican ideas and attitudes and does not attack her directly as he did Howard.

In contrast to Moore, Lovecraft is at his finest in these letters near the end of his life. The letters to Moore are Lovecraft at his most progressive, where he rejects his previous veneration of the past and mocks the formerly praised Nazis and Ku Klux Klan. If Lovecraft had lived a few more years he would have become even more liberal and tolerant, if the Moore letters show anything in comparison to the other exchanges.

Conclusion

Many conclusions can be drawn from this summary of the contemporary political content in the correspondence between H. P. Lovecraft and four of his most important correspondents: Robert E. Howard, Clark Ashton Smith, Robert H. Barlow, and C. L. Moore. When we read these letters in chronological order, we can to some extent track Lovecraft's political evolution. Though he is already a committed leftist at the beginning of this period, his cynicism begins to be replaced with idealism. In this early period, he is still feeling the effects of the Depression, and how it has shattered his previous political paradigm. Herbert Hoover is still the president, and though he views Roosevelt as the lesser of two evils, he does not think that Roosevelt will do much more than

Hoover did to alleviate the Depression, and the best he can say of the Democrats is that unlike the Republicans, they are not *wholly* controlled by corporate interests. By the end of this period, in 1937, he has fully committed to Roosevelt's New Deal and argues its merits to C. L. Moore. Over the course of his first term as president (1933–37), Franklin D. Roosevelt has won Lovecraft over as more than a reluctant supporter.

Lovecraft's correspondence was of course double-sided, and his friends revealed much about their own political views. Robert E. Howard went on at length about his own opinions, which were largely populist and economically leftist. Howard may or may not have been a socialist, but had a very strong opposition to corporations, banks, and other entities that caused hardship for the common man. There was always a strong regional bent to Howard's views; the large financial institutions were often from the East Coast, and often victimized (in Howard's view) hard-working Texas farmers and the like. Howard and Lovecraft may have had acrimonious disagreements about civilization and barbarism, about aristocracy and the common man, and about intellectualism; but Howard was Lovecraft's main source for political opinions to exchange in this time period (the end of the Hoover years and Roosevelt's first term), and it seems very likely that Howard's forgotten-man populism rubbed off on Lovecraft, who would be very anti-corporate in his later letters to other correspondents, though of course putting his own socialistic and culturally elitist spin on the topic.

Clark Ashton Smith does not appear to have been very political, and Lovecraft's correspondence with him does not have much political content. However, Lovecraft's apparent failure to convince him to support Upton Sinclair in the 1934 California gubernatorial election shows that he was skeptical of Lovecraft's views, at least at the time; and that he objected to socialism and Sinclair's program on individualistic, anti-communitarian grounds, perhaps reflecting his isolated and rustic lifestyle. Smith may have lived in poverty, but he valued his freedom as well.

Robert H. Barlow was very young at the time of his friendship with Lovecraft, and Lovecraft's views had a strong influence on his own. Extrapolating from Lovecraft's letters to him, he appears to have enthusiastically opposed the Republicans; and Lovecraft would speak of how Barlow was influenced by Frank Belknap Long and other more Marxist members of the Lovecraft circle. Barlow was an impressionable youth who sought out the political opinions of all around him, as shown in a letter from Lovecraft in late 1936 where Lovecraft responds to an apparent request for information on the political views of E. Hoffmann Price[5] (*OFF* 381).

C. L. Moore was also fairly young at the time of her correspondence with Lovecraft, and her political views at the time appear to have been largely undeveloped. She supported capitalism and the Republican Party, conventional politics for her region and social class, and essentially disregarded Lovecraft's long arguments against her positions. Most of the arguments she made were anecdotal and based on what she had experienced in her workplace. She would latch on to minor points to prove her arguments, showing an unwillingness to engage more deeply on issues. Politics does not appear to have been an important subject of thought to her at the time, and she did not offer any response to Lovecraft's impassioned arguments (even when they challenged beliefs based on her personal life, i.e., "nice bankers"), dismissing each of them by stating in effect, "You have your views and I'll have mine." Moore shows, and hopefully showed Lovecraft, that some people simply are not passionate about politics. Other than their flare-up of politics centering on the 1936 presidential election, Lovecraft and Moore largely focused on other matters that they could actually communicate on, such as writing.

All these correspondents engaged with Lovecraft on the subject of contemporary politics, and Lovecraft would engage with them. Lovecraft seemed to learn from those with differing political views, and attempted to engage them on an individual level, even if he was not always gentle with his assessment of their opinions. Lovecraft and his correspondents lived in an interesting time, arguably one of the periods in American history with the most social unrest and economic upheaval. The Great Depression and the New Deal shaped the views of H. P. Lovecraft and his correspondents, and in turn these views shaped their interactions with one another.

---

5. Quoted in Appendix B.

Appendix 1:
Letter to J. K. Plaisier, 8 July 1936 (*SL* 5.279–80).

Dear J. K. P.

... The background surrounding me (despite some wavering on my aunt's part in response to my repeated arguments) is solidly old-guard Republican, whereas I myself have been increasingly a left-winger ever since the advent of the depression began to force me into real thought on the subject of economic and political trends.

I used to be a hide-bound Tory simply for traditional and antiquarian reasons—and because I had never done any real *thinking* on civics and industry and the future. The depression—and its concomitant publicisation of industrial, financial, and governmental problems—jolted me out of my lethargy and led me to reëxamine the facts of history in the light of unsentimental scientific analysis; and it was not long before I realized what an ass I had been. The liberals at whom I used to laugh were the ones who were right— for they were living in the present while I had been living in the past. They had been using science whilst I had been using romantic antiquarianism. At last I began to recognize something of the way in which capitalism works—always piling up concentrated wealth and impoverishing the bulk of the population until the strain becomes so intolerable as to force artificial reform. Sparta before Agis and Cleomenes. Rome before the Gracchi and Caesar. Always the same story. And now accelerated a thousandfold through the unprecedented conditions of mechanised industry. Well—I was converted at least, and in the spring of 1931 took the left-wing side of social and political arguments for the first time in a long life. Nor has there been any retreat. Instead, I have gone even farther toward the left—although totally rejecting the special dogmatisms of pure Marxism, which are certainly founded on definite scientific and philosophical fallacies. I am all for *continuous development* and revolutions—and it seems to me that the nations with a naturally orderly and liberal tradition have a very fair chance of developing in the proper direction without any cataclysmic upheavals. Great Britain and the Scandinavian countries are far ahead of the United States, but even the latter is coming along despite is ingrained tradition of harsh acquisitiveness. So today I am a New Dealer—

perfectly conscious of the waste and bungling necessarily connected with experimentation, but convinced that open-minded experiment with all its faults is vastly better than efficient and economical progress toward the *wrong goal.*

Appendix 2:
Letter to R. H. Barlow, 11 December 1936 (*OFF* 381)

Cook's politics? I can't dope 'em out myself, but I believe they aren't so very far left of the New Deal. They are, I think, more emotional than logical. He feels a vague identification with the "working class"—whatever that is—whereas I simply fail to find a logical justification for capitalism & its results. I've never talked politics with Sultan Malik [E. Hoffmann Price], but imagine he must be pretty liberal. Back in '32, when my anti-bolshevik feeling was a good deal stronger than it is now, we were discussing Robert S. Carr's migration to Russia—& in reply to some contemptuous allusion of mine he said that we ought not to be too sure that the Soviets haven't many useful lessons to teach the western world, or that they aren't perhaps on the right track in a more or less blundering way. While I haven't asked him, I'd be willing to bet a dime or two that he didn't vote for Lampton or Langford or whatever stalking-horse the plutes put forward!

Works Cited

Arkham House Transcripts of H. P. Lovecraft's Letters. John Hay Library, Brown University. [Abbreviated in the text as AHT.]

Egan, Timothy. *The Worst Hard Time.* Boston: Houghton Mifflin Harcourt, 2006.

Joshi, S. T. "Barbarism vs. Civilization: Robert E. Howard and H. P. Lovecraft in Their Correspondence." *Studies in the Fantastic* No. 1 (Summer 2008): 95–124.

Lovecraft, H. P. *O Fortunate Floridian: H. P. Lovecraft's Letters to R. H. Barlow.* Edited by S. T. Joshi and David E. Schultz. Tampa, FL. University of Tampa Press, 2007. [Abbreviated in the text as *OFF.*]

Lovecraft, H. P., and Robert E. Howard. *A Means to Freedom: The Letters of H. P. Lovecraft and Robert E. Howard.* Edited by S. T.

Joshi, David E. Schultz, and S. T. Joshi. New York: Hippocampus Press, 2009. 2 vols. [Abbreviated in the text as *MF*.]

Sasser, Damon C. "Cecil Lotief and a Gift from the Middle East." "REH: Two-Gun Raconteur." 15 July 15 2011. Accessed Online: http://rehtwogunraconteur.com/?p=11438.

Smith, Clark Ashton. *Selected Letters of Clark Ashton Smith*. Edited by David E. Schultz and Scott Connors. Sauk City, WI: Arkham House, 2003.

Briefly Noted

David Simmons, a lecturer on American literature, film, and TV at the University of Northampton, has edited a substantial volume, *New Critical Essays on H. P. Lovecraft* (Palgrave Macmillan, 2013). The book contains an introduction by Simmons, a foreword by S. T. Joshi, and twelve original essays—by Simmons, Gina Wisker, Sara Williams, Gerry Carlin and Nicola Adams, Robert H. Waugh, Donald R. Burleson, J. S. Mackley, Steffen Hantke, Chris Murray and Kevin Corstorphine, Joseph Norman, Martyn Colebrook, and Mark Jones. The book arrived too late for review, but a review will appear in next year's *Lovecraft Annual*.

For the first time, definitive evidence has emerged of Chinese translations of Lovecraft's work. A volume entitled *Zhan li chuan shuo* (Qui huan ji di, 2004) is a translation of *Bloodcurdling Tales of Horror and the Macabre* (Ballantine/Del Rey, 1982). In another apparent first, the volume *La tuong tu* (Mui Ca Mau, 1997) is a Vietnamese translation of an anthology that contains at least one story by Lovecraft. (Thanks to Stephen L. Walker for this information.)

Letters between H. P. Lovecraft and Orville L. Leach

Edited by Donovan K. Loucks

In April 2013, I was corresponding with Scott Molloy of the University of Rhode Island regarding some geographical matters related to H. P. Lovecraft. Mr. Molloy happened to mention that he had discovered a couple of letters from Lovecraft in some issues of the *Providence Sunday Journal* from 1908. He then mailed to me copies of four letters (one of them incomplete), and from there I tracked down another three letters (and the remainder of the partial letter).

These previously unknown letters comprise an exchange between Lovecraft and Orville L. Leach of Auburn, a village in the township of Cranston, Rhode Island. In all there are seven letters: four from Leach and three from Lovecraft. These all appeared in the "Letters to the Editor" column of the *Providence Sunday Journal* and all appeared in section 2, page 5. These letters were written in June and July 1908, when Leach was forty-eight and Lovecraft was only seventeen.

Orville L[ivingston] Leach (13 August 1859–late December 1921) was an unusual character who engaged in a variety of trades throughout his life. These included Providence city lamplighter in 1879, seller of quack medicines in the 1890s, patented inventor in the 1900s and 1910s, author of a number of pamphlets and of at least one book, and proprietor of a picnic ground from the late 1890s until his death in 1921. In 1886, Leach was married to Theresa Walsh (she was one year his junior), who survived him until at least 1943.

During the 1890s, Leach operated the Dr. Emery Remedy Company. This company dealt in "patent medicines": medicines that were heavily advertised but inefficacious. An advertisement in the *Boston Daily Globe* from 20 April 1892 reads, "AGENTS wanted in every town and city to introduce our celebrated remedies; exclusive territory given; send 25¢ for samples and terms. Dr. EMERY Remedy Co., Providence, R.I." (6).

On 21 December 1893, Leach wrote a letter to James Hathaway, superintendent of the Roger Williams Park Zoo, on office letterhead that read, "Dr. Emery Root and Herb Powder." This letterhead indicated that Leach was proprietor of the company. More unusual is the fact that Leach wrote this letter to superintendent Hathaway because Leach was presenting to the zoo "a very tame American Eagle"! Unfortunately, the letter does not indicate how Leach may have acquired the eagle.

The name "Emery" continues to feature throughout Leach's later endeavors, but its origins are still unknown. Leach founded an organization called the Order of Emorians (also called the "Order of Evergreens" and the "Life & Longevity League"), whose headquarters were at "Emery House"—Leach's consecutive homes in the 1890s at 58 and 102–104 Prairie Avenue. This fraternal organization was probably associated with the Dr. Emery Remedy Company in some way.

For the last twenty or more years of his life, Leach was the proprietor of Emery Park and Picnic Grounds, formerly located at 440 Auburn Street in Cranston, the south corner of Reservoir Avenue and Auburn Street. The park opened sometime in the late 1890s and closed soon after Leach's death in 1921. The site is now occupied by some homes and a parking lot for what until recently was a Bickford's Restaurant.

This site was probably chosen because of its position on the north edge of Blackamore Pond and the presence of the Ponce de Leon Spring. In Gladys W. Brayton's *Other Ways and Other Days*, Leach was quoted as saying:

> This spring water has the property of producing Life and under certain conditions gives out Light. These phenomena have already surprised the world. Sir William Crookes, F.R.S. of London writes, 'I have read the account of the luminosity of the water and its residue with much interest'. When a spring water interests the greatest Scientist in the World, it must be remarkable. Come and try it and get more particulars of this miraculous Spring. (102)

Leach fancied himself an inventor and with three other men founded the Emory Tire Company in 1900 "to manufacture bicycle and vehicle tires" ("Recent Incorporations," 58). Over the next two decades, Leach was granted at least six patents, four of them tire-related: wheel (U.S. patent 33,648, 9 November 1900), cushion-tire (U.S. patent 655,098, 31 July 1900), tire (U.S. patent 669,396, 5 March 1901; Canadian patent 71,923, 25 June 1901), medicinal electrode (U.S. patent 682,089, 3 September 1901), resilient tire (U.S. patent 926,338, 29 June 1909), and storage battery (U.S. patent 1,296,408, 24 April 1918).

Leach's name periodically appeared in newspaper articles discussing the theory of a hollow earth. In the correspondence between the two men, Lovecraft mentions that Leach was "interviewed" in a "local paper" dated 12 August 1907. After some searching, I was able to locate this article in the Providence *Evening Tribune*:

INHABITABLE LAND INSIDE THE EARTH.

———

CONCLUSION REACHED BY AUBURN SCIENTIST.

———

Orville L. Leach Advances New Theory Regarding Structure of Terrestrial Globe.—Thinks Earth is Hollow Sphere, with Land Lining Interior Crust.

Orville L. Leach of Auburn, whose scientific researches along the line of radioactivity have been attended by results that have been read with interest, is out with another discovery. Mr. Leach now comes forth with a new claim based upon the results of a long series of scientific experiments. He finds that when a red hot iron wire is inserted into a jar of pure oxygen gas that the wire burns and shining black hollow globules of oxide of iron fall to the bottom of the jar. Mr. Leach says:

"It will be seen that when a portion of the oxygen gas is taken into the iron that there is a partial vacuum inside the jar and consequently a reduced atmospheric pressure. This fact shows why the hollow globules form.

"Our earth is of course rolling along in a vacuum—in the ether

ORVILLE L. LEACH
Auburn Scientist Who Advances Theory That
Inhabitable Land May Line Interior Crust of Earth.

of the universe, and it is deduced that our earth must be a hollow sphere, as the same laws pertain to the microcosms, or minute parts of the universe, as to the miscrocosms [*sic*] of worlds.

"The ideal of prophets, biologists and optimists has always been above the existing climatic conditions of the exterior of this mundane sphere, where day and night alternate, where gales and cyclones play havoc, where changes of temperature constantly endanger the health and a thousand and one discordant states of existence surround us. It is claimed that all of these incongruities are eliminated from the new land lining the interior of the crust of our earth."

Mr. Leach says gravity is the result of the radio activity of the crust of the earth, that the radiating lines of force are refracted or curled and in passing through the matter of the earth draw the matter toward any surface from which the rays emanate, the same as a corkscrew will draw a cork toward the operator.

While Mr. Leach does not wish to enter into any theological version of his science he suggests that theologists compare the descriptions of "The Golden City" of the book of Revelations to the conditions, size, etc., possible in a land on the inner crust of the earth. That light from electrical conditions on the interior surface exists seems, he says, to be verified by the "Northern Lights," which, it would seem, are a reflection from the interior of the earth.

Mr. Leach says that the earth will not finally lose all its heat and become a dead planet. He says that a vacuum can not conduct heat and consequently the earth will always retain heat; he also says that heat can be made at any time from magnetism, and he propounds the query that if the sun supplies direct heat to the earth why is it that the nearer we get to it the colder it grows?

"The historical data which is adduced to this new claim of an inhabitable land of joy on the interior of our earth's crust is this," continued Mr. Leach. "Antartic [sic] explorers have found butterflies near the south pole, winds which blow from the south in the Antartic [sic] regions are always warm, it is claimed that magneitc [sic] currents flow in at the north pole and out at the south pole, the discovery of the open polar sea by Dr. Kane near the north pole is another fact which seems to prove that there is an opening at the north pole into a region of warmth. The only one who has ever claimed to doubt Dr. Kane's report was a man named Godfrey, who was a disgruntled sailor of the doctor's crew. It remains an undisputed fact that the doctor told the truth and that an open polar sea did exist at the time when he visited the Arctic regions." (7)

Surprisingly, a very similar article titled "Earth's Interior May Be Habitable" appeared *on the very same day* in the Providence *News-Democrat*. Several of the quotations from the two articles are identical, even in punctuation. Given that Leach also wrote pamphlets on such subjects, he must have sent some of them—and probably even photos of himself—to multiple newspapers.

An important point to take away from this article is Leach's statement "that a vacuum can not conduct heat" (7). Leach states in his first letter in the *Providence Sunday Journal* exchange with Lovecraft "that light and heat are conducted by the most perfect vacuum ever made" ("About the Vacuum," sec. 2: 5). Lovecraft catches Leach in this contradiction and points to the article above, which Leach first denies, then ignores.

However, note that Lovecraft's quotation from Leach—"because a vacuum cannot conduct heat"—does not precisely match the quotation in the above article: "that a vacuum can not conduct heat." In addition, the article in the *News-Democrat* reads: "as a vacuum cannot conduct heat" (3). These various combinations of "because/that/as" and "cannot/can not" prompt me to wonder if Lovecraft slightly misquoted Leach or if there are yet other appearances of similar articles in other Providence-area papers.

Leach's hollow earth theories are also mentioned in the *Daily Kennebec Journal* (27 September 1907), *Cedar Rapids Evening Gazette* (8 October 1907), and even the *India Rubber World* (1 December 1907). Leach's efforts to quickly cultivate larger plants by covering the ground (to keep it cool) while allowing the plants themselves to receive maximum sunlight are described in Henry Frank's *The Mastery of Mind in the Making of a Man* (1908). The genesis of Leach's theories about the hollow earth are outlined in Willis George Emerson's *The Smoky God; or, A Voyage to the Inner World* (1908):

> Dr. Orville Livingston Leech [*sic*], scientist, in a recent article, says:
> "*The possibilities of a land inside the earth were first brought to my attention when I picked up a geode on the shores of the Great Lakes. The geode is a spherical and apparently solid stone, but when broken is found to be hollow and coated with crystals. The earth is only a larger form of a geode, and the law that created the geode in its hollow form undoubtedly fashioned the earth in the same way.*" (26–27)

In 1920, Leach (along with five other men) formed a corporation named "The King's Order of Natural Science" to distribute the order's handbook. That same year, Leach published a book titled *The White Spark*, which not only had a lengthy subtitle ("A New Book, giving out a New Philosophy and the Mysteries of the Universe") but a sub-subtitle ("The Handbook of the Millennium and the New Dispensation"). The first paragraph of its "Synopsis of Contents" should suffice to give an idea of its content:

> THIS book is called The White Spark as the white spark or vacuum cell in Nature IS THE RIGHT HAND OF GOD—it is a ubiquitous principle of the universe and is the cause and parent of electricity, combustion, radium, snow-flakes, flowers, trees, leaves, crystallization, wireless telegraphy, animal forms and EVEN LIFE ITSELF. (1)

Leach passed away in late 1921 and is buried in Providence's North Burial Ground. He occupies the same plot as his parents, Elihu Leach (25 April 1812–4 October 1882) and Sarah L. Leach (29 December 1821–5 April 1889), his sister, Louisa A. Leach Skinner (25 May 1842—18 December 1874), and two siblings who died when they were very young. Leach's stone has space on it for the names of a wife and children, but his wife is not buried with him and I have found no evidence that he had any children.

The nature of the debate between Leach and Lovecraft concerns the properties of vacua and extends from there to a discussion of the luminiferous ether. At the time that this exchange took place, the ether theory was being challenged but had not been completely overturned. From reading these letters, it is clear that Lovecraft was very knowledgeable about the ether theory and how it had evolved over time. It is also clear that Leach—with his run-on sentences, hollow earth theories, descriptions of physics textbooks as "old and effete," and notion "that our nerve cells contain vacuo or spaces filled with spirit"—was something of an eccentric. It is especially amusing to note that Leach makes the error that "Lovecraft is a Professor of Astronomy and was formerly at Brown University"—and Lovecraft makes no attempt to disabuse Leach of this notion!

Acknowledgments: I wish to thank D. Scott Molloy, Professor of Labor Relations at the University of Rhode Island, for bringing this exchange to my attention; Marilyn Massaro, curator at the Museum of Natural History and Planetarium at Roger Williams Park, for locating the letter Leach wrote to the zoo; and S. T. Joshi, editor of the *Lovecraft Annual*, for suggesting that I transcribe and annotate these letters for this journal.

About the Vacuum.

To the Editor of the Sunday Journal:

I notice an inquiry in the Evening Bulletin, about the conduction of heat by a vacuum, and beg to say that what your reader has read about the non-conduction of heat by a vacuum is erroneous—all text books on chemistry state that light and heat are conducted by the most perfect vacuum ever made.

I think your reader must have received his idea from the editorial which the Boston American printed some months ago in relation to a "double bottle" with a vacuum or exhausted space about the inner bottle—this editorial, which showed the lack of knowledge of science, explained that a vacuum was a non-conductor of heat and therefore any hot or cold liquid placed in the bottle would remain at the same temperature indefinitely, the editorial explained that this bottle was in imitation of the "cosmic principle of our earth" which did not lose its heat as it was surrounded by a vacuum, this editorial was something like the same paper printed from Ella Wheeler Wilcox once, which stated that "all water contained microscopic animals, and that it would be lifeless and inefficient if it did not," every scientist knows that pure water contains no organic matter whatsoever—and that when it does it is dangerous.[1]

While heat or force will pass through a vacuum it may not be exactly heat while it is in the vacuum, it is again refracted into heat when it impinges on the other side—the sun emits warm rays, but they are reduced by the vacuum or the interstellar space—thus mountain tops are cold but when the rays are refracted by our atmosphere they become warm again—the varying sensations of force or rays are from different wave lengths, caused by rarefaction or refraction.

While a vacuum will transmit light and heat a galvanic current can not pass through a vacuum and an electric spark from the positive terminal in passing into a vacuum forms into rivulets of light while the negative terminal send [sic] a luminous glow into a vacuum.

A vacuum is always cold as all heat is produced by a twisting of rays of force in passing through or around the molecules of matter, and as no matter exists in the ether or a vacuum, there is nothing to refract straight magnetic rays into heat, but practically the result is just the same as if heat passed through the vacuum unchanged as we can not produce a vacuum except by having matter on all sides of it.

I have made a study of vacuo, in my radio-active investigations and it is ap-apparent [sic] that much interest is manifested by the public in regard to the subject.

ORVILLE L. LEACH.

Auburn, June 1.

Notes

First publication: *Providence Sunday Journal* (7 June 1908): sec. 2: 5.

1. The *Boston American* was a daily newspaper published from 1904 to 1961. Over the years it merged with various other papers; these mergers trace to today's *Boston Herald*. Ella Wheeler Wilcox (1850–1919), an American author best-known for her poem "Solitude," which includes the lines, "Laugh, and the world laughs with you; Weep, and you weep alone." Wilcox believed in spiritualism and theosophy.

Heat and Radiant Energy.

To the Editor of the Sunday Journal:

In the Journal for June 7 I notice a letter on heat and the vacuum, written by an Auburn man named Leach, who has recently been identified with many speculations of a more or less scientific nature. In the course of his letter he makes two statements so incorrect that I take the liberty of rectifying them. First, it is stated that the difference between the temperature of a mountain top and of the earth's surface is due to the different wave lengths of the radiant heat at the two places. This is manifestly untrue, as it is a well-known fact, taught in any high school, that the wave length of any certain form of radiant energy is constant and invariable.

Radiant energy consists, in general, of undulations or waves in the ether of space. There are many different forms, depending on the wave lengths. Thus radiant energy resulting from very slow vibrations in ether and consequently having very long waves, produces electrical effects (relating to the conductivity of certain metals) upon striking an obstacle. These waves are the undulations upon whose existence wireless telegraphy depends. Another form of radiant energy gives out somewhat shorter waves, which generate heat when intercepted. It is, therefore, called radiant heat. The amount of heat depends upon the wave length, but when one wave motion is sent out into the ether, its length never changes, and cannot be made to do so. Heat waves of short length are identical with long light waves, i.e., they produce both light and heat. Waves of a somewhat shorter length are wholly luminous, affecting chemical substances such as photographic plates, hence being called "Actinic" waves of light.[1] The shortest waves are the Roentgen or X rays.[2] Now the sun transmits to space waves of various lengths, mainly as light and radiant heat. Some of these reach the earth, where the radiant heat is stopped, raising the temperature. At all parts of its course, however, the wave length of each kind of energy remains unchanged. When thermal rays strike a mountain top, its temperature is raised, but since there is not enough air present to receive any large amount of heat, a person there feels very little warmth. At the surface the comparatively dense air is itself heated, hence persons surrounded by it experience a sensation of heat. In both cases, each wave length is, of course, the same. In connection with this point, where the Auburn "scientist" asserts that the "different wave lengths are caused by the rarefaction or refraction" (of the air) it must be said that no amount of refraction can alter the wave length of any form of radiant energy. If this were so, no telescope could be constructed that will show objects in their natural colors, as color depends on the wave length of light.

The second error in Mr. Leach's letter is still more ridiculous. This is the statement that "all heat is produced by a twisting of rays of force in passing through and around the molecules of matter." As nearly everyone knows that ordinary heat consists of rapid motions on the part of the molecules themselves, it would be interesting to know just what this Auburn gentleman's apparently hazy idea of force and matter is.

Finally, it is amusing to see how absolutely Mr. Leach now contradicts a statement which he published through a local paper not quite a year ago, at the time when he so widely promulgated his now notorious "hollow earth" theory, which was recently described in the Journal.[3] He then asserted that the earth will never lose its thermal energy "because a vacuum cannot conduct heat." Since then, it is evident that the Auburnite's knowledge of radiation has increased, and it is to be hoped that it will continue to do so.

H. P. LOVECRAFT.

Providence, June 9.

Notes

First publication: *Providence Sunday Journal* (14 June 1908): sec. 2: 5.

1. The word "actinic" derives from the Greek word for ray or beam, and refers to solar rays that produce photochemical effects.

2. Wilhelm Röntgen (1845–1923), German physicist who in 1895 discovered X-rays, also called Röntgen (or Roentgen) rays.

3. The article in "a local paper" refers to the one that appeared in the Providence *Evening Tribune* on 12 August 1907 (7) and which is printed in full earlier in the present article.

Scientists at War.

To the Editor of the Sunday Journal:

I notice that my letter in the Sunday Journal of June 7 has brought forth a protest from a much-perturbed individual who signs his name as "Lovecraft." He refers to my "apparently hazy idea of force and matter," but there is nothing "hazy" about this gentleman's ideas; they are decidedly ancient.

He says: "Finally, it is amusing to see how absolutely Mr. Leach now contradicts a statement which he published through a local paper not quite a year ago, at the time when he so widely promulgated his now notorious 'hollow earth' theory which was recently described in the Journal. He then asserted that the earth will never lose its thermal energy, 'because a vacuum cannot conduct heat.' Since then it is evident that the Auburnite's knowledge of radiation has increased, and it is hoped that it will continue to do so."

This statement is untrue. I have never published any such statement in any local paper. Perhaps Mr. Lovecraft means to refer to a statement made in a Boston newspaper, but this was not a publication of my own, and in publishing a reprint from this paper I corrected this statement.

I learned from a textbook on chemistry, written by Edward Yeomans [sic], in my youth that heat and light would pass through the most perfect vacuum ever made, or that its equivalent would do this.[1]

Mr. Lovecraft is a disciple of Count Rumford, who claimed that heat was not a material, but simply a motion; but he has had many opponents to his theory, and Dr. Samuel Metcalfe wrote two large volumes on "Caloric," in which he disproved the Rumford theory and proved that heat was a material "fluid."[2]

Mr. Lovecraft says: "As nearly everyone knows that ordinary heat consists of rapid motions on the part of the molecules themselves." Again, he says: "Radiant energy consists in general of undulations or waves in the ether of space."

I would like to know who contradicts themselves if this erudite gentleman does not. Surely there are no molecules in the ether.

The most ridiculous statement made by this gentleman is this: "The wave length of any certain form of radiant energy is constant and invariable." All textbooks state that the forces are corelative, and heat, light and electricity can be transmuted into one another. Mr. Lovecraft impugns the knowledge of Sir Oliver Lodge.[3] There was recently published in a Boston Sunday paper a description of Sir Oliver's discovery of condensing the fogs of London by sending rays of force into the fog from an electrical device and a diagram was printed showing that the rays were nearly straight when they started, but were refracted into long, deep waves when they had passed through the fog.

My critic finds trouble with my statement that the sun's rays are cold or straight on mountain top [sic] and refracted into heat in the valleys. He hatches up a funny idea that on mountains "there is not enough air present to receive any large amount of heat," and anyone knows that there is but very little difference in the amount of air on a mountain from what is found lower down. People live and breathe on mountains; our air extends upward for

250 miles, and the mountain tops penetrate only a short distance into this— there is more dust and moisture near the surface, and consequently more refractive power.

Aeronauts who have ascended into high altitudes in balloons say that it grew dark and the sun appeared like a red ball—again the proof of the fact that magnetic rays from the sun or ether are refracted into light by our low atmosphere.

Because the telescope shows objects in their natural colors, my opponent thinks that no amount of refraction can alter the wave length of any form of radiant energy, but does he forget that the spectrum can be produced by glass prism?

This "judge and jury" of his own appointment says: "Radiant energy from very slow vibrations in ether, and consequently having very long waves, produces electrical effects," and then he says: "Another form of radiant energy gives out somewhat shorter waves, which generate heat when interrupted [sic]."

The most commonplace scientists know that this is incorrect; the red rays or hot rays of the spectrum are the longest and slowest, while the violet rays or electrical rays are the quickest and shortest.

He says: "When one wave motion is sent out into the ether, its wave length never changes." Again, this gentleman shows that he has not emerged from his incubus—a ray will always go in a straight line except from some obstruction, and as there is no obstructing power to the intangible ether, there is nothing to cause a heat ray or any other ray to go in any way but straight—the sun may send out warm rays, but when they strike the ether, they immediately become cold and straight.

ORVILLE L. LEACH.

Auburn, June 17.

Notes

First publication: *Providence Sunday Journal* (21 June 1908): sec. 2: 5.

1. Edward L. Youmans (1821–1887), American writer who founded the magazine *Popular Science*. The book to which Leach refers is probably *A Class-Book of Chemistry: In Which the Principles of the Science Are Familiarly Explained and Applied to the Arts, Agriculture, Physiology, Dietetics . . .* (1859).

2. Sir Benjamin Thompson, Count Rumford (1753–1814), inventor and

physicist best known for creating the more efficient Rumford fireplace. Samuel L. Metcalfe (1798–1856), an American physician and chemist who wrote the two-volume work, *Caloric: Its Mechanical, Chemical, and Vital Agencies in the Phenomena of Nature* (1843).

3. Sir Oliver Lodge (1851–1940), British physicist and pioneer in wireless telegraphy. He was also a dabbler in spiritualism and occultism.

Vacuums, Wave Lengths, Etc.

To the Editor of the Sunday Journal:

In your issue of the 21st I observe that Orville L. Leach, the scientific gentleman from Auburn, has made a valiant endeavor to refute some facts which I expressed in my letter of June 14, hence I am again forced to correct some of his statements.

In regard to the Auburnite's assertion that my reference to his publication, through a local paper, of the statement that a vacuum will not conduct heat, is "untrue," and that he never published such a statement save through an error in a Boston paper, I must simply say that the article referred to appeared, with a portrait, in the form of a direct interview, in a local paper Aug. 12, 1907. I have the cutting in my possession at present, and if Mr. Leach desires to see it at any time he may do so.

The next statement in Mr. Leach's reply is that he learned, in his youth, from Youman's Chemistry, that heat and light would pass through the most perfect vacuum ever made, or that its equivalent would do so. This is correct, in fact, my letter of the 14th did not contradict it, although the Auburn gentleman seems to labor under that impression.

Following directly upon this, Mr. Leach asserts that Rumford's theory of heat "has had many opponents." He is wise in using the perfect tense, since the theory is now accepted without question, as can be seen by consulting any modern textbook of physics.

As to the assertion that I "contradict myself" in stating that heat is molecular motion and that radiant heat is ether vibration, the sage of Auburn evidently errs in his conception of the nature of ether. Ordinary heat, it is true, cannot exist without the presence of molecules, that is, ordinary matter, but it must not be forgotten that according to every modern authority, ether is itself a certain form of matter, not molecular, but continuous, and capable of sustaining wave motions or vibrations. Radiant heat is the name applied to vibration of a wave length greater than that of red light, giving thermal phenomena when intercepted. In no part of my letter of the 14th do I confuse this form of energy with ordinary or molecular heat.

Mr. Leach observes that "his critic finds trouble with his statement that the sun's rays are cold and straight on a mountain top, and refracted into heat in the valley, and hatches up the funny idea that on mountains there is not enough air to receive any large amount of heat." His critic does find trouble. The density of the air decreases with the altitude, owing to the lesser gravity, as can be shown by the fall of mercury in a barometer taken up a mountain. Aeronauts, and those first going to high altitudes, find difficulty in living and breathing, so insufficient is the supply of air. At the tops of mountains the density of the atmosphere is so small that not enough molecules of its component gases are present to form an obstruction sufficient to transform the radiant heat, or obscure radiations, into ordinary heat. This is why the air is cooler than at low altitudes. This is not a theory "hatched up" by myself, but a fact well known to all who study physics. (See Brocklesby's Meteorology, p. 25 section 36.)[1]

Mr. Leach states that his "opponent" forgets that a spectrum can be produced by a glass prism. His "opponent" does not forget, but the spectrum does not show that the wave length of light can be changed. White light (as sunlight) is composite, being a mixture of many colored lights, that is, is composed of different forms of radiant energy. The prism simply breaks up the beam of white light into the different forms of radiant energy of which it is composed, the wave length of each being the same as before the dispersal. The only change is in the direction of the wave fronts.

Mr. Leach tries to dispute the fact that "when one wave motion is sent into the ether its length never changes." In refutation (?) he informs us that "a ray will always go in a straight line, except from some obstruction, and as there is no obstructing power to the intangible ether, there is nothing to cause a heat ray, or any other ray, to go in any way but straight." While all this is true, I fail to see how such a statement has any bearing on the well-known truth which Mr. Leach attempts to contradict.

H. P. LOVECRAFT.

Providence, June 30.

Notes

First publication: *Providence Sunday Journal* (5 July 1908): sec. 2: 5.

1. John Brocklesby (1811–1889), author of *Elements of Meteorology* (1849), a copy of which HPL owned. "36. We thus perceive, what all observations have proved, that the upper regions of the atmosphere must be colder than the lower. It is not, however, to be forgotten, that the rarefaction of the superior strata contributes to this condition" (25).

Holes in the Ether.

To the Editor of the Sunday Journal:

I again receive the very kind of attention of Prof. Lovecraft in the Sunday Journal of July 5, and for fear that he might feel slighted if I did not respond I will ask you for space for this letter.

I understand that H. P. Lovecraft is a Professor of Astronomy and was formerly at Brown University. He is one of "the old schoolers," who still holds to the idea of the "persistence of wave lengths of force." He has also been an advocate of "the persistence of matter" and the "immutability of the elements," but the latest discoveries by Prof. Ramsey [*sic*] and others prove one element can be changed into another, and Sir Oliver Lodge says: "Atoms can be broken up into electric discharges."[1]

My "strange ideas" are not the result of ignorance of the tenets of the old textbooks. I have studied the same books as the professor, but I have discarded them as old and effete.

I notice that in the professor's letter in the Sunday Journal of July 5 he practically corroborates the statement in my first letter which was the "bone of contention" of his letter in the Sunday Journal of June 7. In my letter I claimed that the reason why the surface of the earth was warmer than mountains was because of the obstructing power of the denser materials in the atmosphere of the surface.

In his letter in the Sunday Journal of June 14 he says: "When thermal rays strike a mountain top, it (temperature) is raised, but since there is not air enough present to receive any large amount of heat, a person there feels very little warmth."

Now in his letter in the Sunday Journal of July 5 he says: "At the tops of mountains the density of the atmosphere is so small that not enough molecules of its component gases are present to form an obstruction sufficient to transform the radiant heat.["] This is exactly my idea, as I expressed in my first letter.

Prof. Lovecraft in his last letter says: "Mr. Leach tries to dispute the fact that when one wave motion is sent into the ether its length never changes."

["]In refutation (?) he informs us that "a ray will always go in a straight line except from some obstruction, and as there is no obstructing power to the intangible ether there is nothing to cause a heat ray or any other ray to go in any [way] but straight."

"While all this is true, I fail to see how such a statement has any bearing on the well-known truth which Mr. Leach attempts to contradict."

It is evident that the professor has a constriction on the word refract. Webster's Dictionary defines the word in this way: "To bend a ray out of its course." But the professor seems to think refraction means simply a bending from a straight trend, the same as a bow is bent; but is not a wave or a spiral a lateral bending out of its course?

An ostrich may go in a "bee line" from Providence to Boston, but he goes zig-zag, and this is not straight. His path is refracted just as much as if he went to Boston by way of Worcester or in a half circle.

The professor will not deny that the forces are correlative. I am sure, and if one force can change into another it positively must be from a changing of its wave lengths, for if heat retained its regular wave lengths it would still remain heat and the same with any force.

Prof. Lovecraft says I am wise in using the perfect tense in saying that the Rumford theory has had many opponents, but I will say now that it has many opponents, and the new stellar photography proves that the orbits of the planets are great paths of moving force or ether, like streams of water, and on these paths the planets are floated or borne along—not by any undulation or wave motion, but by great moving ribbons of force. Has the professor heard of this, and does he ridicule the idea?

He states one great fundamental principle of my scientific creed when he says: "Ether is itself a certain form of matter, not molecular, but continuous." This means, of course, unparticled matter or spirit, which I claim is the only matter in the universe. I was the first man to give out the theory that matter was simply space spots, outlined by a moving wall of spirit. I was in correspondence with Sir William Crookes several years ago and sent him my theories and received his acknowledgment of the data.[2] At the same time I sent the same data to Sir Oliver Lodge. The ideas were discussed before the British Association for the Advancement of Science, and Sir Oliver averred that the theories were correct.[3] The English papers published the reports and they came back to America and Prof. Serviss wrote an article for a Boston paper, explaining that Sir Oliver averred that the ether was the only real thing in the universe, and Prof. Serviss in the same article says: "One savant (this is myself) says matter is simply a hole in the ether—we are holes in the ether—a mountain is a hole in the ether," etc.[4]

I claim that the matter of our bodies is "a hole in the ether," but that our nerve cells contain vacuo or spaces filled with spirit, which has consciousness and a potential of motion.

It will be seen that I am a Pantheist, but if science proves that I am right, who can deny my claims?[5]

The truths of God and nature are ever open to the Auburnite as well as to a Brown Universityite, and the professor may fight as he retreats, but he cannot release himself from the iron grip of truth and progress.

ORVILLE L. LEACH.

Auburn, July 7.

Notes

First publication: *Providence Sunday Journal* (12 July 1908): sec. 2: 5.

1. Sir William Ramsay (1852–1916), Scottish chemist who received the Nobel Prize in Chemistry in 1904 for his discovery of inert gases in earth's atmosphere.

2. Sir William Crookes (1832–191), British physicist who worked in the area of spectroscopy and performed pioneering work with vacuum tubes. The Crookes tube is named after him and is mentioned in HPL's "The Shunned House" (1924).

3. The British Association for the Advancement of Science was founded

in 1831 and is now known as the British Science Association.

4. Garrett P. Serviss (1851–1929), American astronomer. HPL owned Serviss's *Pleasures of the Telescope* (1901), *Astronomy with an Opera-Glass* (1906), *Astronomy with the Naked Eye* (1908), and a Barrett-Serviss Star and Planet Finder (planisphere). The quotation ascribed to Serviss appeared in the *Metaphysical Magazine* 23, No. 5 (November 1908): 325, though it is not clear from the context if it is actually by Serviss.

5. A pantheist believes that everything in the universe composes God.

Waves in the Ether.

To the Editor of the Sunday Journal:

Once more I observe that Mr. Orville L. Leach has favored the public with a contribution on ether physics, in which he again makes some statements that compel me to contradict them. In his letter he asserts that I am an "advocate of the persistence of wave length, persistence of matter and immutability of the elements." The first statement is true, for every student knows that the length of an ether wave cannot be changed save by absorption and re-emission by a fluorescent body. The second is not quite so correct, because, as with all modern readers, I recognize the fact that certain observations slightly tend to discredit the law of the conservation of mass. According to the electrical theory of matter, the mass of a body depends on the velocity of the electrons or corpuscles which compose its atoms, hence, should their energy diminish or increase, the mass of the body would correspondingly diminish or increase.

I am also conversant with the claim of Heydweiler that cupric sulphate and water have a different weight when taken separately from that of their solution; and with that of Walace [*sic*] that water changes weight with freezing, yet after all, are these meagre theories and claims sufficient to overthrow such a well-established idea as that which holds matter uncreatable and indestructible?[1] As to the transmutation of elements, neither I nor any other student, so far as I am aware, now contradicts the fact that elements may be degraded into others of lesser atomic weight. The change of copper into lithium, as made by Sir William Ramsay in his recent radium experiments, would be sufficient to establish such a belief.

Mr. Leach states that he has cast aside as "old and effete" the textbooks which I have studied. Does he refer to Mumper's Physics (1907), The New Knowledge (1907), or others of similar date?[2]

He also says that in my letter of June 14 I "corroborate the statement in his first letter, which was the 'bone of contention.'" If I read correctly, Mr. Leach stated in his first letter that "mountain tops are cold, but when the (sun's) cold rays are refracted by our atmosphere they become warm again, the varying sensations of force of [sic] rays being from different wave lengths, caused by rarefaction or refraction."

In no place do I concur to this peculiar statement. In my letter of June 14 I stated the recognized facts, and on July 5 gave the explanation, showing that the heat felt at any place is due not to the radiations directly, but to the molecular heat caused by their interception by the air, the amount of which, of course, determines the amount of heat formed. The radiations themselves can, of course, produce no sensations.

My objection to Mr. Lynch's [sic] statement lay in the fact that he assumed a change of wave length due to refraction, a manifestly impossible thing. In discussing wave motion Mr. Leach falls into the error of supposing that the bends of the wavy line which a transverse wave describes are the results of refraction. In physics, the direction of a wave is considered as the direction of the vibratory impulse, or line of propagation, which is, of course, a straight line. Refraction, in its scientific sense, is defined as "the bending of the line of propagation of a wave" (Avery's Physics).[3] Thus the Auburnite's interesting comparison to the ostrich on his weary journey from Providence to Boston falls flat. When luminous rays are ordinarily transformed into heat, the wave length is not changed, but lost, because heat is molecular, not wave motion. Light cannot be transformed into radiant heat except in the phenomenon of absorption and re-emission. In speaking of the Rumford theory of heat, it is almost unnecessary to state that it is now accepted without question as being the only possible explanation of the observed facts. Mr. Leach construes my statement that the ether is continuous and not molecular into an expression of one "great fundamental principle of his scientific creed.["] I must, however, remark that the continuity of the ether has been assumed almost ever since the existence of the medium itself was acknowledged. As to any theory that matter consists of "space spots, outlined by a moving wall of spirit," I must say that nothing of the kind has ever been accepted by the scientific world. Sir Oliver Lodge, J. J. Thomson, and other eminent investigators have outlined the new electric theory of matter, assuming that all masses are aggregations of, and not holes in, the ether.[4] According to this theory, all matter is electrical, the ether being "bound" by moving electrons or corpuscles which compose atoms. If the "holes in ether" theory be the "iron grip of truth and progress" from which Mr. Leach asserts that, although I may "fight as I retreat," I cannot release myself. I have great doubts as to the efficiency of the "iron grip."

H. P. LOVECRAFT.

Providence, July 13.

Notes

First publication: *Providence Sunday Journal* (19 July 1908): sec. 2: 5.

1. Adolf Heydweiler (1856–1925), adjunct professor at Breslau from 1895 to 1901, professor at the Universität Münster from 1901 to 1908, and professor of experimental physics at the Universität Rostock from 1908 to 1921. "Cupric sulphate" is simply another term for "copper sulfate." "Heydweiler claims that copper sulphate and water do not have the same collective weight before and after solution. Wallace claims that a mass of water does not have the same weight before and after freezing. Altogether, both from theoretical and experimental considerations the absolute validity of the law of the conservation of mass is certainly challenged" (Kennedy 250). From this context it is not clear who "Wallace" is, though it may be Alfred Russel Wallace (1823–1913), British biologist and explorer.

2. William N. Mumper (1858–1931), professor of physics and chemistry and author of *A Text-Book in Physics for Secondary Schools* (1907). Duncan R. Kennedy (1868–1914), author of *The New Knowledge: A Popular Account of the New Physics and the New Chemistry in Their Relation to the New Theory of Matter* (1905).

3. Elroy M. Avery (1844–1935), historian and author of *School Physics* (1895) and *Elementary Physics* (1897). However, this exact quotation appears in neither of these two books, though very similar quotations do.

4. J. J. Thomson (1856–1940), British physicist, discoverer of the electron, inventor of the mass spectrometer, and recipient of the 1906 Nobel Prize in physics.

Matter the Deficiency of Mass.

To the Editor of the Sunday Journal:

In answer to a very courteous letter of inquiry from A. E. Williams, I would say that I claim the molecules of matter are caused to rotate by impinging lines of force, and taking to greater orbits cause matter to expand.[1]

It was not my intention to pay any more attention to H. P. Lovecraft, but he says: "As to any theory that matter consists of 'space spots outlined by a moving wall of spirit,' I must say that nothing of the kind has ever been accepted by science. Sir Oliver Lodge, J. J. Thomson and other eminent investigators have outlined the new electric theory of matter, assuming that all masses are aggregations of and not holes in the ether."

Prof. Serviss quotes from the report from the British Association for the Advancement of Science, saying that "matter instead of being, as we innocently believe on the evidence of our senses, the only real and solid thing in nature is, in fact the absence or deficiency of mass."[2]

And again: "Inside the solidest substances we should find emptiness."[3]

ORVILLE L. LEACH.

Emery Park, Auburn, July 20.

Notes

First publication: *Providence Sunday Journal* (26 July 1908): sec. 2: 5.

1. The letter from A. E. Williams was sent either directly to Leach or through the *Providence Sunday Journal*, as it does not appear in the "Letters to the Editor" column.

2. This quotation may be found in the *Metaphysical Magazine* 23, No. 5 (November 1908): 325. From the article's context, it seems as if it may not be by Lodge, but by Osborne Reynolds (1842–1912), British innovator in fluid mechanics.

3. This slightly paraphrased quotation also appears in the *Metaphysical Magazine* 23, No. 5 (November 1908): 325.

Works Cited or Consulted

Acts and Resolves Passed by the General Assembly of the State of Rhode Island and Providence Plantations at the January Session, A.D. 1920. Providence, RI: E. L. Freeman Co., 1920.

Annual Report of the Park Commissioners of the City of Providence. Providence, RI: The Providence Press (Snow & Farnham, City Printers), 1895.

Avery, Elroy M. *Elementary Physics.* New York: Butler, Sheldon & Co., 1897.

———. *School Physics.* New York: Sheldon & Co., 1895.

Brayton, Gladys W. *Other Ways and Other Days.* Cranston, RI: Globe Printing, 1975.

Brocklesby, John. *Elements of Meteorology.* New York: Pratt, Woodford & Co., 1849.

Daily Kennebec Journal 38, No. 228 (27 September 1907): 6.

Dr. Emery Remedy Co. Advertisement. *Boston Daily Globe* 41, No. 111 (20 April 1982): 6.

"Earth's Interior May be Habitable." [Providence] *News-Democrat* 3, No. 89 (12 August 1907): 3.

Emerson, George Willis. *The Smoky God; or, A Voyage to the Inner World.* Chicago: Forbes & Co., 1908.

Frank, Henry. *The Mastery of Mind in the Making of a Man.* New York: R. F. Fenno & Co., 1908.

"Inhabitable Land Inside the Earth." [Providence] *Evening Tribune* 2, No. 190 (12 August 1907): 7.

Kennedy, Duncan R. *The New Knowledge: A Popular Account of the New Physics and the New Chemistry in Their Relation to the New Theory of Matter.* New York: A. S. Barnes & Co., 1905.

Leach, Orville L. *The White Spark.* Providence, RI: Oxford Press, 1920.

Lepore, Lisa. "Query: Order of the Emorians." Online posting. 26 April 2002. Ancestry.com. <http://archiver.rootsweb.ancestry.com/th/read/RIGENWEB/2006-04/1146109059>

———. "Query: Order of the Emorians." Online posting. 30 April 2002. Ancestry.com. <http://archiver.rootsweb.ancestry.com/th/read/RIGENWEB/2006-04/1146420661>

Metcalfe, Samuel L. *Caloric: Its Mechanical, Chemical, and Vital Agencies in the Phenomena of Nature.* London: William Pickering, 1843.

Mumper, William N. *A Text-Book in Physics for Secondary Schools.* New York: American Book Co., 1907.

"Recent Incorporations." *Bicycling World and Motocycle [sic] Review* 42, No. 3 (18 October 1900): 58.

Serviss, Garrett P. *Astronomy with an Opera-Glass.* New York: D. Appleton & Co., 1906.

———. *Astronomy with the Naked Eye.* New York: Harper & Brothers, 1908.

———. *Pleasures of the Telescope.* New York: D. Appleton & Co., 1901.

"The Solidest Thing on Earth." *Metaphysical Magazine* 23, No. 5 (November 1908): 324–25.

"'Symmes's Hole' Recalled." *India Rubber World* 37, No. 3 (1 December 1907): 85.

"Where Missing Explorers Go." *Cedar Rapids Evening Gazette* 25, No. 232 (8 October 1907): 2.

Youmans, Edward L. *A Class-Book of Chemistry: In Which the Principles of the Science Are Familiarly Explained and Applied to the Arts, Agriculture, Physiology, Dietetics . . .* New York: D. Appleton & Co., 1859.

Lovecraft's Rats and Doyle's Hound: A Study in Reason and Madness

Robert H. Waugh

> dea, magna dea, Cybebe, dea domina Dindymi,
> procul a mea tuos sit furor omnis, era, domo:
> alios age incitatos, alios age rabidos.

> [Goddess, great goddess, Cybebe, goddess and mistress of
> Dindymus,
> Far from my house be all your madness, Lady,
> Make others enraged, make others mad] (Catullus 63.91–93)

At the conclusion of my essay on Lovecraft's flamboyant story "The Hound" I wrote, "This story, like 'The Rats in the Walls,' concerns a supernatural, bestial destroyer, but the vision of that destroyer in 'The Hound' is more difficult to discover given the scope of the story's allusions" (83). One of those allusions I spent a good deal of space investigating was Sir Arthur Conan Doyle's *The Hound of the Baskervilles*. In retrospect, however, it must have seemed to some readers of the essay rather obtuse of me that I did not also investigate a possible connection between Lovecraft's rats and that novel. Gavin Callaghan must have thought me especially obtuse, since he had just published his encyclopedic essay tracing the broad influence of Doyle on Lovecraft. In this essay I mean to make up for my obtuseness and pursue that connection of the hound with the rats. In the process we shall learn that we need to allow the Magna Mater into our considerations, for she will not be ignored.

When we consider the bare bones of the two stories the similarity between them must seem obvious. In England, around the time of the English Civil War, two disasters occur that leave two noble families and their dwellings damaged; this background of war is extended to the American Civil War, World War I, and the Boer War. Various legends attest to the nature of the two disasters, and both families have manuscripts that describe the disaster in detail, though the Delapore manuscript has been burned. Now, in the present day (circa 1888, 1901, and 1923), an heir has returned from the colonies to refurbish and re-establish the home and family. Unfortunately, the past disasters still exist as present, bestial evils that, when they strike once more, leave the two heirs maimed, whether mad or verging upon madness, or dead. Though in both cases the bestial evils seem to have been exterminated some doubt remains; a rational approach to such evils appears to be insufficient.

Such—once we have scraped away various subplots of a romantic or a mythic nature, to which we will return—seems to be the central story of the two works, which originates in the two manuscripts. When Holmes gives his final directions to Watson at Paddington Station, he asks the good doctor "simply to report facts [. . .] and leave me to do the theorizing" (*The Complete Holmes* 817). When Watson asks what he means by facts he becomes rather vague, and when Watson later says that the landscape he meets in Devon presents "a strange jagged summit, dim and vague in the distance, like some fantastic landscape in a dream" (819), I believe we shall agree that these words may be as factual as any that Holmes originally intended or that he can expect. As Lovecraft argued, atmosphere is important and may be a guide to the truth.

Using these various remarks as a framework for our investigation, let us turn first to the two disasters as they are recounted in the manuscripts. Dr. Mortimer reads to Holmes an account written in 1742, the same year as *The New Dunciad*, giving us perhaps little trust in the account. It introduces Hugo Baskerville, "a most wild, profane, and godless man," but even more a man possessed by "a certain wanton and cruel humour" (789), who has become enamored by a yeoman's daughter and who steals her away one Michaelmas. He does her no harm at first, because he and his friends must sit down to "a long carouse as was their nightly custom" (789). For this man, apparently, woman waits upon wine and song. When she escapes he utters the Faustian bargain, to give his soul to the devil if he captures her, and then pursues her, let-

ting loose his hounds upon her trail on the advice of one of his
friends. He is, however, himself pursued by a black mute hound,
all the more horrifying in not letting loose the great howl as
should be its nature. In the climax of this account his friends discover the hound plucking at Hugo's throat and lifting "its blazing
eyes and dripping jaws" (790) upon them, sending them shrieking
across the moor and dying later of shock, not presumably before
relating what they have seen. Oddly, the style of this sober manuscript shifts in tone here to a participation in the horror—
"dripping jaws" indeed! The writer concludes piously, asking his
sons to say nothing of this to their sister. In a patriarchal society
the request is not surprising.

At this point we should turn our attention to a point that Callaghan emphasizes: both narratives picture the various beasts leaping at the jaws or throats of their victims (210–11). Why should
that attack be important? Callaghan connects it with the attack on
the father, but I wonder whether the nature of the attack may lie
in its being directed at the throat, to prevent the victim from
speaking and presenting his own case. What does Hugo Baskerville have to say for himself, now that the girl is dead? Delapore's
cat is leaping for his throat, but Delapore, who has now the mind
of a rat or the atavistic mind of his ancestors, has already killed
and partially devoured the amiable and plump Capt. Norrys.
What, then, did Norrys have to say for himself, the man who initi-
ated the action of the story by telling Delapore's son of Exham Priory and exciting his interest and then his father's? Would he plead
to be forgiven for helping the Delapores take the Priory off his uncle's hands? Was there not something shady about that financial
deal? These questions are unanswerable, but that is my point. They
and other questions like them must not be raised, neither in Doyle's
world nor in Lovecraft's. The hound in the manuscript is mute, and
the rats never appear in the contemporary world.

The Delapore manuscript has been lost in the fire of the narrator's family plantation, but he believes he can reconstruct its message, just as he believes he can reconstruct Exham Priory, the
English home of his family. Lovecraft gives readers sufficient information to believe, with perhaps too much confidence, that
they can reconstruct the manuscript better than this character.

Once upon a time the place of the priory became the prehistoric site of a cannibalistic ritual, long before humans became humans; and on that site other rituals, whether belonging to the Druids or to those who worshipped the Magna Mater, settled and adopted the local rite—murder and cannibalism—adapting these rituals to their home in the caverns beneath the site where the Saxons and the Normans built the priory. In the time of James I one of the sons of the family discovered his family in their rituals and killed them in a nice polite bloodbath, "father, three brothers, and two sisters" (*DH* 32), with no great disapproval of his neighbors or of the king, and fled to Virginia where he became an honored albeit reclusive plantation owner. Thus matters remained until the letter and the plantation, and all the past they contained, were burned during the Civil War, leaving the protagonist of the story ignorant, utterly ignorant, of his family and of himself. There is no reason why the rats should be mentioned in this letter, since their legend arises later than these events and the narrator believes that their story is mere legend.

The basic similarity in these two manuscripts is the admission that the two families are much too liable to outbursts of violence, in both cases treating their neighbors as much less than their equals, much less in fact than swine. To use the word repeated often in Doyle's book, both families are "masterful," regarding the people of Devon and Anchester as no more than a herd from which they can pick and choose at their pleasure. And the family of the de la Poers goes further than this, regarding their own family as prey if they do not agree that the peasantry is subhuman; violent and patricidal as Walter de la Poer's action is, there is little doubt that he acts because he has discovered the murderous intentions of his father. The true message of the manuscripts, if read aright, is that each family is liable to be murderous and they must be careful to restrain themselves—if they wish to.

One further point should be made about these stories—the degree to which one should believe in them. Stapleton, the dissembling cousin of the family, sees in Sir Charles's belief in the hound an opportunity to kill him; he rationally exploits the story of the manuscript, in which he does not himself believe; and the rational Holmes does not believe in it either. The original trespass, the rape of the girl, is itself a part of the legend and nothing more. The original trespass in Lovecraft's story, however, the ritual of murder and cannibalism, must be believed in; if Delapore regards it as no more than a legend he becomes liable to an eruption of his own murderous unconscious; and the story of the rats, which as we have seen is not a part of the manuscript that was burned, becomes the form of that unconscious. In this regard the two stories approach the theme of reason and madness from two very different directions.

Yet the two stories are very similar in so many ways. Let us examine the backgrounds of war, the mass murders at which the two stories gesture. In "The Rats in the Walls," as I have already argued in "'The Rats in the Walls,' the Rats in the Trenches," the patricidal and filicidal madness of the World War is played out in the sub-cellars of Exham Priory. It is, however, significant that the other two wars of the story are civil wars, which are often wars of brother against brother; and this is something of the way that Lovecraft, at one point early in the war, viewed its cataclysm. "Englishmen and Germans are blood brothers," he wrote in 1915 in his peroration to his essay "The Crime of the Century" (CE 5.14). Though he was to change his attitude, we should keep in mind that for him the conflict began as a civil conflict, with closely related peoples at war. Some of this material, of course, characterizes Delapore, the bland Boston business man, as a man divided; we do not expect him to become a rat.

What happens in Doyle's fiction? The English Civil War is important as background to his story. The first trespasser, Hugo Baskerville, is without doubt a Cavalier, as the lace of his formal portrait indicates; yet his face, as painted there and revealed in the face of Stapleton, a.k.a. Rodger Baskerville, is "prim, hard and stern, with a firm-set, thin-lipped mouth, and a coldly intolerant eye" (879), a description we might take as that of a Roundhead. It is not a face that Holmes expects nor that the reader expects. This is also a man divided against himself, who probably represents a psyche divided against itself, a division portrayed at large by the English Civil War.

Is there any other presence of war in *The Hound of the Baskervilles*? Sir Charles Baskerville has made "large sums of money," according to the *Devon County Chronicle*, "in South African specula-tion"; but "[m]ore wise than those who go on until the wheel turns against them, he realized his gains and returned to England with them" (791). More frankly, Watson describes the lodge of Baskerville Hall as "the first fruits of Sir Charles's South African gold" (821). A person reading these passages in 1902 might have a complex relation to it. It was indeed a wise act to realize one's gains and return to England when you remember the very recent Boer War, from 1899 to 1901. But the story may well occur in the fall of 1888, if we are to accept Baring-Gould's chronology of the Holmes saga (2.3), though this interpretation is not asserted ex-plicitly in the text. In any case, it would have taken Sir Charles a considerable time to amass the riches that made him not only generous throughout "the whole countryside" (791) of Devon, the riches would have enabled him to renovate the considerable pile of Baskerville Hall, as his nephew still intends. To do all this Sir Charles must have been rich indeed. South Africa, with its re-cently exploited seams of gold and diamonds, the profits of which were doubling every few years during the 1890s ("Transvaal," *EB* 27.190–91), was a lucrative colony that Britain was not willing to lose, even at the cost of a colonial war.

What did Doyle think of this situation? Though he voluntarily served as a doctor for the English forces during the war, he wrote this scathing account of his views to his mother: "Now about the Boers. [. . .] They want to spread into Bechuanaland we promptly 'head' them out of that—Gold the root of all evil is found & dia-mond mines & the riff-raff of the world swarms down and settles & keeps on *increasingly* swarming and settling. Now can you imagine the *disgust* of those Burghers! [. . .] They would actually rather let the gold alone than work it!" (*Doyle: A Life* 435). Though Sir Charles is certainly not "riff-raff," it is difficult not to believe that he has returned to England with tainted wealth through the old dispossession of the natives.

And what are we to think of Delapore's wealth? Presumably, after the family loses everything in the destruction of the planta-tion Carfax and the loss of their slaves, the wealth has its roots in his father's activity in wisely moving to the North, though Dela-pore would have us think that the move was made because his mother came from the North. He writes that "I grew to manhood, middle age, and ultimate wealth as a stolid Yankee" (*DH* 27), which is to say that most of his life was spent enjoying the excesses and clever exploitations of the Gilded Age. I believe that his career would be described in greater financial detail than in his bland words, "I merged into the greyness of Massachusetts business life" (*DH* 28). How could he have come to England with his great plans without owning tainted wealth? Callaghan persuasively points out a similarity here between Lovecraft's story and Doyle's story "The Five Orange Pips" (212–13); but the wealth of that character lies in a plantation that does not burn down. He is not as alienated as Delapore, the would-be Englishman who is a would-be Southern gentleman and a would-be Northern magnate.

We need to notice one other detail about these heirs who are coming from the colonies to claim their home. They are doubled and redoubled, in that Sir Charles from South Africa is followed by Sir Henry from Western Canada, often talking like a man from the North-American West (810), but both are accompanied if they but knew it by their cousin Rodger from Central America. This doubling is mirrored in Stapleton's relations to his women and in the first letters of their names; he has beaten his wife Beryl, whose proper name is Beryl Baskerville, and lied to his lover, Laura Lyons. Delapore is coming from Virginia and from Massachusetts, though he has been preceded by his son. He writes and talks in a studied fashion as though he were an Englishman, as Lovecraft did his best to do, but Delapore is not at all an Englishman by birth. All these men must to some extent strike the English natives as outsiders, but they are as intimate as insiders as anyone, a true Baskerville and a true de la Poer, the name that Delapore has now assumed. Exham Priory has two towers, as has Baskerville Hall.

One of their aims in their return is to renovate the home. This aim of Sir Charles is immediately taken up by his nephew, who says upon coming up to the Hall, "It's no wonder my uncle felt as if trouble were coming on him in a place like this. [. . .] I'll have a row of electric lights up here inside of six months, and you won't know it again with a thousand-candle-power Swan and Edison right here in front of the hall door" (821), as though American electricity and Saxon know-how were sufficient guard against melancholia. In the view of Watson, all that is necessary after the renovating and refurnishing will be a wife, who he has no doubt will be Beryl Stapleton (840); a wife, then, is a part of the furnishings. Delapore has no wife and indicates no intention to find one. He does, however, have electricity, realized in "the electric bulbs which so cleverly counterfeited candles" (*DH* 34). In both cases the electric lights are an attack on the dark corners and ancient aggressions that now come to life and attack. It is as though the two men flirt with the magic world of Gothicism at the same time that they deny it—to their danger. They renovate the past at the same time as they attempt to erase it.

It is possible, however, that more than the renovation qua renovation lies at the heart of the attack on the two ancient halls. In the sixth circle of Dante's *Inferno* where the violent are punished, the violent against themselves include the spendthrifts, who are pursued by black hounds: "Dietro a loro era la selva piena / Di nere cagne, bramose e correnti, / Come veltri che uscisser di catena" [Behind them was the forest full of black / She-mastiffs, ravenous, and swift of foot / As greyhounds, who are issuing from the chain.] (13.124–26). Not one hound, note, but a forest full of them. I don't think that we can gauge the amount of money that Sir Charles or Sir Henry had spent or were about to spend on Baskerville Hall. Sir Charles had already spent a good deal in charity, but that is not the sort of outlay that causes us to accuse or judge a Christian gentleman; still, since so many people know of his charity, it does smell of ostentation. Much more extremely Delapore is spending an immense amount of money on the renovation of a building from the ground up—though not he believes from the cellar down. If little of that money goes to anyone in the neighborhood, *tant pis;* it is their own fault because of their superstitious recalcitrance. Delapore, of course, is not pursued by black hounds; he is pursued by himself, an id manifesting itself as an army of rats. Dante would not have minded the image, though he would probably have held to his pack of black mastiffs. Bestial, instinctual rapaciousness is the point of the two stories.

After the disaster of the family plantation, a result of the institutional violence of slavery, Delapore came north to gain a wealth sufficient to buy what was left of Exham Priory after centuries of neglect, and not simply to renovate it but to rebuild it from the shell of walls that is all that remains. He has no idea of furnishing it with a wife; he need not, since he has bought a home that at one time was under the patronage of the Magna Mater; and he does not bother to overcome the animosity of the countryside with any acts of generosity. Letting "no expense deter [him]" (*DH* 26), his attention is totally focused on the priory that is to be, not upon any social connections he might make in the neighborhood. True, he becomes a friend of Capt. Norrys, the friend of his son— but Norrys is later to be his feast. He confesses that he comes of a "somewhat reserved and unsocial Virginia line" (*DH* 27).

The rats in Lovecraft's story, invisible as they are, seem to be an army, a word that appears ten times for reasons that are clear in my earlier essay. The word "rats" appears twenty-nine times, never in the singular; of these uses, the word appears ten times in the last two pages, creating the crescendo and climax of the story. The word "vermin" appears only two times, perhaps because of its abstraction; and the word "rodent" appears seven times, always as an adjective. The hound is only one, both in the legendry and in fact, but he has a large supporting cast. Often with great force, the word "hound" occurs several times in the novel, by my count fifty-three times; a bit less, twenty-two times in fact, half as often as "hound," we find the word "dog," most often in the purposive participle "dogging," but a number of times it appears in quite innocuous forms such as the "iron dogs" behind which a comfortable fire burns. It is not applied to the hound until the creature is dead. And then there are the rhymes, "bog" and "fog." In the climactic fourteenth chapter the word "fog" appears ten times, and the fifteenth chapter back in London begins with a diminuendo "foggy" (892). The word "bog" appears only five times, but crucially associated with the hound and in a dramatic scene with the death of two ponies (828–29); and once in the last chapter Watson refers perhaps ineptly to the "bogy hound" (899); it is not so important as the other words.

To pursue these forms further, the hound never dogs its prey but runs and bounds after it; a dog that dogs is persistent but does not break into a run. It is as though the hound were accompanied by its own entourage of dogs and bogs and fogs, accompanied by its own shadows. When it springs upon Sir Henry out of the fog "fire burst from its open mouth," running, says Watson, "with long bounds, [. . .] leaping down the track, following hard upon the footsteps of our friend" (887). Like the rats, the hound is the incarnation of energy.

The rats are their own shadow. As a horde they move in a different manner than does the hound, yet they also like the hound pursue their prey in a rush; in one legend they are a "scampering army of obscene vermin which had burst forth from the castle" and "swept all before it" (*DH* 31). On the other hand, since it is quite possible that Delapore is the only rat in Exham Priory, he has some sympathy with "the hapless rats" that were trapped in sub-cellars; and in Doyle's tale, once we understand that the hound is a real hound that has been brutalized by Stapleton, a reader must have some sympathy with it also; the rats and the hound behave as they do because they are starved. Neither work believes that the animals are evil; they are so only in the manuscripts and legends that project human fears.

At the conclusion of the stories no heir is left in very good shape. Stapleton, who was certainly in line to inherit Baskerville Hall, vanishes in the Grimpen Mire and is presumably dead. In describing the attempt he and Holmes made to find the man, Watson writes, "[I]t was as if some malignant hand was tugging us down into those obscene depths, so grim and purposeful was the clutch in which it held us" (891). Here we realize the irony of the name of Stapleton's home, Merripit. These obscene depths and pits are like the caverns in Lovecraft's story. Stapleton's cousin Sir Henry has shattered nerves and the morning after the attack is delirious, with a high fever. Though we are assured that a trip around the world with Dr. Mortimer will restore him, we do not see the result, and wedding bells with Beryl are doubtful. Thus the fates of both Stapleton and Sir Henry are never narrated explicitly.

The fate of Delapore is ambiguous also. After his adventure in the caverns beneath the priory, caverns that have no bottom, he is penned in an insane asylum where he suffers a madness of regression. This regression or atavism is also a theme of Doyle's novel, made explicit when Holmes demonstrates that Hugo Baskerville, the original instigator of evil in the family line, and his descendent Stapleton look remarkably alike; Stapleton is "a throwback" (879). This theme is one reason that so much of the novel is devoted to Watson's meditations on the people who inhabited the Neolithic huts and burrows on the moor, "some unwarlike and harried race who were forced to accept that which none other would occupy" (834). It is no surprise, then, that Selden the convict is forced to hide there, himself a throwback, whose face, according to Watson, "might well have belonged to one of those old savages who dwelt in the burrows on the hillsides" (849). Callaghan has cogently argued that Doyle draws an implicit connection between Baskerville Hall and the ancient stone burrows that surround it and thus a spiritual connection between historic and prehistoric horrors, a connection that Lovecraft makes explicit (215–16).

Given how close the two stories are, we must ask why they seem to differ so much in the matter of romance. In part, of course, it is a question of genre; if there is any romance in Lovecraft's canon it is disastrous. Each of Doyle's four novels devoted to Sherlock Holmes has a romance. Two women, Beryl and Laura, are very important to the plot of *The Hound of the Baskervilles*, and Mrs. Barrymore is not unimportant, but no woman is of importance to the plot of "The Rats in the Walls." Delapore is a widower who mentions his former wife in one sentence. What has happened? The answer lies, I believe, in the indication that one of the stages of the cult of the priory was the worship of the Magna Mater, whose chariot is drawn by lions and whose worship consists of self-castration. Lovecraft is quite aware of these matters, having read enough of Virgil, Ovid, and Catullus, as has his protagonist, who shudders at the discovery of her name.

But though Delapore has read the classics and Stapleton is merely an amateur naturalist, Stapleton is much more aware, much more conscious, of the various social threads that he is so adroit at playing upon and of his own nature that he is careful to suppress. Delapore has little experience of the social world or of his own unconscious and is therefore much more liable to be driven by it. As I discuss this further I want it to be clear that I am using Erich Neumann's treatment of the archetype of the Magna Mater, a symbol of the unconscious mind that bears a grudge against the conscious mind, opposed to the unconscious mind out of which it has grown because it cannot admit its dependence (147–48). This structure is apparent in the landscapes of the two stories. No home except the Neolithic burrows is built on the moor, much less on the devouring Grimpen mire; though it is rather solitary, Baskerville Hall does exist in the middle of a far-flung community. Exham Priory seems to be built securely upon a limestone cliff overlooking "a desolate valley" (27), but that superiority is fallacious since the foundation is riddled by caverns that seem to have no end.

Signs of the Magna Mater can be easily read in Doyle's story. Laura's married name is Lyons, and the hound looks to Watson "as large as a small lioness" (888); the hound that Stapleton thought to command belongs in fact to the feminine world of the Magna Mater (Neumann 170). Beryl from Costa Rica represents the foreign aspect of the Magna Mater; her worship was brought to Rome during the Republic, but she was always viewed askance, as we can see in Catullus' poem, which represents Atys as an exile. What are we to say of Mrs. Barrymore, "a large, impassive, heavy-featured woman with a stern set expression of mouth" (824)? Doesn't this description recall the appearance of late-Neolithic fertility goddesses, something like that which Neumann presents (plate 22)? Watson notes that Mrs. Barrymore has been weeping. She has no children, but she has acted like a mother to her younger brother whom she had indulged and thus was responsible in part for the brute he became. Of his crimes only murder is specified, but the language suggests that other crimes were much worse in their ferocious, unspeakable manner; he has a whiff of Jack the Ripper about him. But outcast as he is, his maternal sister still cares for him and weeps for him, unable to control the hound that in retrospect we see as expression of the goddess. The weeping that Watson remarks on is neither for Sir Charles nor for Sir Henry, excellent examples of the conscious world, but for her regressive brother. He is the double of Sir Henry in that he can wear the baronet's clothes and dies in his place.

Given the power of the goddess and the several similarities between the two stories that we have been tracing, what I find remarkable about "The Rats in the Walls" is the absence—some might say the suppression—of the goddess. She is mentioned, a fragment of her name in a Roman inscription is copied, Delapore shudders at the thought of Catullus' poem, and that is all until Delapore screams her name in his madness. I do not think that his scream simply records a stage in his regression, whipped through the whirlpool of his shattered self. It is an admission that he has failed in his life and that his culture has failed also, taking part with such enthusiasm in the death-wish of the World War.

What the Magna Mater commands of us we necessarily perform. To the length of self-castration? What else are we to think of the World War? I earlier argued that the army of the rats transcends personal psychosis (67–68). I do not believe that this is so, at least so profoundly, of *The Hound of the Baskervilles*, but it is interesting that the novel concerns several Baskervilles, not simply one: There is Hugo, who committed the original transgression, Hugo, who penned the manuscript warning his children of the curse, Rodger and his son Stapleton (under his several pseudonyms), Sir Charles, Sir Henry, and Selden, wearing the clothes of Sir Henry and thus, as far as the hound is concerned, assuming his identity. The guilt of being a Baskerville is spread wide, just as the guilt of being a de la Poer is spread wide. So the Magna Mater commands Stapleton, who has played with the materials of the unconscious, the legends of the painted hound, to flee to the center of the Grimpen Mire, a symbol of the terrible Mother, and there she devours him. She commands Delapore, because he has suppressed her in the name of reason, to regress (note how little credence he gave to his family's legends); he castrates his consciousness and becomes a slave of the unconscious, devoured by the deep caverns and mouths of his line.

This theme of self-castration cannot be ignored. According to Neumann, it arises within "a male immature in his development, who experiences himself only as male and phallic" (172). Upon occasion he captures a butterfly, but more often Stapleton is seen in the story as the failed naturalist, his phallic net trailing behind him; his wife is, as Watson puts it, the furnishing of the house, an object to be manipulated. Delapore, despite his age, is most concretely characterized by his erection of the priory. The inhibited agony of this situation is expressed in Wagner's *Parsifal* when

Klingsor, who has laid a "Frevlerhand" [sinful/bold hand] upon himself (5.195), cries out at Kundry's mockery, "Furchtbare Not" [fearful need]! (5.207). What is the need that is so fearful? The answer lies in Alberich's words which almost echo Klingsor's, "schmählicher Not" [humiliating need]! (4.57). The castration, which seems like a capitulation to holiness in the manner of Origen, is actually a capitulation to the Magna Mater, an admission that the man cannot live a full life without an intimate, carnal relationship with a beloved. Alberich forthrightly curses love, and Klingsor renounces it; thereby they each earn a magical power that, however, proves illusory. These remarks trace the trajectory of Stapleton's and Delapore's lives. The one man dies in the mire; the other man abases himself to the goddess in his descent to the animal, and in this descent he is no longer a horde. He is only one weak, unintelligible rat: "chchch . . ." (*DH* 45). These are not his last words in the story, but I think he will chitter again.

No doubt the story of the hound, long after the death of Stapledon and his hound, its jaws smeared with phosphorus, will live on also, just as the peasants on the moor tell it. The peasants below the ruins of Exham Priory will tell such stories too.

Works Cited

Baring-Gould, William S., ed. *The Annotated Sherlock Holmes*. New York: Wings Books, 1992. 2 vols.

Callaghan, Gavin. "Elementary, My Dear Lovecraft: H. P. Lovecraft and Sherlock Holmes." *Lovecraft Annual* No. 6 (2012): 198–228.

Catullus, C. Valerius. *Carmina*. Ed. R. A. Mynors. Oxford: Oxford University Press, 1960.

Dante Aligheri. *La Divina Comedia*. In *Tutte le opere*. 3rd edition. Ed. E. Moore. London: Oxford University Press, 1904.

———. *The Divine Comedy*. Trans. Henry Wadsworth Longfellow. Boston: Houghton, Mifflin. 1884.

Doyle, Sir Arthur Conan. *The Complete Sherlock Holmes*. Preface by Christopher Morley. Garden City, NY: Garden City Books, n.d.

———. *A Life in Letters*. Ed. Jon Lellenberg, Daniel Stashower, and Charles Foley. New York: Penguin Press, 2007.

The Encyclopaedia Britannica. 11th ed. Edinburgh: A. & C. Black, 1910–11.

Neumann, Erich. *The Great Mother: An Analysis of the Archetype.* Bollingen Series 47. Trans. Ralph Manheim. Princeton: Princeton University Press, 1991.

Wagner, Richard. *Gesammelte Schriften.* Ed. Julius Kapp. Leipzig: Hesse & Becker, 1914. 14 vols.

Waugh, Robert H. *A Monster of Voices: Speaking for H. P. Lovecraft.* New York: Hippocampus Press, 2011.

Briefly Noted

New editions of Lovecraft continue to appear. In 2010, Dover quietly released a volume, *Lovecraft's Best Short Stories*, edited by Mike Ashley, containing some rather surprising selections, including "Beyond the Wall of Sleep" and "The Lurking Fear." Sterling Publishing (the parent company of Barnes & Noble) released Lovecraft's *Great Tales of Horror* in 2012 and is about to issue a volume of Lovecraft's complete Cthulhu Mythos tales, including several ghostwritten tales. In September Penguin will issue S. T. Joshi's edition of Lovecraft's *The Thing on the Doorstep and Other Weird Stories* (2001) in hardcover, as part of a six-volume series, Penguin Horror (general editor Guillermo del Toro). Among the other volumes in this series is a compilation of Poe's horror tales and poems, *The Raven*, and S. T. Joshi's anthology *American Supernatural Tales* (2007). Joshi, incidentally, has compiled a volume of Clark Ashton Smith's tales, prose poems, and poems for Penguin Classics, under the title *The Dark Eidolon and Other Fantasies*. It is expected to be published in the spring of 2014.

Lovecraft's Travelogues of Foster, Rhode Island

Kenneth W. Faig, Jr.

In Memory of Foster Historian Margery I. Matthews (1923–2000)

Introduction

Most readers will associate the name of Howard Phillips Lovecraft with stories of cosmic alienage and the supernatural. It is proper that his fame should rest primarily upon these works, since, as he wrote to the members of the Transatlantic Circulator in 1920–21, his creative impulse was limited to this domain.

But there was another aspect to Lovecraft the writer—the private world of his letters, of which a very generous selection was published by Arkham House in five volumes between 1965 and 1976. More letter groups have since been edited by S. T. Joshi and David E. Schultz, for publication by Necronomicon Press, Hippocampus Press, and Night Shade Books. In his letters, Lovecraft may be seen as a "whole man," with interests ranging far beyond the outré to encompass literature, philosophy, and the physical and social sciences.

The mind of Lovecraft the private man was never very far from his native city of Providence, Rhode Island. Here his maternal grandfather, Whipple V. Phillips, had come in the mid-1870s to pursue his business career, and here he himself was born in his grandfather's house at 454 Angell Street on 20 August 1890. He developed an extensive knowledge of the antiquities of his native city, buttressed by reading the complete file of the *Providence Journal* at the Providence Public Library. His neighbor Addison P. Munroe, who served in the Rhode Island General Assembly, commented to

Winfield Townley Scott that the young Lovecraft knew more of
the issues before the Assembly than most of its members. Lovecraft's knowledge of the antiquities of his native city can be appreciated by any reader of his great short novel, *The Case of Charles
Dexter Ward*. Fittingly, the marker on Lovecraft's grave at Swan
Point Cemetery bears the legend: "I Am Providence."

However, if there was a second topographical locus which fascinated the author, it was certainly the western reaches of rural
Rhode Island where his mother's family, the Phillipses, settled in
the latter portion of the eighteenth century. Sarah Susan (Phillips)
Lovecraft's great-grandfather Asaph Phillips (1764–1829) had purchased property on Howard Hill in the newly established town of
Foster between 1788 and 1790. Here he farmed on a property
which remained in the family through its Cole and Henry lines
well into the twentieth century. Asaph and his wife Esther
Whipple, married in 1787, raised a family of four sons and four
daughters born between 1788 and 1807. Their son Jeremiah Phillips (1800–1848) purchased the Blanchard Mill on the Moosup
River from the estate of William Blanchard at auction on 22 December 1834,[1] and died when caught in its machinery fourteen
years later. Since his wife, Roby (Rathbone) Phillips (1797–1848),
had died the previous summer, their two surviving sons, James
Wheaton Phillips (1830–1901) and Whipple Van Buren Phillips
(1833–1904), and two surviving daughters, Susan Esther Phillips
(1827–1851) and Abbie Emeline Phillips (1839–1873), were left as
orphans to be cared for by their relative Nancy Stanton when the
1850 census was recorded. Both sons eventually married into the
Place family: James married Jane Ann Place (1829–1900) in 1853
and Whipple married Robie Alzada Place (1827–1896) in 1856.
James and Jane inherited the Johnson Road farm of Jane's uncle
Abraham (whose wife was another Rathbone sister Nabby),
which they farmed through the end of the century, while
Whipple and his family removed to Greene, in Coventry, Rhode
Island, after several years of keeping store in Foster.

---

1. Jeremiah Phillips was the winning bidder for the mill property at $280. Com-
municated to the editor by Margery I. Matthews, 31 May 1994, citing Foster
Town Records, Book 9, p. 228.

Howard Phillips Lovecraft first came to know Foster when he and his mother Sarah Susan (Phillips) Lovecraft (1857–1921) spent two weeks as boarders in the Johnson Road farmhouse of his great-uncle James Phillips around the time of his sixth birthday in August 1896. The boy must have been impressed with this new rural domain; for a number of his memories of his great-uncle's farmhouse and the surrounding countryside are clearly etched in his fine story "The Silver Key," written shortly after he and his aunt Mrs. Gamwell paid a one-day visit to Foster in October 1926. He was probably a less willing visitor to Moosup Valley Church, where his great-uncle was one of the elders, but doubtlessly sat politely through the sermons of his remote relation, Rev. George W. Kennedy (1824–1900), then in his final years of service. Lovecraft and his mother returned again to Foster for a brief one-day visit in 1908, and there is a surviving photograph of fifty-year-old Sarah Susan in front of the James Phillips farmhouse, then owned by James's elder son Walter Herbert Phillips (1854–1924).

Lovecraft was not to return to Foster until the autumn of 1926. By this time, Sarah Susan (Phillips) Lovecraft was dead, and Lovecraft was accompanied by his younger aunt, Annie Emeline (Phillips) Gamwell (1866–1941). Having learned that the original Asaph Phillips farmhouse had been destroyed by fire earlier in the century, Lovecraft and his aunt resolved upon a program of tracing the family roots and visiting ancestral burial grounds. His own interest in family history, originally evinced in his 1905 copying of paternal records compiled by his great-aunt Sarah Allgood, had been reawakened by his young friend Wilfred Blanch Talman, an ardent devotee of genealogical research. The development of motor coach service from Providence to western Rhode Island and points beyond finally facilitated the pursuit of Lovecraft's interest, and with Annie Gamwell he traversed the Plainfield Pike westward from Providence to the hamlet of Rice City on an October day in 1926. Through the graciousness of one of their local relatives, Lovecraft and Annie Gamwell were able to visit not only Tyler and Place sites in the Moosup Valley vicinity but also the village of Greene, where Whipple V. Phillips got his start as a businessman and served as first master of the Masonic lodge. Talking to old-time residents like Squire G. Wood, who had known

Whipple V. Phillips personally, and viewing the portrait of Whipple V. Phillips still on display in the Masonic lodge must have made a pleasant ending to a day's exploration for Lovecraft and his aunt.

They were not to return to western Rhode Island for nearly three years. Their second expedition occurred on Wednesday, 26 August 1929, when they disembarked from the motor coach in the tiny hamlet of Mount Vernon and ascended Howard Hill Road to explore their more direct Phillips ancestry. Here Lovecraft viewed for the first time the graves of his great-great-grandparents, Asaph Phillips (1764–1829) and Esther (Whipple) Phillips (1767–1842). Providence engineer William A. Henry (1867–1941) and his wife Emma Isadore (Phillips) Henry (1866–1929) had erected a summer home in colonial style on the Asaph Phillips farmstead, which they inherited through Mrs. Henry's grandmother Esther (Phillips) Cole (1807–1881), the youngest daughter of Asaph and Esther (Whipple) Phillips. Mrs. Henry had died the April before the visit of Lovecraft and Annie Gamwell, who were greeted by her daughter Maud Esther (Henry) Shelmerdine and her young sons. After enjoying "coffee, cordiality and pears from a tree planted by Asaph Phillips" at the Henry home, Lovecraft and his aunt departed to revisit the Stephen Place homestead in Moosup Valley. Lovecraft's account of his own and his aunt's traversal of the "Moosup Valley short-cut" (shown as "Whippoorwill Lane" in *Foster Map 1971)* is surely his most lyrical paean to the Foster countryside. Despite some rough going through swampy lowland on the abandoned Moosup Valley side of the road, Lovecraft and his aunt emerged in the vicinity of the Job Place and James Phillips farms on Johnson Road, and made their way again to the Stephen Place home. During this visit, Lovecraft and his aunt had the good fortune to see not only the exterior but the interior of the home in which Sarah Susan (Phillips) Lovecraft, her mother Robie Alzada (Place) Phillips, and her grandfather Stephen Place, Jr., had been born. This home, which passed from the Place family to the Battey family after the death of Stephen Place, Jr.'s widow Sarah (Rathbone) Place in 1868, was of great sentimental value to the author. For many years, a crayon drawing of the home that his mother had made after a painting by her aunt Sarah Place Vaughan adorned his study. Lovecraft liked to imagine the peaceful rural existence of Stephen Place, Jr. (1783–1849), and his father, Stephen Place, Sr. (1736–1817). Doubtless, there was much more hard work and toil than he imagined; but more reliably he appreciated the understated beauty of the rural countryside that had formed an important part of his ancestors' lives.

It is our misfortune that Lovecraft never carried out his stated intention of exploring even earlier ancestral sites in Foster and elsewhere in Rhode Island. It is possible that he was frustrated by the lack of reliable information relating to his direct paternal line. It is known that Asaph Phillips's father was James Phillips, but his burial place is not known and his date of death (1807) as provided by Lovecraft unproven. Pardon Tillinghast Howard (1839–1925), a great-grandson of Asaph Phillips through his daughter Betsey (Phillips) Howard, believed that James was the son of Jeremiah (1695?–1779) of Glocester, the grandson of Joseph (1669?–1719) of Providence, and the great-grandson of Michael (1630?–before 1676) of Newport. Lovecraft himself, however, believed that Asaph's father James was the son of James and the grandson of Michael, thus skipping a generation. Further, by 1929, Lovecraft was claiming that Michael was himself the son of Rev. George Phillips (d. 1644) of Watertown, Massachusetts—a claim not supported by any genealogical evidence known to the editor. The persistence of the given name "Jeremiah" in Lovecraft's branch of the Phillips family provides some circumstantial evidence in favor of Pardon Tillinghast Howard's account of Asaph Phillips's ancestry. Lovecraft expressed an intention to consult with his remote relation Frank Darius Phillips (1872–1958) of Potterville, Scituate, R.I., on the matter of the earlier Phillips generations and their burial places, but is not known to have pursued his expressed intention. Mrs. Gamwell's increasing age and ill health in the 1930s may have also militated against further explorations in her company, while Lovecraft's natural modesty may have militated against solo expeditions which would have required social calls.

Thus, we are left with Lovecraft's accounts of his one-day expeditions of 1926 and 1929. While we certainly wish that the author had had further opportunity to explore his western Rhode

Island origins in Foster, we must also be appreciative of the wonderful accounts that he left of his two actually accomplished expeditions. These accounts are not unmarred by the author's prejudices: The hard-working Finnish immigrants who helped Foster maintain its viability as an agricultural community in the twentieth century come in for their share of criticism—perhaps Lovecraft recalled his friend Edith Miniter's account of Polish immigrants in *Our Natupski Neighbors* (Henry Holt, 1916)—and there is one unfortunate reference to the "mongrel" Jewish population of New York City (where Lovecraft lived in 1924–26), which he would surely have lived to regret had he survived the Second World War to become familiar with Hitler's Holocaust. Lovecraft's racial prejudices are an unfortunate part of the man, but we should not allow them to detract from his appreciation of his family origins in the Rhode Island countryside.

The editor does not believe that Howard Phillips Lovecraft would have found the Foster of 1825 of his great-grandfathers Jeremiah Phillips (1800–1848) and Stephen Place, Jr. (1783–1849), a very congenial place. The author, like most of the rest of us, had become very dependent upon the comforts provided by modern "machine" civilization. But setting aside the harsh practicalities of making a living in a nineteenth-century agricultural environment, one can contemplate Lovecraft's identification with the cultural and emotional heritage that he received through his ancestors. Lovecraft had some twenty of the books of his great-grandfather Stephen Place, Jr., in his own library, including the 1797 Alden Aldrich *Reader* that so influenced his own development as a writer. His collection of the *Farmer's Almanack* began with issues collected by his great-great-grandfather Stephen Place, Sr., who had made marginal notes in some of his copies. While his immediate family had ceased to be direct owners of real estate with the sale of Whipple V. Phillips's Providence home following his death in 1904, Lovecraft continued to hold (with pride) throughout his life a small mortgage on a Providence quarry, which Whipple V. Phillips may have acquired from his nephew Jeremiah Wheaton Phillips (1863–1902); the mortgage, in fact, was the only asset listed in the inventory of Lovecraft's estate made by his executor Albert A. Baker (1862–1959). In the 1920s, Lovecraft's friend

James Ferdinand Morton, Jr. (1870–1941), became the curator of the Paterson, New Jersey, museum, and Lovecraft took "squirearchical" delight in presenting Morton with rock specimens from the family quarry, then operated by Mariano de Magistris.

One may well dream of the life that might have been Howard Phillips Lovecraft's had he not died prematurely of cancer in 1937 but lived to witness the Second World War and subsequent events. While his grandfather Whipple Phillips and his great-uncle James Phillips both died at about seventy, Lovecraft's Place ancestors were long-lived. Had he attained economic success as an author of science fiction in the postwar world, one wonders if he might have acquired the Whipple Phillips house at 454 Angell Street before its ultimate demolition and restored it to its former grandeur. Had Lovecraft lived to witness the celebration of his centenary in 1990, perhaps he might have been a resident of Halsworth House, able to look out from the window of his room onto his beloved St. John's Churchyard on the steep hillside ascent. But would Providence have been his most likely "retirement" haven? The sunny south with its cultural traditions and warm climate—particularly Charleston, South Carolina—would certainly have beckoned. Of course, there would always be the New England villages where his ultimate cultural roots and personal sympathies lay. His regret for the American Revolution, while idiosyncratic, was nevertheless real.

From the editor's perspective, however, it is difficult to envision a more appropriate retirement haven for Lovecraft than the farmhouse of his great-uncle James Phillips in Foster, Rhode Island[2]—where he awakened to view the dewy morn from the small-paned windows of his bedroom and rose to explore the beautiful countryside with a boy's energy and fascination for two glorious summer weeks in 1896. Perhaps in later life a hired female helper from Moosup Valley might have made life comfortable for the author in the James Phillips farmhouse. Perhaps he might have taken his exercise on each clement day by strolling

---

2. Regrettably, this farmhouse on the west side of Johnson Road was destroyed by fire in the first decade of the twenty-first century and was replaced by a modern structure.

from his home along the country lanes, visiting family burial grounds and other familiar sights. Doubtless, he would have ranged as far as the energies of old age would allow, for in middle age he was a walker of great endurance, especially if motivated by an antiquarian, topographical, or aesthetic quest. It is indeed possible than an "alternative universe" life of Howard Phillips Lovecraft might have ended in quiet retirement in Foster, Rhode Island. His life of course did not end in the Foster he so loved, but the Foster travelogues of 1926 and 1929 that the author left to us permit us to reconstruct and to participate in part in his cultural identifications with this ancestral topography.

The editor wishes to thank S. T. Joshi for granting him access to the full texts of the 1926 and 1929 travelogues and for making arrangement for their publication in the *Lovecraft Annual*. The 1926 travelogue was earlier published in part in *Selected Letters* 2.81–89 and the 1929 travelogue was earlier published in part in *Selected Letters* 3.15–20.[3]

The editor has not provided full citations for vital records. The vast majority, with exceptions as noted, have come from the An-cestry.com, FamilySearch.org (LDS), and AmericanAncestors.org (NEHGS) websites. The editor wishes to thank the Rhode Island State Archives, the late Margery I. Matthews, the late Violet E. Kettelle, and other individuals and institutions who assisted him in his research; however, he retains full responsibility for all errors and opinions contained in his annotations. All occurrences of the Rathbone surname have been normalized to that form; however, the author has let stand variations of the Harrington surname like Herenden, etc.

---

3. The 1929 travelogue as excerpted in *SL* 3 derives from the holograph letter to Maurice W. Moe, rather than the typed letter to Frank B. Long, both dated 1 September 1929. The typed letter to Long is the source for the text in this edition.

10 Barnes Street,[4]
Providence, R.I.,
Octr. 26, 1926.

Young Man[5]:—

In replying to your keenly appreciated communication, I must begin in something of my old-time travelogical vein; for the past week has witnessed a pilgrimage on my part, more impressive than any I can recall taking in years. This excursion, on which I was accompany'd by my youngest daughter Mrs. Gamwell,[6] was to these rural reaches of Rhode-Island from whence our stock is immediately sprung; and is design'd to be the first of several antiquarian and genealogical trips covering the Phillips-Place-Tyler-Rathbone-Howard country, and including inspection of as many of the original colonial homesteads as are yet standing. This devotional survey is naturally a recreation of the keenest interest; covering as it does those forms of landscape whose images are permanently burnt into my pastoral soul, and those whose spirit and atmosphere are ineffably stamped on the quintessential germ-plasm bequeathed to me down a long line of rustick progenitors. I had previously been in that region but twice in my life; in 1896, when I spent two weeks at the colonial farmhouse of my great-

---

4. HPL lived at 10 Barnes Street from his return to Providence in 1926 until he removed to 66 College Street to form a common household with his younger aunt Annie Emeline (Phillips) Gamwell in 1933. His elder aunt Lillian Delora (Phillips) Clark also had a room at 10 Barnes Street until she died in 1932.

5. Frank Belknap Long, Jr. (1901–1994), a close friend and correspondent of HPL, resident for all his life in New York City.

6. Annie Emeline (Phillips) Gamwell (1866–1941) was the youngest child of Whipple V. Phillips (1833–1904) and his wife, Robie Alzada (Place) Phillips (1827–1896), having been preceded in birth by Lillian Delora Phillips (1856–1932) [m. 1902 Franklin C. Clark (1847–1915)], Sarah Susan Phillips (1857–1921) [m. 1889 Winfield S. Lovecraft (1853–1898)], Emeline Estella Phillips (1859–1865), and Edwin Everett Phillips (1864–1918) [m. 1894 & 1903 Martha H. Mathews (1868–1916)]. In 1897 Annie Phillips married Edward Francis Gamwell (1869–1936), a Brown graduate and Cambridge, Massachusetts, newspaperman, but she had long been separated from him by the time she accompanied her nephew to Foster in 1926 and 1929. The couple had two children who died early, Phillips Gamwell (1898–1916) and Marion Rhoby Gamwell (1900–1900).

uncle James Phillips,[7] and in 1908, when I took a very casual single day's jaunt with my mother;[8] this infrequent visiting being due to difficulties of transportation only just solved by means of one of those new-fangled motor stage-coach lines.

On this occasion we started at 9 a.m. from the Eddy Street coach terminal over the antient Plainfield Pike, noting in due time the historick Fenner farmhouse (1677)[9]—homestead of one of Rhode-Island's greatest old families—and later on the region devastated to create the new Scituate reservoir.[10] In less than an hour we reach'd the general section associated with our lineage, and were delighted with some of the late Georgian doorways around Clayville.[11] At length we disembarked at the quaint hilltop village (with a *gorgeous* view!) oddly known as "Rice City",[12] and struck

---

7. James Wheaton Phillips (1830–1901) was the elder brother of HPL's grandfather Whipple V. Phillips (1833–1904). In 1853 he married Jane Ann Place (1829–1900), daughter of Job W. Place (1795–1879) and Asenath (Pierce) Place (1793–1881). Jane's uncle Abraham Place (1800–1852) and his wife, Nabby (Rathbone) Place (1794–1854), were childless, so James and Jane took over their farmhouse on Johnson Road and farmed there through the end of the century.

8. Sarah Susan (Phillips) Lovecraft (1857–1921), who married Winfield Scott Lovecraft (1853–1898) in Boston in 1889.

9. The Thomas Fenner house is located at 43 Stony Acre Drive in Cranston, R.I., less than 500 feet south of R.I. Route 14 (Plainfield Pike). HPL may have had a less obscured view from the Pike in 1926 than is available today. With the Clemence-Irons house in Johnston and the Eleazar Arnold house in Lincoln, the Thomas Fenner house is one of three surviving seventeenth-century "stone-ender" houses in Rhode Island, and is the least altered of the three. See *Jordy* 184–85 [item CR12] and *Isham and Brown* frontispiece, 31–35 and plates 12–18.

10. The Scituate Reservoir covered 14,800 acres and was constructed 1915–25 (*Wolf-3* 7).

11. The village of Clayville is situated on the Foster-Scituate town line on R.I. Routes 14–102. Clayville was a mill village but lost its two mill buildings in 1923 during the construction of the Scituate Reservoir (*Jordy* 263, *Downing* 35). An 81-acre historic district, admitted to the National Register of Historic Places in 1988, is still preserved in the village.

12. In the late eighteenth century, Samuel Rice kept a tavern in the vicinity and named the hamlet "Rice City." Elder Douglass Farnum preached a revival in Rice City in November 1812, and in January 1813 Samuel Rice and others received baptism. Rice later removed to Ohio, where he named another hamlet after himself. The Christian Church in Rice City continued to thrive, and in 1870 forty-six

northward along a back road[13] across the town line from Coventry into Foster, and toward the brookside hamlet of Moosup Valley, "metropolis" of our hereditary region.

As we followed the antique highway past copse and mead, cottage and stream, gentle slope and shady bend, I was destin'd to be surpris'd by the loveliness of the countryside. I had known before that it was pretty, but having seen it only twice—once thirty and once eighteen years ago—I had never properly appreciated it. Now, in my old age, I was forcibly struck with its comparably graceful lines of rolling hill and stone-walled meadow, distant vale and hanging woodland, curving roadway and nestling farmstead, and all along the route the crystal convolutions of the upper Moosup River, cross'd here and there by some pleasing rustick bridge. At one bend in the stream I paus'd with proper pensiveness; for there in 1848 my great-grandfather Capt. Jeremiah Phillips met an untimely end in his own mill (now demolish'd),[14] being dragg'd into the machinery by the skirts of his voluminous frock coat as a malign wind blew them against some wheel or belt. Whenever we enquir'd the way we found that our names were well known to the inhabitants, and I doubt if any person we saw was not related to us in some more or less distant fashion—such being the universal consanguinity of an antient pastoral community. Finally we beheld across the meadows at our left the distant roofs and white church belfry of Moosup Valley,[15] and were soon descending to it

---

members received dismissal to join the Moosup Valley Church founded by Elder George W. Kennedy in 1868. See *Matthews-3* 28 et seq. and *Jordy* 339–40 [CO13].

13. HPL and Mrs. Gamwell probably took Vaughan Hollow Road north from Rice City, and then the right fork where Vaughan Hollow Road divides into Barb's Hill Road (left fork) and Potter Road (right fork). They would have followed Potter Road to Moosup Valley Road and then proceeded west to the hamlet of Moosup Valley.

14. Jeremiah Phillips (1800–1848), the father of Whipple V. Phillips, purchased the mill on the Moosup River originally constructed (c. 1796) by William Blanchard following Blanchard's death in 1833 and operated it until his own accidental death in its machinery on 20 November 1848. A new mill was built on the site in 1867 by Leonard Hopkins and destroyed by a freshet in 1886. The ruins of both mills may still be seen at the sharp bend of Potter Road. See *Downing* 69.

15. This meeting house for Moosup Valley Christians was originally erected in

past the idyllick farmhouse at the bend of the road—once the seat
of "Aunt 'Rushy"—Jerusha Foster[16]—who used to give candy to
my mother and aunt[17] when they came to see her back in the
early 'sixties—but now occupy'd by a fashionable Providence
man[18] who has married into the old local stock—Arthur Dexter's
daughter,[19] who lived a piece up the hill.

1864–65. The Moosup Valley Christian Church was organized in 1868 under
Rev. George W. Kennedy (1824–1900), who served as its first pastor for thirty
years until retirement in 1898. See *Matthews-3* 49–56 and *Downing* 64.

16. Rusha (Potter) Foster (1800–1867) was the wife of Otis Foster (1808–1887)
(*Faig-1* 81). In *Foster Map 1870*, O. Foster was located on the east bank of the
Moosup River, south of Moosup Valley Road. William Kennedy was at this loca-
tion in *Foster Map 1895*.

17. The reference is to HPL's elder aunt, Lillian Delora (Phillips) Clark (1856–1932).

18. Margery I. Matthews wrote to the editor on 29 February 1992: "#2 house
which HPL says was occupied by the scion of a well-connected Providence family—well that was true. However 'Nick' was an easy-going, unambitious fellow
not well regarded by the high society branch of the family." The editor wishes he
had asked Mrs. Matthews for the surname of the Providence gentleman, but he
did not. He has not been able to determine which of Arthur Dexter's three
daughters was his wife. In *Foster Map 1971* R. Salisbury resides on the southeast
corner of Potter and Moosup Valley Roads.

19. Arthur Barry Dexter, the son of Henry Oscar Dexter (1836–1868) and Mercy
[Mercie] Ann (Griffiths) Dexter (1837–1902), was born in Providence, R.I., on
8 July 1859. His father was the son of Stephen Dexter, and his mother was the
daughter of Mahala Potter (1802–1885), who married Charles Griffiths [Griffis]
(1805–1880) in Providence on 11 October 1829. (Mahala and Charles Griffiths
separated in 1852 and Mahala and her children resumed the Potter surname. Mahala was the daughter of Reuben Potter.) Arthur Dexter lost his father on 27 October 1868 and thereafter lived with his mother in Greene, Foster, and West
Greenwich, where he removed after his mother's marriage to Olney William
Arnold (1827–1907) on 1 December 1875 (*Wood* 51–52). Arthur Dexter's future
wife, Annie Marie Potter, the daughter of Alvah D. Potter (1820–1889) and
Hannah M. (Shippee) Potter (1827–1918), was born in Putnam, Conn., on 21 May
1859. Arthur Dexter and Annie Potter married in Foster on 5 October 1879.
Their children (all born Foster) were: (1) Everett Henry Dexter, born 12 January
1881, died 23 September 1922, Providence, R.I., married Minnie Florence
Spaulding; (2) Carrie M. Dexter, born 21 March 1882; (3) Leon Arthur Dexter,
born 7 April 1884, died August 1966, Foster, R.I., married Ruth Maybelle Johnson (1902–1971); (4) Frank Will Dexter, born 20 [or 30] April 1887, died June
1969, Foster, R.I., married Ruth —— (1904–1986); (5) Charles Alvah Dexter, born

Crossing the rushing Moosup by another of those deliciously
Arcadian bridges, we were soon in the pine-shaded village cemetery,[20] where for some time the colonial slate slabs kept us busy.

---

10 January 1892, died November 1974, Foster, R.I., married Pearl F. ——; (6) Herbert Albertus Dexter, born 8 [or 9] September 1895, died August 1972, Foster,
R.I., married Helen M. —— (1906–1975); (7) Nettie P. Dexter, born 10 July 1897;
(8) Ralph Edgar Dexter, born 16 May 1899, died 10 November 1921, Providence,
R.I.; (9) Eva M. Dexter, born 12 December 1901. In *Foster Map 1895*, A. B. Dexter
occupied the household on the northwest corner of Moosup Valley and Johnson
Roads, previously occupied in *Foster Map 1862* by George Place and in *Foster Map
1870* by George Place Estate. *Downing* 64 describes this house as follows:

Place-Dexter Farm (Moosup Valley) (c. 1760 et. seq.) (#232): This much altered, lengthened, 1½-story, south-facing house, with its large, ramshackle, 19th-
century barn at the rear, has long been a landmark in Moosup Valley, located as
it is at the corner of Moosup Valley Road and Johnson Road (originally called the
Moosup Valley "North Road"). The house may have been built as early as c. 1760
by Enoch Place who bought land here from Stephen Harrington in 1751. Enoch's
grandson George Place owned the farm in the mid-1800s; the Dexter family acquired it about 1880 and ran a general store here in the early 20th century.

In *Foster Map 1971*, E. Bennis, A. Williams, and W. Hirst are on the north side
of Moosup Valley Road west of Johnson Road; F. Kennedy and F. W. Dexter on
the north side east of Johnson Road. R. Dexter and H. A. Dexter are on the south
side of Moosup Valley Road east of Johnson Road. The editor has not found marriages for the three daughters, Carrie, Nettie, and Eva, of Arthur B. and Annie M.
Dexter. *Colwell* (25, 39) prints group photographs including the young Eva Dexter—the first as a student at Moosup Valley School and the second as a Camp Fire
girl in 1917. Annie Marie (Potter) Dexter died on 14 March 1917, aged 57. The
daughters remained in the home of their widowed father Arthur B. Dexter in the
1920 U.S. census. (It is possible that Nettie was also enumerated in that year as a
bookkeeper boarding in the home of Emma A. Potter in Providence Ward 3.) Carrie Dexter lived in the Foster home of her brother Herbert A. Dexter in the R.I.
1925 census. Eva M. Dexter lived in the Foster home of her brother Herbert A.
Dexter in the U.S. 1930 census. None of the sisters were living the Foster homes of
Herbert A. Dexter and Leon A. Dexter in the 1940 U.S. census. Arthur B. Dexter, a
staunch Republican politically, served several terms as Foster representative in the
R.I. General Assembly (*Wood* 51–52). He eventually removed to Greene, R.I., and
took Mrs. Alpine E. Tanner as his second wife. He died in Greene on 5 April 1927.
20. Moosup Valley Cemetery (Foster Historical Cemetery #83) lies immediately
east of Moosup Valley Church on the north side of Moosup Valley Road. In addition to the persons mentioned by HPL, Clarke Howard Johnson (1851–1930)
and Casey B. Tyler (1819–1899) are also buried there.

There were scores of our kindred there—Tylers, Howards, Fryes, Hopkinses, Rathbones, and Places—although our closest relatives all rest in private burying grounds near their respective homesteads. We now walkt through the "civick centre" of the village, noting the church, schoolhouse, grange, and publick library—all of which is family 'property' through association. A distant relative— the Rev. George Kennedy[21]—built the church and was its first

---

21. Rev. George Waldron Kennedy (1824–1900) was the founding pastor of Moosup Valley Church. In October 1852, he married Mercy Battey (1827–1860), the daughter of Daniel and Priscilla (Briggs) Battey. The only child of this marriage (the first of Rev. Kennedy's four) was Alvero A. Kennedy (1853–1936), who married Nabby Emogene Tyler (1854–1945) in Warwick, R.I., on 17 January 1883. The editor has not found a common ancestor for HPL and George W.(4) Kennedy [George(3) Alexander(2) Hugh(1)]. Hugh(1), the progenitor of the Kennedy line, was born at sea and settled in Voluntown, Conn. His son Alexander(2) (1745–1826) married Mary Edmunds (1742–1820) and removed to Foster. Alexander's son Capt. George(3) (1789–1868) married Celinda Parker (1787–1866) and with her had a large family including in addition to George Waldron(4) Kennedy, Alexander(4) (1816–1873), William E.(4) (1819–1908), Theodore Parker(4) (1825–1913), William (1827–1896), and other children, some short-lived. Capt. George(3) Kennedy's wife, Celinda Parker, was the daughter of Col. Thomas Parker (1755?–1814) and Rosanna (Tyler) Parker (1756?–1832). See *Faig-1* 68 for Casey B. Tyler's assertion that Rosanna Tyler was "a descendant of William Tyler, who first settled in what is now Foster in 1729 and owned and occupied a portion of the first Tyler purchase." *Sherman* 224 does not show a daughter Rosanna of William(4) Tyler [John(3) Lazarus(2) John(1)], born 4 April 1718 in Warwick or East Greenwich, R.I., the son of Foster settler John(3) Tyler. William(4) Tyler and his first wife Lydia Herenden had children Sarah (b. 1743), Elizabeth (b. 1747), Martha (b. 1749), and William(5) (b. 1750). William(4) Tyler and his second wife Elizabeth Reynolds had children Rebecca (b. 1754) and Lydia (b. 1756). Some family historians show Rosanna [Rosannah] Tyler as the first child of William(4) Tyler by his second wife Elizabeth Reynolds. *Sherman* 223 shows only a daughter Freelove (b. 1708–18) for John(3) Tyler's brother William(3) Tyler, who died at Portsmouth, R.I., between 15 March and 14 April 1718, ten years before John(3) Tyler settled in Foster. One Ancestry Family Tree Maker line, otherwise undocumented, shows Rosanna Tyler as the daughter of Samuel Tyler, Jr. and Elizabeth Hill and as the granddaughter of Samuel Tyler and Lydia Herendon, which conflicts with the first wife claimed for William(4) Tyler by *Sherman*. Descendants of James(4) Tyler (1736–1813) do share common ancestry with HPL through James(4) Tyler's first wife Mary(4) Place (d. 1787), the daughter of HPL's ancestor Enoch(3) Place (1704–1789). There are other links by marriage

pastor, whilst my grandmother's cousin[22] Casey B. Tyler (a local writer and historian, also notary publick, town clerk, and State Senator 1850–51)[23] left his private library to the village to form the present Tyler Free Library—which has some 5,000 volumes and is annually aided by the state.[24] The village formerly contain'd a smithy, two shops, a slaughter-house, and a tannery; but commerce declin'd when the old stage route left, and the omnipresent Ford has driven out all that could support a blacksmith. Beyond the "civick centre" we climbed the hill to the old Casey Tyler house[25] where my aunt Mrs. Clark was born,[26] and here we were

---

between the Kennedy and Place families. Capt. George(3) Kennedy's sister Betsey(3) Kennedy (1787–1855) married Christopher(5) Place (1780–1855) [Rufus(4) Enoch(3) Thomas(2) Enoch(1)]. They were the parents of Christopher Perry(6) Place (1820–1897), whom HPL probably met during his 1896 visit to Foster. Finally, Jessie Helen Kennedy (1889–1974) and Bertha Tyler Kennedy (1893–1974), the granddaughters of Rev. George Waldron Kennedy and the daughters of Alvero A. Kennedy and Nabby E. Tyler, married Albert John Bennis (1887–1971) and Ellis Blake Bennis (1890–1976), grandsons of Christopher Perry(6) Place and sons of James M. Bennis (1851–1912) and Jennie Foster (Place) Bennis (1859–1948).

22. Robie Alzada Place (1827–1896) and Casey B. Tyler (1819–1899) were third cousins through common descent from Adam(2) [Thomas(1)] Casey. Robie Alzada Place was the granddaughter of Sarah(4) Casey (1755–1813) [John(3) Adam(2) Thomas(1)] and John Rathbone (1750–1810). Casey B. Tyler was the grandson of Nehemiah Potter (1739–1812) and Eunice(4) Casey (1745–before census date 1790) [Edward(3) Adam(2) Thomas(1)].

23. For the relevant vital statistics on Casey B. Tyler, see *Holman* 24–26. *Faig-1* 60–113 reprints Tyler's "Historical Reminiscences of Foster."

24. Since the time of HPL's visit, the Tyler Free Library, originally built on the north side of Moosup Valley Road in 1900, was moved (1965) across the street and joined to the Moosup Valley Schoolhouse (originally built in 1811) (*Downing* 64 [#236]). The entire structure is now operated as the Tyler Free Library. Many of the publications of the Foster Preservation Society are available for purchase at the Tyler Free Library.

25. This is the Tyler Store on Plain Woods Road, which runs west from Moosup Valley Road (*Downing* 68 [#244]). Photographs of the house may be found in *Colwell* 64 and *Wolf-1* 88. This section of Foster was known as Tylerville, from the Tyler family, which settled there by 1728. Casey B.(6) Tyler [John(5) James(4) John(3) Lazarus(1) John(1)] was the son of John Tyler (1784?–1860), the grandson of James Tyler (1736–1813), and the great-grandson of John Tyler (b. 1688–93, Portsmouth R.I., d. 21 September 1778, Foster, R.I.), who settled in Foster

literally enchanted with the beauty of the landscape. Across the road a wooded valley dips magnificently to the lower meadows, while to the east and north are incredibly lovely vistas of stone-walled rolling pastures, clumps of forest, bits of stream, and purple ranges of hills beyond hills. The house itself, a large three-story structure, is of the early 19th century origin; but beside it is the still intact (though inhabited by a newcomer named Dunbar[27] who has only lived there twenty-five or thirty years) colonial homestead of a story and a half which housed James Tyler (Casey's father)[28] before he built it. The house of Casey[29] was estab-

---

c. 1728. William(4) Tyler (b. 4 April 1718, Warwick or East Greenwich, R.I.) came with his father John(3) to Foster in 1728. See *Holman* 1–7 and *Sherman* 220–25.

26. Lillian Delora Phillips was born here on 20 April 1856. Whipple V. Phillips operated the Tyler Store for about two years commencing in 1855 (*Faig-1* 101).

27. Albert Jarvis Dunbar was born 16 November 1892 in Eastham, Mass., the son of George E. Dunbar and Mary (Hartley) Dunbar. In 1900 he was one of nine siblings in his parents' household in East Providence, R.I.; in 1910 he was in his parents' household in Providence Ward 2. He married Grace Agnes McCord (born 27 October 1894, Providence, R.I.), the daughter of William McCord and Agnes (Gibson) McCord, in Providence on 31 March 1915. Their children (all born R.I.) were: (1) Jarvis G., born 5 September 1915; (2) Paul M., born 8 July 1917; (3) Christine G., born 28 September 1919; (4) Albert M., born 28 August 1921; (5) Maurice A., born 3 December 1922; (6) Ruth A., born 4 September 1925; (7) Enid, born 21 May 1930; and (8) David, born 23 November 1934. When he registered for the draft on 12 January 1918, Albert J. Dunbar was an unemployed mechanic living with his wife and two children at 696 Chalkstone Avenue in Providence. By 1920, the family had relocated to Warwick, R.I., where Albert worked as a vulcanizer in an auto shop. By 1925, the family had relocated to Moosup Valley Road in Foster, where they remained through the 1940 census. Albert J. Dunbar was working as a public road inspector when the 1935 R.I. census was enumerated. Albert J. Dunbar died on 4 March 1942, age 49, in Rutland, Worcester County, Mass. At the time of his death his residence was Greene, R.I.

28. James(4) Tyler (1736–1813) [John(3) Lazarus(2) John(1)] was actually Casey B. Tyler's grandfather. Casey's father was John(5) Tyler (1784?–1860), the son of James(4) Tyler. The Captain James Tyler House (c. 1794 and c. 1830) on Plain Woods Road (*Downing* 68 [#243]) was built on the site of the house of James Tyler's father John(3) Tyler (b. 1688–93, d. 1778), originally built c. 1728 and burned in 1790. John(3) Tyler was the original Tyler family settler in Foster (then Scituate), R.I., c. 1728.

29. Thomas(1) Casey (1637?–1711) settled in Newport as early as 1658 (*Casey* 1).

lish'd in the patriarchal Narragansett Country, where large slave-holding was the rule, and was connected with the great Newport house of Wanton, which gave the Province three Royal Governors and some spectacular privateer captains.[30] The marriages of James Tyler and of John Rathbone (to Caseys)[31] give us an interesting

---

HPL had two streams of Casey blood, since his great-grandmothers Sarah Casey Rathbone (1787–1868) (m. Stephen Place, Jr.) and Robie Rathbone (1797–1848) (m. Jeremiah Phillips) were both daughters of John Rathbone (1750–1810) of Exeter, R.I., and his wife Sarah(4) Casey (1755–1813) [John(3) Samuel(2) Thomas(1)]. HPL loved to tell the story of Samuel(3) Casey (1724?–1770+), the brother of his four-times great-grandfather John(3) Casey (1723–1794). Samuel(3) Casey vanished from history when his neighbors disguised in blackface freed him from the Kingstown, R.I., jail after he had been sentenced to death for counterfeiting. Samuel(3) Casey was a silversmith of note and his story, which HPL loved to retell, may be found in *Miller* 1–9. Silas(6) Casey (1807–1882) [Wanton(5) Silas(4) Thomas(3) Adam(2) Thomas(1)], the father of Casey family historian Thomas Lincoln(7) Casey (1831–1896) (*Casey*), inherited the summer farm originally built (c. 1750) by Daniel Coggeshall on Boston Neck Road in North Kingstown. In 1955, Thomas Lincoln Casey's son Edward Pearce(8) Casey (b. 1864) gave this farm to the Society for the Preservation of New England Antiquities. Although not owned by the Caseys until the nineteenth century, the Silas Casey farm (*Jordy* 364 [NK44]) is one of the last surviving examples of the plantation-style economy which existed in the Narragansett country in the eighteenth century.

30. William Wanton (1670–1733) and John Wanton (1672–1740) were brothers who served as Governors of Rhode Island in 1732–33 and 1734–40, respectively (both died in office). Gideon Wanton (1693–1767), son of Joseph Wanton and nephew of Governors William and John Wanton, served as Governor in 1747–48. Joseph Wanton (1705–1780), son of William, served as Governor in 1769–75. Philip Wanton (1719–1779), son of Philip and Hannah (Rodman) Wanton, married Elizabeth(4) Casey [John(3) Thomas(2-1)] on 28 December 1749. She was the daughter of John Casey and Elizabeth Hicks (*Casey* 3).

31. John Tyler (1784?–1860) married 20 December 1807 Abigail (Nabby) Potter (1787–1838), the daughter of Nehemiah Potter and Eunice(4) Casey [Edward(3) Adam(2) Thomas(1)]. (*Casey* 7). Eunice was born in Warwick, R.I., on 7 July 1745, the daughter of Edward and Hannah (Bowen) Casey. Her husband Nehemiah Potter was born 13 April 1739 in Coventry, R.I., the son of Job Potter (born 4 March 1720), and grandson of Abiel and Martha Potter. The couple married in 1763 and Eunice was apparently deceased by the time of the 1790 U.S. census. Nehemiah Potter died on 12 September 1812 in Scituate, R.I. In addition to daughter Abigail (b. 1787), Nehemiah and Eunice (Casey) Potter had daughters Rhoda (b. 16 July 1764), Rachel (b. 18 October 1766) and Eunice (1771–1848) and

link with the Newport Tories—God Save the King! (One branch
of Samuel Casey's[32] descendants left the U.S. at the close of the
Revolution & is still existent at Colbourne, Ontario, Canada.) I
told my aunt upon reaching home that she had certainly chosen
an ideal spot to be born in!

From there we retraced our steps to the village, this time
stopping to see a cousin, Mrs. Nabby (Abigail) Tyler Kennedy,[33]
whom Mrs. Clark asked us to look up, and who lives in the oldest
homestead of all—the antient Judge Tyler Tavern[34] whose oldest
parts date back to 1729 (according to some, 1728), when William
Tyler, Gent.,[35] made the region his family seat, and took up most

---

sons Russell (1769–1832) and Nehemiah, Jr. (1773–1810). In 1776 John Rathbone
(1750–1810) married Sarah(4) Casey (1755–1813) [John(3) Samuel(2) Thomas(1)]
(Casey 27). Their daughter Sarah ("Sally") Rathbone (1787–1868) married HPL's
great-grandfather Stephen Place, Jr. (1783–1849). Their daughter Rhoby
Rathbone (1797–1848) married HPL's great-grandfather Jeremiah E. Phillips
(1800–1848). Another daughter, Abigail (Nabby) Rathbone (1794–1854), married
Abraham Place (1800–1852).

32. Casey 34-35 notes that William(4) Casey [Samuel(3) Samuel(2) Thomas(1)]
and his brother Willett(4) Casey, the sons of silversmith Samuel(3) Casey, settled
in Adolphustown, Canada. Perhaps the fact that these two sons located in Canada may point to the ultimate destination of their father after he was freed from
the Kingstown, R.I. jail on 3 November 1770. Willett(4)'s son Samuel(5) Casey
continued to reside in Adolphustown, Canada and served as a member of the
Canadian parliament (Casey 39).

33. Nabby Emogene (Tyler) Kennedy (1854–1945) was a third cousin of Lillian
Delora (Phillips) Clark (1856–1932) through common descent from Enoch(3)
Place. Nabby descended from Enoch(3)'s daughter Mary(4) Place (d. 1787), who
was the first wife of James Tyler (1736–1813). Lillian descended from Enoch(3)'s
son Stephen(4) Place (1736–1817), who married Martha Perkins (1747–1822).

34. The Tyler Tavern Stand on Moosup Valley Road (Downing 64 [#239]) was
erected by William Tyler, Jr. [William(5) Tyler (b. 1750)] about 1780. It was
damaged and rebuilt following the Great Gale of 1815. HPL claims that the oldest part of the house was built in 1728 or 1729. The oldest Tyler house (Downing
68 [#246]) stands on the south side of Plain Woods Road and is dated to c. 1740
by Downing and her researchers. It was reconstructed from a shell in 1972.

35. William(4) Tyler [John(3) Lazarus(2) John (1)] was born in Warwick or East
Greenwich, R.I., on 4 April 1718 and was the son of original Foster settler John(3)
Tyler. Casey B. Tyler erroneously described early Foster settler William Tyler as
the brother, rather than the son, of original Foster settler John(3) Tyler (Faig-1 60).

of the land in sight. That land, call'd the "Tyler Purchase", was later divided amongst other colonial proprietors; and a hearteningly large part of it still remains in the hands of blood descendants. The region is the most truly American and wholesomely colonial I have ever seen; for there seems to be no break or alteration in the steady stream of hereditary habits and traditions which date back to the times when Col. Thomas Parker[36] married 'Squire Tyler's daughter and knocked the local raw recruits for the French and Indian Wars into shape on the training-field back of the old Tavern. The reigning Tyler of Revolutionary times was a magistrate, and in his day a formidably businesslike whipping post stood in front of the house. Much of the Tavern, by the way, was blown down in the great gale of 1815; so that the house at which we stopt is really a composite, with its final form dating from 1816. The room in which we sat, however, was part of the original house; and had the immense floor-boards, exposed corner-posts, and panelled overmantel which told authentically of the early Georgian period. Our cousin, tho' only 72 years of age, is now the oldest inhabitant;[37] and I was astonish'd at the amount of family lore she has preserv'd. She has much better genealogical records than ours, and will be a mine of information if I ever start the research I have long plann'd. She reaches the time of William the Conqueror direct through two lines, Tyler and Foster;[38] and be-

---

36. A Thomas Parker was born to George and Warwick Parker in R.I. on 20 May 1725. Another Thomas Parker, possibly his son, married Rosanna Tyler (1756?–1832). This Thomas Parker (1755?–1814) died in Foster on 7 May 1814 in his sixtieth year. His widow Rosanna (Tyler) Parker died in 1832, in her seventy-seventh year. See *Faig-1* 68.

37. HPL refers specifically to the hamlet of Moosup Valley. Nabby Emogene (Tyler) Kennedy (1854–1945) did survive long enough to hold the *Boston Post* gold-headed cane as the oldest inhabitant of the town of Foster. She was presented with the cane by the Foster Town Council on 3 June 1944, following the death of Caroline Johnson Carroll, and held it until her own death on 16 March 1945 at the age of ninety. Her successor as holder of the gold-headed cane was Jennie Foster (Place) Bennis (1859–1948), the daughter of Christopher and Nancy (Blanchard) Place and widow of James M. Bennis (1851–1912). For the *Boston Post* cane, see *Matthews-6* 24–25 and *Wolf-1* 121–27.

38. Nabby E.(7) Tyler (1854–1945) [James E.(6) John(5) James(4) John(3) Lazarus(2) John(1)] was the daughter of Casey B. Tyler's brother James E. Tyler

lieves she could do so through others with a little additional compiling. Her mother[39] was my grandmother's closest confidante and associate in the 1840's, so that she knows as much about my particular branch as about her own. All in all, I was very glad to run across this manorial family Sibyl, with whom my immediate kindred had been wholly out of touch since the 'seventies, when she attended seminary with my elder aunt.[40] She was, indeed, able to unlock the present as well as the past; being custodian by right of seniority and ancestral position of all the keys in the village.

(1817–1879) and his wife Waity Ann (Foster) Tyler (1815–1869). She married Alvero A. Kennedy. The editor does not know how Nabby E. (Tyler) Kennedy traced her Tyler and Foster ancestry to the time of William the Conqueror. The standard Foster family genealogy *Pierce* ties R.I. senator Theodore Foster (1752–1818) to the line of original settler Reginald Foster of Ipswich, Mass., but the editor has not found Waity Ann Foster in this genealogy.

39. Waity Ann Foster was the wife of James E. Tyler (1817–1879), brother of Casey B. Tyler (1819–1899). Waity Ann Foster was the sister of Albert T. Foster (1803–1856) [m. Cynthia C. Potter (1799–1869)] and Otis Foster (1808–1887) [m. Rusha Potter (1800–1867)]. She and her brothers were the children of John Foster (1779–1860) and Polly King (1787–1860), who joined the Shakers in Enfield, Conn., in April 1826 and are buried in the Shaker yard in Enfield. (The Shaker society in Enfield operated between 1787 and 1915.) John Foster was the son of Samuel Foster (d. 1816, aged 70) and Waity (Wells) Foster (b. 1757, d. 11 April 1841, Enfield, Conn.). Casey B. Tyler states that the wife of Samuel Foster was Waity Place, but both Violet E. Kettelle (letter to the editor, 24 January 1993) and an Internet source agree that Samuel's wife was Waity Wells, the daughter of James Wells (b. 27 March 1734, North Kingstown, d. 4 September 1823, Foster). Samuel Foster was the son of Stephen Foster (fl. 1783) (who married Lydia Blanchard) and the grandson of Thomas Foster (Scituate, R.I., freeman, 1738) (*Faig-1* 81). The editor has not linked this Rhode Island Foster family branch to the descent of Reginald Foster of Ipswich, Mass., described in *Pierce*.

40. Nabby Emogene (Tyler) Kennedy (1854–1945) was a member of the graduating class of the Rhode Island Normal School in June 1875. The editor does not find the name of Lillian Delora Phillips among the graduates of the Rhode Island Normal School listed in Thomas W. Bicknell's *A History of the Rhode Island Normal School* (1911). Lillian Delora Phillips and her sister Sarah Susan Phillips attended the Wheaton Seminary in Norton, Mass. This institution was founded as a female seminary in 1834 and became Wheaton College in 1912. It is possible that Nabby Emogene Tyler attended Wheaton Seminary before she went to the Rhode Island Normal School.

Kindly enough, she took us through the old church—where her husband's father[41] had preach'd sulphureous damnation—the grange in which she is an active worker, and the Tyler Free Library, which her kinsman founded and of which her daughter[42] (who now lives in my grand-uncle James Phillips' homestead where I visited in 1896) is the present librarian. The latter building is simple, but the collection is astonishingly good. I have a new respect for the taste of my bygone cousin, whose old desk occupies a place of honour at the end of the main room. He used to have historical and antiquarian articles in the papers, "cutely" signed "K.C."[43] Many specimens repose in our old family scrapbooks, but I can't truthfully say that the Gibbonesque style impressed me overpoweringly. The recent library accessions are as well chosen as Casey Tyler's original private stock, and if the na-

---

41. Rev. George W. Kennedy (1824–1900), founding pastor of Moosup Valley Church and father of Alvero A. Kennedy (1853–1936), husband of Nabby Emogene (Tyler) Kennedy (1854–1945). It seems likely that HPL and his mother heard Rev. Kennedy preach during their two-week visit with James Phillips (1830–1901) and Jane Ann (Place) Phillips (1829–1900) in August 1896. In 1891 *Bayles* 635 noted the following officials of the Moosup Valley Church: Reverend G. W. Kennedy, pastor; J. W. Phillips, clerk; Deacon Tillinghast, treasurer; A. B. Dexter, Sabbath school superintendent.

42. Jessie Helen (Kennedy) Bennis (1889–1974), the wife of Albert John Bennis (1887–1971), served as librarian of the Tyler Free Library between 1907 and 1965 (*Holman* 136–37). Jessie's sister Bertha Tyler Kennedy (1893–1974) married Ellis Blake Bennis (1890–1976), the brother of Albert John Bennis. The editor is not sure whether Albert and Jessie Bennis or Ellis and Bertha Bennis were the occupants of the James W. Phillips farmhouse when HPL and his aunt visited in 1926. Vivian E. (Phillips) Kinnecom, a granddaughter of James W. Phillips, wrote to Lyman T. Place on 15 December 1947: "After my grandmother and grandfather died, my father [Walter Herbert Phillips] had the place and then my brother [Ellston Corey Phillips], who later sold it to Ellis Bennis and his wife, so it is still in the Place family" (*Faig-2a* vi). It is possible that Ellis and Bertha (Kennedy) Bennis were the occupants of the James W. Phillips farm in 1926, in which case HPL mistakenly stated that Bertha was the librarian of the Tyler Free Library. It seems equally possible that Albert and Jessie (Kennedy) Bennis were the occupants of the James W. Phillips farm in 1926, in which case HPL correctly stated that Jessie was the librarian of the Tyler Free Library. In *Foster Map 1971* the households of both Albert and Ellis Bennis are on Moosup Valley Road.

43. Tyler's "Historical Reminiscences of Foster" was reprinted in *Faig-1* 60–111.

tives read many of them, they will be in no danger of retrograding toward a state of yokelry.

Now leaving Moosup Valley, we climb'd another hill past "Aunt 'Rushy's" homestead (which them city folks a-stayin' thar dew keep up in right peart shape!) and enter'd the especial territory of the Places[44]—encountering on our right the well-beloved homestead[45] whose crayon picture by my mother you may have noticed on my wall.[46] I had seen this twice before—in 1896 and 1908—but had really never given it the appreciation it deserves. Now, in my sunset years, I can accord greater credit to that vanish'd Place who built it—or its predecessor—for truly, I never saw an house so intelligently adjusted to make the most of all the aesthetick features of the landscape. In front, across the road, one sees on the right the ascent of rocky meadow extending to the James Phillips house and later to the Job Place[47] estate atop the

---

44. The stretch of Moosup Valley Road around the intersection with Johnson Road was in fact often called "Placetown" because of the predominance of the Place family in the vicinity. Enoch Place (1704–1789) first settled in this vicinity in 1751. For the name "Placetown," see *Matthews-2* 31 and *Faig-2a* xxiii [letter of Vivian E. (Phillips) Kinnecom to Lyman T. Place, 15 December 1947].

45. The Place-Battey farmhouse on Moosup Valley Road (1769 et seq., *Downing* 64 [#234]). Originally constructed by Stephen Place, Sr. (1736–1817), it was the birthplace and subsequent home of his son Stephen Place, Jr. (1783–1849). HPL's mother Sarah Susan (Phillips) Lovecraft (1857–1921) and maternal grandmother Robie Alzada (Place) Phillips (1827–1896) were both born in this house, which probably accounts largely for its sentimental importance to the author. The house was purchased by Henry Battey (1832–1919) after the death of Stephen Place, Jr.'s widow Sarah [Sally] (Rathbone) Place (1787–1868).

46. The editor does not believe that this crayon drawing is among the HPL relics preserved in the Lovecraft Collection in the John Hay Library at Brown University. Whether it survives in family or other hands is not known to the editor. The editor is unable to ascertain whether the crayon drawing can be detected in the photographs of HPL's study at 66 College Street taken by Robert H. Barlow following HPL's death in 1937, which were reproduced in *Marginalia* (Arkham House, 1944).

47. Job W. Place (1795–1879) and his wife Asenath (Pierce) Place (1793–1881) were the parents of James Phillips's wife Jane Ann Place (1829–1900). After their deaths, their home became the residence of their son Henry Lester Place (1839–1902). The house on Johnson Road (*Downing* 63 [#269]) was originally constructed c. 1760 by Stephen Place, Sr.'s brother Benajah Place (1742–1815), the

hill; this slope is balanc'd by a breathlessly lovely valley panorama on the left, in which the stone-wall'd meadows descend in terraces to the gleaming bends of the river, wilst the white village belfry peeps alluringly thro' embowering verdure (now turn'd to the riotous red and gold of autumn) and sets off the endless undulations of purple hills beyond. Behind the house and its attendant orchard a sparsely wooded ravine winds gently down to lower pastures, and forms a background worthy of any artist's brush. Altogether, I was prodigiously imprest with the beauty of the whole picture; and wisht ardently that I might buy back the place, which pass'd from the family some half-century ago. The Vale of Tempe[48] here finds its reincarnation, and the very birds pipe Theocritus[49] and the Eclogues and Georgicks of Maro.[50] The house, in which my own mother and her mother and mother's father[51] before her were born, is of the prettiest New-England farm type; and dates from a late colonial period when the larger Georgian homestead on the same site was burn'd down. It is now tenanted by the parvenu newcomers who took it fifty years ago (anyone around Moosup Valley is a stranger and newcomer unless his family has a good two centuries of settlement there!) and has quite sadly deterio-

---

father of John Place (1763–1846), and the grandfather of Job W. Place and Abraham Place (1800–1852).

48. The Vale of Tempe is a valley in northern Thessaly which runs from Olympus on the north to Ossa on the south, through which the river Pineios (Peneus) flows to the Aegean Sea. Its length is ten kilometers; its width is as narrow as twenty-five meters. The poets of antiquity described the vale as a beautiful location as noted by John Lemprière in his *Classical Dictionary* (1788). In mythology, it was noted as the domain of Apollo and the Muses. Laurels for the winners of the Pythian games were gathered in a temple dedicated to Apollo which stood on the banks of the Pineios. Here Aristaeus, the son of Apollo and Cyrene, pursued Eurydice, the wife of Orpheus, until she was killed by a serpent's bite. The cities of Tempe, Arizona (USA), and Tempe, New South Wales (Australia), are named after the Vale of Tempe.

49. Theocritus was a Greek poet of the third century B.C.E. He was most noted as a writer of pastoral or bucolic poetry.

50. HPL refers to the Roman poet Publius Vergilius Maro (70–19 B.C.E.), most commonly known as Virgil or Vergil.

51. Sarah Susan (Phillips) Lovecraft (1857–1921), Robie Alzada (Place) Phillips (1827–1896), and Stephen Place, Jr. (1783–1849).

rated since our forbears had it. I can even see a marked falling-off since 1908, when I was last there. We paus'd at length in the family burying-ground,[52] separated by a bank wall and iron gate from the roadside, and admir'd several comely skulls and cheerful cherubs—to say nothing of urns, fountains, and weeping willows—on the many slabs of slate and marble. No fragments, unfortunately, were *conveniently loose;* (I *do* want a paperweight of New-England slate instead of New-Jersey red sandstone!) tho' I was strongly tempted by an entire slab of the 1840 period, remov'd from the grave of Stephen Place Jr. in 1903, when a Western relative erected a finer stone, and now lying against the wall at the rear of the enclosure. Epitaphs were abundant, but I found nothing really quaint or grotesque. The rural 'squires of that region were too much in town, and to well train'd in taste at the village academies, to blossom forth with the engaging illiteracy found in other parts of New-England. Time has not been kind to the antient slate, and moss has play'd its obscuring part; so that the earliest epitaph I could read was that of my great-great-grandfather Stephen Place (there were endless Stephens![53]) who died in 1817. His stone (topt by a willow weeping over an urn) reads thus:

> "The dust must to the dust return,
>   And dearest friends must part and mourn;

---

52. The Place-Blanchard lot (Foster Historical Cemetery #90) stands next to the Moosup Valley Fire Station (*Downing* 64). It contains the graves of Stephen Place, Sr., Stephen Place, Jr., and their wives, among others.

53. HPL refers to Stephen(4) Place (1736–1817) [Enoch(3) Thomas(2) Enoch(1)], who married Martha Perkins (1747–1822) and had a large family. Another contemporary Foster, R.I., Stephen Place was Elder Stephen(4) Place (1745–1827+) [Nathan(3) Peter(2) Enoch(1)], a Baptist preacher who married Martha Warren (d. 1805) and also had a large family (*Faig-2* 277–87). Elder Stephen Place's branch of the family shared the longevity of HPL's branch of the Place family: his father Nathan(3) Place (1719–1817) died at the age of 98 years 12 days, and his mother Desire (Tucker) Place (1714?–1805) in her ninety-second year. The last Stephen Place in Foster appears to have been Stephen W. Place (1837?–1907), the son of Anthony Place of Glocester, R.I. Stephen W. Place was a Union Civil War veteran and married Emeline (Randall) Simmons (1826–1903), the widow of George Simmons, in 1871. They had no children. Stephen's occupation was given as shoemaker in the U.S. 1870 census. For Stephen W. Place, see *Faig-2* 288 *and Faig-2a* xxi.

The gospel faith alone can give
A cheering hope, the dead shall live."

Inane, but hardly *quaint* in the truest sense. His wife Martha,[54] who departed this life in 1822, revels in equal inanity:

"Hail, sweet repose, now shall I rest,
No more with sickness be distress'd;
Here from all sorrows find release,
My soul shall dwell in endless peace."

We now proceeded to the old James Phillips place,[55] scene of my 1896 visit, and here again I was astonisht by the beauty of the landskip. The antient white house nestles against a side hill whose picturesque rocks and greenery almost overhang the north gable end, while across the road is a delicious combination of hill and vale—hill to the left, with the Job Place estate and its burying ground at the top (James Phillips, having married Job Place's daughter Jane, lies there)[56] and to the right the exquisite "lower meadow"

---

54. Martha (Perkins) Place (1747–1822).

55. The Place-Phillips farmhouse (c. 1810, *Downing* 63 [#270]). However, the house, constructed for Abraham Place, probably dates to 1826 or later, since a deed of that year describes the 30-acre property as vacant (letter of Margery I. Matthews to editor, 22 July 1992, citing Foster Deed Book 8, p. 226). John(5) Place (1763–1846) [Benejah(4) Enoch(3) Thomas(2) Enoch(1)] deeded the property to his son Abraham(6) Place (1800–1852) in this 1826 deed. This house on the west side of Johnson Road was burned to the ground in the first decade of the twenty-first century and replaced by a modern dwelling. The editor had the good fortune to examine the interior of the original Place-Phillips farmhouse with Marc A. Michaud, Daniel W. Lorraine, and others in 1990, when the property was offered for sale.

56. The Place-Phillips lot is Foster Historical Cemetery #86. An enumeration of the burials there, abstracted from the records of James N. Arnold and Grace G. Tillinghast, may be found in *Faig-2* 231–34. James W. Phillips (1830–1901) and his wife Jane Ann (Place) Phillips, three of their early-deceased children, and their son Walter Herbert Phillips (1854–1924) are all buried in this lot. In addition, Jane Ann's parents Job Wilcox Place (1795–1879) and Asenath (Pierce) Place (1794–1881) and paternal grandparents John Place (1763–1846) and Lydia (Wilcox) Place (1773?–1856) and numerous other Place relatives are buried here. Janet (McCallum) Phillips (d. 1987), the widow of James W. Phillips's grandson Ellston Corey Phillips (1890–1977), left a bequest for the maintenance of Foster Historical Cemetery #86.

with its musical winding brook. The only flaw in the picture is a
recent social-ethnic one—for FINNS, eternally confound 'em, have
bought the old Job Place house![57] This Finnish plague has afflicted
North Foster for a decade, but has hardly secured a real foothold in
Moosup Valley, only two families marring the otherwise solid colo-
nialism. They are seldom seen or heard—but it does make me
crawl to think of those bovine peasants in the house where my
great-uncle's wife was born—and tramping about an antient Place
graveyard! Maybe a *hand* will reach up thro' the rocky mould some
day. . . . Well—after this I fancy people will be careful how they
dispose of their real estate![58] Entering the James Phillips house—
which has not alter'd since 1896—we were welcom'd by its present
inhabitants—a distant kinsman (whose mother was Christopher
Place's daughter) named Bennis, and his wife, daughter of Nabby
Tyler Kennedy and librarian of the Tyler Free Library.[59] News of
our presence in the region had travelled ahead of us; and I was

---

57. *Grass* 30, 32, 38, 39 notes four Finnish households on Johnson Road: Oscar
and Ida Johnson (with children Taimi, Arno, Anne, Arnie and Art); Vaino and
Minnie Lehto (with children Sylvia and Onni); Minnie (Lehto) Taskinen; Sylvia
(Basset) Taskinen (with two daughters). The editor does not know which of
these families farmed the former Job W. Place farm on Johnson Road.

58. Actually the Finnish settlers added significantly to the value of Foster agriculture when fifty families settled in the western part of the town between 1919
and 1926. There are still a significant number of families of Finnish descent resident in Foster. For the Finns in Foster, see *Grass* and *Downing* 41.

59. Jennie Foster Place (1859–1948) was the only daughter of Christopher Perry
Place (1820–1897) and his second wife Nancy (Blanchard) Place (1824–1911). She
married James Matthew Bennis (1851–1912) in 1876 and had six children. Two of
their sons, Albert John Bennis (1887–1971) and Ellis Blake Bennis (1890–1976),
married Jessie Helen Kennedy (1889–1974) and Bertha Tyler Kennedy (1893–
1974), daughters of Alvero A. Kennedy (1853–1936) and Nabby Emogene (Tyler)
Kennedy (1854–1945). Jessie Helen (Kennedy) Bennis was librarian of the Tyler
Free Library between 1907 and 1965. If HPL is correct, Albert John Bennis and
his wife Jessie Helen (Kennnedy) Bennis were the occupants of the James W.
Phillips farmhouse on Johnson Road when HPL and his aunt visited in 1926.
Since Vivian E. (Phillips) Kinnecom states in a 1947 letter to Lyman T. Place that
her brother Ellston Corey Phillips sold the James W. Phillips farmhouse to Ellis
B. Bennis, it is possible that HPL mistakenly identified Ellis's wife Bertha (Ken-
nedy) Bennis as the librarian of the Tyler Free Library.

greeted with two bygone letters of my mother's, which Mrs. Bennis had found among Uncle James's old papers in the attick! This pastoral "grapevine telegraph" (or rather Bell Telephone) is really quite amusing—for we were heralded in advance wherever we went. Even our first casual inquiry at Moosup Valley caused us to be overtaken at the Tyler Tavern by an honest housewife bearing a newspaper cutting of my grandfather's obituary, which the village thought might be of interest! At Uncle James's place I continued some observations on the feline part of the population which I had begun in Moosup Valley, and decided that the prevalence of tailless Manx cats was mark'd enough to constitute a distinct local feature. Evidently the breed—about which you must tell Felis[60]—secur'd a strong foothold at an early date; diffusing its blood throughout the continuously settled territory adjacent, but stopping when the distances became extreme. These uncaudal creatures are lively and graceful, and one soon forgets the handicap impos'd upon them by Nature—an handicap, indeed, which we poor featherless bipeds are not sham'd to share! (Yet how would Felis look without that glorious vulpine bush?) The house pleas'd me as much as it did in 1896, and I envy'd afresh the rag carpets and the wealth of colonial furniture.[61] The Dyckman cottage[62] in New-York will illustrate the atmosphere of the place better than anything else in your benighted metropolitan reach—allowing of course for the difference betwixt Dutch and New-England designs. I was permitted to revisit the corner room where I slept thirty years ago, and where I used to see the green side hill thro' the archaick small-pan'd windows as I awoke in the dewy dawn. Certainly, I was drawn back to ancestral sources more vividly than at any other time I can recall; and have since thought about little else! I am infus'd and saturated with the vital forces of my inherited being, and re-baptis'd in the mood, at-

---

60. Latin for "cat"; also the name of the then-current feline pet in the household of Frank Belknap Long, Jr.

61. Some elements of the James Phillips farmhouse are reflected in HPL's description of the Randolph Carter house in "The Silver Key," which HPL wrote shortly after his 1926 visit to Foster (*Connors* 30 et seq.).

62. Located at Broadway and 204th Street in Inwood section of Manhattan, the Dyckman Cottage was built in 1784 and deeded to New York City in 1910.

mosphere, and personality of sturdy New-England forbears. A pox on thy taowns and decadent modern notions—one sight of the mossy walls and white gables of true agrestick America, and pure heredity can flout 'em all! An health to His Majesty's Province of Rhode-Island and Providence-Plantations! GOD SAVE THE KING!

Later in the afternoon my good 333d cousin Bennis[63] took us in his car to another scene of our family history—the village of Greene,[64] across the town line in Coventry, where my grandfather established himself and his enterprises in early manhood, and where his last two children (including Mrs. Gamwell) were born. He found the place a tiny crossroads hamlet call'd "Coffin's Corner", but at once proceeded to build a mill, a house, an assembly hall, and several cottages for employees—finally renaming the village after Rhode Island's arch-rebel, Genl. Nathanel Greene.[65] All his edifices are still standing, tho' some of them are diverted from their original uses. The house—a capacious Victorian affair of 16 rooms—remains in the hands of those distant kinsfolk (the Tillinghasts, descendants of old Pardon Tillinghast who founded the Providence sea-trade in 1681) to whom it pass'd when my grandfather came to Providence for good in the seventies;[66] whilst the mill is broken up

---

63. Albert John Bennis (1887–1971) and his wife Jessie Helen (Kennedy) Bennis (1889–1974) and Ellis Blake Bennis (1890–1976) and his wife Bertha Tyler (Kennedy) Bennis (1893–1974) were all HPL's fourth cousins, through common descent from Enoch(3) Place [Thomas(2) Enoch(1)]. Jessie's and Bertha's great-great-grandfather James(4) Tyler (1736–1813) married for his first wife Mary(4) Place (d. 1787), the daughter of Enoch(3) Place. The editor is not sure whether Albert John Bennis or Ellis Blake Bennis greeted HPL and his aunt at the James W. Phillips farmhouse and took them to visit Greene.

64. Greene and vicinity are discussed extensively in *Wood.* See particularly p. 35 for Whipple V. Phillips's business enterprises, p. 12 for his home, and pp. 61–66 for his Masonic connections. Whipple V. Phillips and his wife Robie Alzada (Place) Phillips originally attended the Rice City Christian Church. In the 1880s Robie Phillips and her daughters became members of the First Baptist Church in Providence, R.I.; however, Whipple V. Phillips and his son Edwin E. Phillips never joined the First Baptist Church.

65. Nathanael Greene (1742–1786) was a major general of the Continental Army during the Revolutionary War.

66. Daniel Tillinghast purchased Whipple V. Phillips's home and lived there until his death. It was subsequently owned by Albert W. Cleveland. See *Wood* 12.

into shops and tenements. The hall retains its pristine impressiveness; its lofty rooms forming the present home of Ionick Lodge, the Masonick branch founded by my grandfather, and of which he was the first Grand Master. It did me good to see his picture there, enshrin'd in proper state.[67] All the population speak of him with affection, and I was especially pleas'd to talk with those who knew him in person—the old folks like 'Squire Gardner Wood,[68] and Col. Brown the local G.A.R. leader,[69] and the antient cracker-box senate in the gen'ral store, many of whose bearded or stubbly patriarchs worked for him some sixty years ago. One old boy named George Scott[70] shed actual tears of sentimental reminiscence at being confronted with Whipple Phillips' darter an' gran'son!

---

67. Whipple V. Phillips was the first Master (1870–71) of Ionic Lodge No. 28. His portrait still hangs in the lodge hall.

68. Squire G. Wood 3rd was born on 11 March 1861, the son of Caleb Thomas Wood and Ellen P. (Tillinghast) Wood. He died in 1932. He was the author of *A History of Greene and Vicinity*, published posthumously in 1936.

69. HPL probably refers to Curnel Seth Brown, born 17 June 1845, who served in the Navy during the Civil War and married Sarah Jane Case (1847–1927) in 1864. He was recorded in Voluntown, Conn., in the 1870 U.S. census and in West Greenwich, R.I., in the 1880 U.S. census. Brown arrived in Greene in 1882 and opened a grocery (*Wood* 12). Beginning in 1885, he served as postmaster of Greene for twenty-seven years, with one gap of eighteen months (*Wood* 30). (The gap apparently ended when Brown was reappointed to the office by the Cleveland administration on 14 October 1893.) Brown died in 1935. Curnel S. Brown and his wife had at least two sons: Elmer E. Brown (1871–1875) and Irving Elmer Brown (1890–1959) [m. Amy Martin Barrows (1890–1981)]. They are all buried in Woodland Cemetery, Coventry, R.I. (*Edelman and Sterling* CY066 AE0016). G.A.R. refers to Grand Army of the Republic, a Union Civil War veterans' organization.

70. George W. Scott was born June 1856 in R.I., the son of Lyman Scott (1813–1894) and Olive (——) Scott. In the 1900 U.S. census, he was living with his wife Sarah W. (born January 1866, R.I.) and his son Harold W. (born December 1892, R.I.) in Cranston, R.I., working as a grocer's clerk. By 1920, he was divorced from his wife and living with his sister Sarah Smith in Greene, R.I., where he worked as a farm laborer. His situation remained the same in the 1930 U.S. census, except that his former spouse Sarah Scott, 64, single, was also living in his household in that year. In the 1940 U.S. census, he was living in the home of his son Harold W. Scott (1891–1947), a postal clerk, and his daughter-in-law Ellen F. Scott (1898–1983) in Greene. George W. Scott died later in 1940 and was buried in Hopkins Hollow Cemetery (*Edelman and Sterling* CYO12 A0054).

Well, by that time it was night, and we had to take the 6:12 stagecoach home. We had had a great day, but even so had hardly scratched the surface of what we wish to see. The territory cover'd was more Place and Tyler than Phillips or Rathbone country, and a first sight of the antient Phillips burying ground (near the old Asaph Phillips homestead—which my aunt has just learned by telephone was burned down some five years ago[71]) still lies ahead of me. As-aph Phillips, by marrying Esther Whipple of Providence,[72] brought us the blood of that damn'd prophane ruffian Capt. Abraham Whipple,[73] ringleader in the lawless burning of His Majesty's arm'd schooner *Gaspee* on Nanquit Point in 1772. I hope to take this Phil-lips pilgrimage before winter—but if I don't, I shall have something to live till next summer for. Anyway, I have definitely adopted the bucolick squirearchical ideal—or confirm'd myself in its adoption—and am already acquiring a distinctly provincial accent—such as Foster folks ought to use, although they don't seem to. Had I not renounc'd literature, I shou'd compose a pastoral poem in the hero-ick couplet, intitul'd "Moosup-Valley; an Eclogue".[74]

Well—be a reasonably good young man.

Yr obt GRANDPA THEOBALD.[75]

---

71. This reference dates the burning of the Asaph Phillips farmhouse (c. 1788–90) about 1921. However, note that HPL's 1929 travelogue dates the burning of the farm-house fifteen years earlier (c. 1914). The editor does not know which date is correct.

72. Esther Whipple (1767–1842) was the daughter of Benedict Whipple (1739–1819) and Elizabeth (Mathewson) Whipple (1736–1802) of Scituate, R.I. Scituate separated from Providence as early as 1731.

73. Captain Abraham(5) Whipple (1735–1819) [Noah (4) Noah(3) Samuel(2) John(1)] was most famous as one of the leaders of the group of Rhode Island co-lonials who burned the grounded ship HMS *Gaspée* on 9 June 1772. Numerous individuals commented that HPL resembled the portrait of Captain Whipple (now lost) once owned by Brown University; however, HPL was not a descen-dant of Captain Whipple but rather a third cousin at four removes. His great-great grandmother Esther(5) Whipple (1767–1842) [Benedict(4) Benjamin(3) Benjamin(2) John(1)] was a third cousin of Captain Abraham Whipple through common descent from John(1) Whipple (1618-1685) of Providence.

74. Insofar as the editor is aware, no such work by HPL has survived. An eclogue is a poem in traditional form on a pastoral subject.

75. HPL took the pseudonym Lewis Theobald, Jun. in remembrance of Alexander Pope's literary foe Lewis Theobald (1688–1744). Pope and Theobald published rival

Providence, Rhode-Island,

Septr. 1, 1929.

Young Man[76]:—

Well, Sir, once more you must prepare your sophisticated soul for boredom; for your grandpa hath another travelogue coming on! This will be really a direct continuation of one
which I writ you three years ago next month; for like that it deals
with a day's journey into my ancestral countryside of Foster, in
western Rhode-Island. You may recall that my treatise of 1926
dealt wholly with the Place-Tyler-Casey region of Moosup-
Valley—representing my grandmother's rather than my grandfather's streams of heredity—and that I outlin'd therein a design of
making further ancestral pilgrimages to cover the more predomi-
nantly Phillips regions. Little did I think that three years wou'd
elapse ere I took the next trip of the series; but such hath been
the crowded programme of an indolent old gentleman that this
indeed turn'd out to be the case! Incidentally, I presume I told you
last month, as I guided your gaudily painted Essex on the Plainfield Pike, that you went directly through that antient Theo-
baldian countryside on your way from Providence to your next
pausing-place. Had you but diverged on some of the winding, rut-
ted roads which cross the Pike beyond Clayville, you might have
seen all that I describ'd in 1926 and shall describe today—yet I
doubt not but that the beaches of Connecticut offer'd many more
attractions to spirited youth than the stone-wall'd meads and em-
bower'd farmhouse gables of archaick Foster cou'd have done!

My own trip was made last Wednesday,[77] in the company of that
selfsame aunt Mrs. Gamwell who shared the memorable trip of
1926. The day was glorious, and as our scene of action we selected
the region next to Moosup-Valley—Howard Hill, where the later
Phillipses and Howards are thickest—in order to follow out our plan
of working backward through our ancestral stream. The lovely

---

editions of the works of William Shakespeare and were severely critical of each
other's editorial work. Pope parodied Theobald as Dulness in his *Dunciad.*

76. The addressee was Frank Belknap Long, Jr. (1901–1994).

77. 26 August 1929.

slopes of Howard Hill do not form the oldest Phillips country; for that terrain, containing the very antient homestead now falling to ruin, lies to the south, on the old abandon'd section of the Plainfield Pike,[78] and is being sav'd by me as a climax. In the graveyard there I shall find the cherub-carven slate slab of my great-great-great-grandfather James Phillips (d. 1807)[79] and probably that of his father James (d. 1746)[80] as well; things I have never seen, but whereof I have heard accounts. For this present trip we chose a region easier of access (known to my aunt, but never beheld by me) where between 1788 and 1790 my great-great-grandfather Asaph Phillips (1764–1829) settled, and where his descendants are represented both by permanent residents and by persons who spend only their summers there for old heritage's sake. Catching the stagecoach in good season, we travers'd a route at first lying along the old Danielson Pike and including the pleasing village of North-Scituate, but later reaching the Plainfield Pike at Clayville—a small hamlet which you may re-

---

78. The Plainfield Pike originally ran more or less directly southwest from Providence, R.I., to Plainfield, Conn. The construction of the Scituate Reservoir in 1915–25 necessitated the rerouting of a section of the pike. The modern pike is designated as R.I. Route 14 in Rhode Island. The Old Plainfield Pike runs from Route 14 in Foster, R.I., eastward to Route 12 (Tunk Hill Road) in Scituate. (A gated private roadway that forms part of the reservoir property runs further eastward until it submerges in the reservoir.) Foster historian Marjorie I. Matthews wrote the editor that there are no Phillips burial grounds along the Foster section of the Old Plainfield Pike. Perhaps the road that HPL was referring to was a completely different one. HPL's hoped-for informant on earlier Phillips family burials, his remote cousin Frank Darius Phillips (1872–1958), lived in the village of Potterville, on the Scituate section of Old Plainfield Pike. Like Tylerville and Placetown in Moosup Valley, Potterville was doubtless named because of the onetime predominance of the Potter surname in its immediate vicinity. See *Faig-2* (241–59) for a discussion of HPL's beliefs concerning his Phillips ancestry. For Potterville, see *Scituate Map 1964* and *Jordy* 269–70.

79. HPL's letters appear to be the only source for the year of death of James Phillips. The editor is not aware that any James Phillips matching this year of death is recorded in John Sterling's cemetery database.

80. No son James is recorded for James(2) Phillips (d. 1746) [Michael(1)] of Smithfield, R.I. Pardon Tillinghast Howard (1839–1925), a great-grandson of Asaph and Esther (Whipple) Phillips, recorded Asaph(5)'s ancestry as James(4) Jeremiah(3) Joseph(2) Michael(1) (*Faig-2* 241–59).

call as lying just beyond the extensive reservoir country, and strag-
gling up an hill from the water, with two abandon'd factories along
the shoar. Thereafter we duplicated your route of last month as far
as Mount Vernon—a semi-abandon'd settlement of two or three
houses whose chief edifice[81] has a splendid Georgian doorway with
festoon'd fanlight (I hope you notic'd it!) and which still harbours
the crumbling cellar walls of the ruin'd bank of which my great-
uncle Raymond Place[82] was cashier in the 1830's. Helpful rusticks—
who remembered my grandfather well—directed us to the proper
road toward Howard Hill,[83] and we were soon rambling northward
along one of the loveliest country lanes I have ever seen—a lane
which now and then dipt into dark coppices, and now and then
emerg'd to grassy heights whence one might survey the countryside

---

81. HPL probably refers to the Mount Vernon Tavern (*Downing* 68 [#224]). It is
curious that he does not mention that this edifice was in the Fry family from
1842 until 1888, when George Fry (1824–1899) and his family removed to Ore-
gon. George Fry was the son of Richard Fry (1789–1855) and Waite (Phillips) Fry
(1791–1883); his mother was the second daughter of Asaph and Esther
(Whipple) Phillips. See *Faig-2* 49–52 and 302–4.

82. Raymond Gardiner Place (1813–1902) was the son of Stephen Place, Jr.
(1783–1849), and his wife Sarah (Sally) (Rathbone) Place (1787–1868) and the
brother of HPL's maternal grandmother Robie Alzada (Place) Phillips (1827–
1896). He married Eliza Lyon Fry (1813–1894), the daughter of Richard Fry
(1789–1855) and Waite (Phillips) Fry (1791–1883), the second daughter of Asaph
and Esther (Whipple) Phillips. Raymond G. Place was appointed cashier of the
Mount Vernon Bank in 1844 and continued in that office after the bank removed
to Providence about 1855. He succeeded Judge Daniel Howard, Jr. (1787–1879),
husband of Asaph's and Esther's eldest daughter Betsey (Phillips) Howard, as
Foster town clerk in 1852 and continued in that office until 1854. He subsequently served as cashier of the Westminster Bank (1858–61) in Providence and
served three terms as a city councilman representing the Eighth Ward. His prin-
cipal business, like that of Whipple V. Phillips, was coal and lumber. When he
died at the age of eighty-eight he was a resident of the Home for Aged Men on
Broad Street in Providence. See *Faig-2* 45–47.

83. HPL and his aunt probably walked north on Howard Hill Road from the Plain-
field Pike (R.I. Route 14) in Mount Vernon. Curiously, he does not mention Foster
Historical Cemetery #87 (*Downing* 62) on the east side of the road. Asaph and
Esther (Whipple) Phillips's daughter Waite (Phillips) Fry (1791–1883), her husband
Richard Fry (1789–1855), and their son Alfred Casey Fry (1816–1836) are buried in
this cemetery. Their headstones can be seen readily from Howard Hill Road.

for miles around, spying distant farmhouse gables, lines of stone walls, winding brooks, and gnarl'd hillside orchards whose combined glamour produc'd a picture finer than anything in any eclogue I ever read. This lane at length debouch'd upon the Howard Hill Road thro' a picturesque farmyard with an old mill and mill-stream close by.[84] Then came a walk along the hill's crest, where every lane ended in a noble prospect of distant horizons and where sentinel elms and pines, stone walls and bars, swinging meadow gates, and a little old white schoolhouse[85] with belfry and small-pan'd windows, help'd to

84. If HPL and his aunt walked north on Howard Hill Road from Mount Vernon, the old mill and mill-stream referred to are probably part of the Randall-Howard wheelwright complex on the west side of the road (*Downing* 61 [#280]). Ray Howard (1848–1942) operated the premises as a carriage maker and blacksmith from 1879 onward. The wagon shop was built over a branch of West Meadow Brook and includes a dam that formerly powered a 12-foot waterwheel. A more famous mill site in the general vicinity is the Phillips-Battey site (*Downing* 64 [#S31]). This was originally constructed about 1862 by David Phillips and may have replaced an earlier mill constructed by Obadiah Fenner (1764–1858) about 1799. In 1882 Henry Battey (1832–1919) purchased this mill and operated it for many years. Battey was also a cattle dealer and operated the Foster poor farm. He purchased the Place-Battey farmhouse on Moosup Valley Road (*Downing* 64 [#234]) after the death of Stephen Place, Jr.'s widow Sarah [Sally] (Rathbone) Place (1787–1868). *Foster Map 1895* depicts a lane which runs north from Moosup Valley Road to the Phillips-Battey sawmill, but there does not appear to be any lane leading east or northeast from the Phillips-Battey sawmill site to Howard Hill Road. However, it is always possible that HPL and his aunt followed an unmarked lane or footpath or traveled "across lots."

85. Not far north of the Randall-Howard wheelwright shop, Howard Hill Road takes a jog to the east; most automobile travelers will miss the jog and continue north on Walker Road. However, if one examines *Foster Map 1895* and *Foster Map 1971* it appears likely that HPL and his aunt followed the eastward jog of Howard Hill Road. This jog soon turns north and the stretch from the northward turn to Briggs Road probably represents the walk along the rim of the hill which HPL describes. At the intersection of Howard Hill Road and Briggs Road formerly stood Foster School no. 5—probably the schoolhouse referred to by HPL. From this point, HPL and his aunt would have followed Briggs Road eastward to its intersection with Luther Road. The home shown as occupied by W. Bennett in *Foster Map 1895* is the site of the original Asaph Phillips farmhouse (c. 1788–90); it was inherited in turn by Asaph's daughter Esther (Phillips) Cole (1807–1881) and her husband Israel Cole (1807?–1886) and by their daughter Waite

promote the pastoral beauty of the scene.

At last the site of the burn'd-down Asaph Phillips homestead hove in sight (recognis'd by my aunt, who had been there before) and we knew we had arriv'd at the focal point of our journey. The old house, built about 1790, perisht some fifteen years ago;[86] but the present owner of the estate, William Henry, Esq., a civil-engineer of Providence (husband of the late great-granddaughter of Asaph Phillips)[87] who dwells there summers, hath erected a new house of antient design, with interior woodwork taken from demol-isht colonial buildings of the region. There are sightly orchards, pic-turesque old barns and byres, rambling stone walls, stately groves, magnificent vistas on every hand; so that, recalling that my grandfa-ther (Whipple V. Phillips) and great-grandfather (Capt. Jeremiah Phillips) were both born here, and that the seat of my Place ances-tors down the slope toward Moosup-Valley is equally beautiful (cf. 1926 travelogue, plus subsequent parts of this) I again assur'd myself that I come naturally and honestly by my pastoral predilections and love of fine bucolick landskips. The old Phillips graveyard,[88] which I

(Cole) Phillips Bennett (1843–1911) (*Faig-2* 225–26). Through Mrs. Bennett the home was inherited by her daughter Emma Isadore (Phillips) Henry (1866–1929) and her husband William Alan Henry (1867–1941). The Phillips-Cole cemetery (Foster Historical Cemetery #73) lies in the meadow immediately east of the site of the Asaph Phillips farmhouse (c. 1788–90).

86. Note the conflict between HPL's 1929 and 1926 travelogues on this point. The 1929 travelogue says the original Asaph Phillips farmhouse burned about fifteen years ago (c. 1914), while the 1926 travelogue says the farmhouse burned about five years ago (c. 1921).

87. William Alan Henry (1867–1941) married Emma Isadore Phillips (1866–1929) on 23 June 1889. Emma Isadore Phillips was the daughter of Waite Anne Cole (1843–1911) and her first husband Harley Colwell Phillips (1843–1911) (*Faig-2* 144–46). Emma Isadore Phillips had died in Providence on 18 April 1929, four months and eight days before HPL and Mrs. Gamwell made their visit to the homestead on 26 August 1929. Arthur Phillips Henry (1892–1967) and Wal-ter Earl Henry (1898–1954), sons of William Alan and Emma Isadore (Phillips) Henry, were operating the farm at the time of the 1920 U.S. census, and the story of their operation was told in the *Providence Sunday Journal* for 9 January 1921.

88. Foster Historical Cemetery #73 (Cole-Phillips lot). The somewhat conflict-ing information from the Benns and Tillinghast transcriptions of this cemetery is reproduced in *Faig-2* 228–30. The cemetery may be approached from the yard of

have long'd to see for years, is situate on the crest of a meadow hill which drops abruptly to an exquisite wooded valley with a brook.[89] It is girded by a low drest-stone wall, and commands a splendid prospect of meads and groves—one particularly impressive cluster of giant trees lying shortly westward. On its hillward side it drops to a lower terrace which juts boldly out from the slope and ends in a high bank-wall—a terrace devoted to the newer interments, and maintain'd in as elegant and sophisticated a state as your own Wood-lawn;[90] with close-shav'd greensward, trim beds of gay flowers, taste-ful urns, and polisht granite monument and markers of the most metropolitan pattern. In this lower terrace area are interr'd many Providence Phillipses who cherish a wish to lie on ancestral soil de-spite their lifetime separation from the ancestral scene. It is very at-tractive in its way, but forms a rather incongruous element in the agrestick Foster landskip. Naturally, my chief interest lay in the up-per and older burying-ground with its Georgian slate slabs bearing weeping-willows, cinerary urns, and glibly rhym'd epitaphs, and its white marble slabs of the 1840's with their brief, pious, and senti-mental observations. This place was much like the old Place ceme-

---

the adjoining home or from a path cut south from Briggs Road.

89. The newer portion of the cemetery is built on an embankment overlooking Westconnaug Brook.

90. Woodlawn Cemetery was founded in the Bronx, N.Y., in 1863. After tempo-rary interment in an indigent grave, Frank Belknap Long [Jr.] (1901–1994) was himself reburied in a family lot [Lot East Middle Part 55 L.L.P. Sec. 57 Plot Pros-pect] in Woodlawn Cemetery on 17 November 1994, and his name subsequently inscribed on the lot's central monument. *Moshassuck Review* (February 1995) contains an account of Long's reburial and a reproduction of the lot plat. Foster Historical Cemetery #73 containing the graves of Asaph and Esther (Whipple) Phillips and other family members is maintained twice a year through a bequest left by their great-great-granddaughter Maud Esther (Henry) Shelmerdine (1893–1958), who with her two young sons entertained HPL and Annie Gamwell when they visited the cemetery and the site of the Asaph Phillips homestead in 1929. When the editor visited this cemetery in 1990, the upper section with the older graves was in poor condition, while the lower, banked section containing later graves was reasonably well maintained. Daniel W. Lorraine took the photographs of Asaph's and Esther's markers that served as the frontispiece for *Faig-2* but con-tracted a serious case of poison ivy in the endeavor. For burials in Foster Histori-cal Cemetery #73, see *Faig-2* 228–30.

tery in Moosup-Valley, which I describ'd in my 1926 travelogue. I now copy'd with great pains several ancestral epitaphs—in some cases having to clear away moss, earth, and creepers in order to reach the bottom lines. I was reminded of my delightful day's trip through the New-Netherland Dutch region of Rockland County with Talman in 1928,[91] when he took me to scores of similar places containing his ancestors. He has all his family burial-grounds at his finger-tips—as indeed I hope to have mine after the completion of my series of expeditions. But here are a few of the Phillips epitaphs:

ASAPH PHILLIPS
(my gt-gt-grandfather; 1764–1829)

The sweet remembrance of the just
Shall flourish when they sleep in dust.

————

ESTHER PHILLIPS, wife of Asaph Phillips (1767–1842)

Blessed are the pure of heart, for they shall see God.

————

CAPT. JEREMIAH PHILLIPS (Asaph's son, 1800–1848.)

(Kill'd in his own mill—he was inspecting it on Nov. 20, 1848, and caught the skirts of his voluminous frock-coat in a whirling belt. This was 4 months after the death of his wife, so that grandfather grew up an orphan.[92])

——————————————

91. HPL visited his friend Wilfred B. Talman at his home in Spring Valley, Rockland County, N.Y., on 24 May 1928 (*Joshi-1* 709).

92. In the 1850 federal census, Nancy Stanton was caring for the four surviving children of Jeremiah and Roby (Rathbone) Phillips in their home in Foster: Susan Esther Phillips (1827–1851), James Wheaton Phillips (1830–1901), Whipple Van Buren Phillips (1833–1904), and Abbie Emeline Phillips (1839–1873). Nancy Stanton was probably a relation by blood or marriage of Roby (Rathbone) Phillips (wife of Jeremiah), Sarah (Sally) (Rathbone) Place (wife of Stephen, Jr.), and Nabby (Rathbone) Place (wife of Abraham), through their sister Ruth Rathbone (1787–1838), who married John Stanton, son of Joseph Stanton, of Voluntown, Conn., in 1812. *Cooley* 181 shows daughters Mary E. Stanton (born 3 May 1812) and Sally Stanton (born 10 February 1820) for this marriage. Perhaps Nancy

This mortal shall put on immortality.

———————

RHOBY RATHBONE (wife of Capt. Jeremiah Phillips; 1797–1848)
(Whose sister Sarah Casey Rathbone,[93] marrying Capt. Stephen
Place Jun., was the mother of my grandmother Rhoby Place—
named for her, and later marrying her son Whipple Phillips.)

> O ye mourners, cease to languish
> O'er the grave of those you love;
> Pain and death and nights of anguish
> Enter not the world above.

———————

SUSAN ESTHER PHILLIPS (dau. of Capt. Jeremiah: 1827–1851)
(My grandfather's favourite sister,[94] who dy'd at 24, and after

———

Stanton was a sister or other relative of John Stanton. Writing to Lyman T. Place
on 15 December 1947, Vivian E. (Phillips) Kinnecom (1884–1963), a granddaughter of Whipple V. Phillips's elder brother James W. Phillips (1830–1901), recalled that the three Rathbone sisters (Sarah, Nabby, Roby) from West
Greenwich, R.I., visited so frequently that they wore paths among their respective homes in Moosup Valley (*Faig-2a* vii).

93. HPL refers to his great-grandmother Sarah Casey Rathbone (1787–1868), the
daughter of John Rathbone (1750–1810) and Sarah Casey (1755–1813). HPL's ancestor John(3) Casey (1723–1794) [Samuel(2) Thomas(1)] was the father of Sarah
Casey (1755–1813).

94. Whipple Phillips also had a younger sister, Abbie Emeline Phillips (1839–
1873), who married Henry D. Dixon (1835–1905) in Sterling, Conn., in 1859.
They had four sons, three of whom lived to maturity, while one son, Whipple
Van Buren Phillips Dixon, died as an infant in a scalding accident in 1872. The
Benns and Tillinghast transcriptions of the Cole-Phillips lot (Foster Historical
Cemetery #73) disagree as to whether there was yet a third sister Anna M. Phil-
lips; Tillinghast lists such a child dying on 10 January 1829 at the age of 3 years 7
months 22 days, while Benns lists no such child but a child Seth dying on 10 January
1829 at the age of 7 months 22 days (*Faig-2* 228–30). It seems clear that Tillinghast
and Benns must have interpreted a worn or fragmentary stone or stones differently.
It seems that barring further evidence HPL's earlier transcription of the stone for
Seth Whipple Phillips ought to have the greatest authority, combined as it is with a
bit of family tradition concerning the boy. The commonplace book of Sarah Susan
(Phillips) Lovecraft as preserved in the Lovecraft Collection in the John Hay Library at Brown University lists yet another child of Jeremiah and Roby (Rathbone)

whom my mother was given her middle name of Susan.)

> Thou art gone to the grave, but we will not deplore thee,
> Tho' sorrows and darkness encompass the tomb;
> The Saviour has pass'd thro' the portals before thee,
> And the lamp of his love is thy guide thro' the gloom.

———————

SETH WHIPPLE PHILLIPS (Son of Capt. Jeremiah: 1825–1829)

(Dy'd at the age of 3yrs. 7mo. 22d., before my grandfather was born. When—in 1833—my grandfather did appear, he was given the first name of Whipple—the middle name of this tiny brother he had never known.)

> Parents, weep not for thy son,
> Who is early call'd away;
> His better life is now begun,
> Where youth will ne'er decay.

———————

ZILPHA ANN PHILLIPS (dau. of James,[95]
the son of Asaph and bro. of Jeremiah)
(died Sept. 23, 1824, aged only 10mo. 20d.)

> Our short-liv'd idol, our sweetest flow'r,
> Is call'd by death's all-conquering pow'r
> To leave a world of grief and pain:
> We part, but soon shall meet again.

Tho' the head of the Henry household[96] was absent in town,

————————————————————————————————

Phillips: a son Wheaton, presumed to have died early.

95. James Phillips (1794–1878) was the second son of Asaph and Esther (Whipple) Phillips. Zilpha Ann Phillips was his daughter by his second wife, Mary Ann Phillips (1803–1852). James and Mary Ann (Phillips) Phillips had another daughter, Emily Esther Phillips (1830–1895), who lived to maturity and married Charles W. Greene (1829–1901). James and Mary Ann Phillips and their family removed in 1844 to Delavan, Ill., where James Phillips prospered and became prominent in local affairs. For James Phillips, see *Faig*-2 13–19.

96. William Alan Henry (1867–1941), widower of Emma Isadore (Phillips) Henry (1866–1929), a great-granddaughter of Asaph and Esther (Whipple) Phillips.

his visiting daughter (my third cousin) from New-Jersey[97] and several grandsons extended pleasing hospitality. I had met none of them before, and was very favourably imprest by their unaffected kindliness and quiet cultivation. They produc'd some genealogical data—books and charts—which help'd me very materially in defining my exact relationship to several collateral Phillips lines, and I in turn was able to tell them much they did not know about various links and coats-of-arms. Here the incentive given me by Talman two years ago bore useful fruit!

Having been regaled with cordiality, coffee, data, and pears from a tree planted by Asaph Phillips, we departed over Howard Hill in quest of a short cut to Moosup-Valley and the Place country, insomuch as I wisht to behold again the antient and sightly birthplace of my mother, grandmother, and Place great-grandfather. At the top of the hill we paus'd at the newer Howard homestead, where we made ourselves known to the gentleman of the estate, Whipple Howard, Jun.,[98] a descendant of Judge Daniel Howard, whose wife

---

97. Maud Esther (Henry) Shelmerdine (1893–1958) was the daughter of William Alan Henry (1867–1941) and Emma Isadore (Phillips) Henry (1866–1929). She married William A. Shelmerdine (1888–1966) in Providence in 1914. They had sons William A. Shelmerdine, Jr. (1916–1978), and Alan Gordon Shelmerdine (born 11 February 1926), undoubtedly the grandsons of William and Emma (Phillips) Henry whom HPL and his aunt met in 1929. For Maud Esther (Henry) Shelmerdine, see *Faig-2* 184–85. Alan Gordon Shelmerdine resided with his parents in Summit, Union County, N.J., when the 1930 and 1940 U.S. censuses were enumerated. He enlisted in the armed forces at Fort Dix, N.J., on 22 March 1944 and subsequently attended Oberlin College in Oberlin, Ohio. He married Betty Jean Stevens, whom he divorced in Marin County, Cal., in November 1975. In 1993 he resided in Bellevue, Wash. It does not seem likely that he would have retained any memory of HPL's 1929 visit, since he was only three years old at the time.

98. Whipple Howard (1834–1910) was the son of Martin Howard (1790–1865) and his wife Ruth Lockwood (Whipple) Howard (1803–1881). Martin Howard and Judge Daniel Howard, Jr. (1787–1879)—whose first wife was Asaph and Esther Phillips's daughter Betsey Phillips—were both sons of Daniel Howard, Sr. (1752–1827), and his wife Dorothy (Clarke) Howard (1758–1843). Whipple Howard lived all his life on his father's farm (c. 1783, *Downing* 62 [#262]) about a mile and quarter south of Foster Center, and his home is readily located on Howard Hill Road in *Foster Map 1895*. Whipple Howard married Esmeralda Evelyn Cole (1853–1904), daughter of George Cole. However, according to *Howard* 69–70,

their son Whipple Howard, Jr. died in infancy in 1873. Perhaps HPL in fact met one of their other sons, Almond Ormond Howard (1881–1954), Everett Martin Howard (1883–1968), or William Albert Howard (1885–1949). Everett Martin Howard married Asaph and Esther (Whipple) Phillips's great-granddaughter Agatha May Cole (1883–1933). Almond Ormond, Everett Martin, and William Albert were the brothers of Gertrude Elizabeth Howard (1872–1949), who married Frank Darius Phillips (1872–1958) in 1891. Frank Darius Phillips was the relation with whom HPL wished to discuss earlier Phillips burials in Foster. *Foster Map 1895* shows a G. Howard homestead (1831, *Downing* 62 [#290]) where Howard Hill Road takes its northward jog shortly after dividing from Walker Road. Visiting the Whipple Howard homestead would have taken HPL and his aunt a mile northward on Howard Hill Road toward Foster Center, whereas the G. Howard household of *Foster Map 1895* was considerably closer to the Asaph Phillips homestead and their ultimate return route to Moosup Valley. This G. Howard was probably George Howard (1817–1898), the son of Gorton Howard (1784–1874), a brother of Judge Daniel Howard, Jr. (1787–1879), and Martin Howard (1790–1865). George Howard had a son Rufus Howard (1852–1928) by his first wife and married for his second wife Esther Lyon (1839–1907), the daughter of Gardner and Ann (Phillips) Lyon. The 1939 typescript of Casey B. Tyler's *Historical Reminiscences of Foster* owned by the Rhode Island Historical Society—perhaps prepared by Nabby Emogene (Tyler) Kennedy—contains the interjected statement concerning the Gorton Howard homestead shown in italics in the following quotation: "Isaac Howard died on the farm now owned and occupied by John Howard, son of Gorton Howard, and great-grandson of the said Isaac, on `Howard Hill,' as it is familiarly called all through that vicinity. *In 1939 this farm is owned by Everett M. Howard, son of Whipple Howard*." Perhaps the farm had passed from Gorton Howard's son John Howard (b. 1826) to his older brother George Howard (1817–1898) by the time *Foster Map 1895* was compiled. The editor believes that HPL and his aunt are more likely to have visited the George Howard homestead (*Downing* #290) than the Whipple Howard homestead (*Downing* #282) as shown in *Foster Map 1895*, simply because of the relative distances from the Asaph Phillips homestead that are involved. While HPL had great stamina as a walker, his aunt was several months past her sixty-third birthday (10 July 1929) at the time of their excursion on 26 August 1929. If Everett Martin Howard (1883–1968) was living on the Gorton Howard homestead (*Downing* #290) as early as 1929, perhaps he was the Howard family member whom HPL misremembered as "Whipple Howard, Jun." Perhaps HPL could remember only that his helper was a son of Whipple Howard, and therefore referred to him as "Whipple Howard, Jun." For Everett M. Howard, see *Faig-1* 105 and *Faig-2a* xii. For Whipple Howard, see *Howard* 69–70.

was Asaph Phillips' next-youngest daughter Anna[99]--my third cousin by that link, and a remoter cousin by an earlier link. He prov'd a man of middle age, wide information, and much affability; who remains on his ancestral soil in the manner of those who went before him. His house is of early 19th century date, and in fine repair—one of the most pleasing New-England rural places I have ever beheld. I am proud to bear his family name as my first. By his directions we found the Moosup-Valley short cut, and at once plung'd into a deserted countryside of utterly dreamlike loveliness.

The lane we follow'd[100] was formerly the main highroad to Moosup-Valley and the country westward, but was abandon'd about the time of the revolution in favour of the present route. During its existence houses had been built upon the Howard Hill half of it, so that the perpetuation of that part as an accessible lane was necessary. The other half, in the valley beyond the Lyon burying-ground[101] and toward the James Phillips place, was suffer'd to fall into desuetude; to such extent that today not a trace remains of it. Entering the still-preserv'd part of the route from the top of Howard Hill, we found ourselves in the most marvellous and magical colonial territory it hath ever been my good-fortune to behold. Other old roads have such signs of modern decadence as telegraph-poles and mail-boxes, but here nothing of the kind had

---

99. HPL errs here. The wife of Daniel Howard, Jr. (1787–1879), was Asaph and Esther (Whipple) Phillips's eldest daughter Betsey Phillips (1789–1848). Their daughter Ann Phillips (1804–1845) married Gardner Lyon (1804–1849). Daniel Howard, Jr., and his wife Betsey (Phillips) Howard are buried in Foster Historical Cemetery #71 across from their home on Howard Hill Road. Gardner Lyon and Ann (Phillips) Lyon are buried in Foster Historical Cemetery #103 (the Lyon lot) located westward from Howard Hill Road (along what is labeled "Whip-Poor-Will Lane" in *Foster Map 1971*). HPL and Mrs. Gamwell skirted, but did not visit, the Lyon lot in their traversal of the "Moosup Valley short-cut" during their 1929 visit to Foster.

100. The editor believes that this lane was almost certainly "Whip-Poor-Will Lane" as shown in *Foster Map 1971*. Note that this lane ends in marshy land just west of the G. Hollis sawmill site and the Lyon lot (Foster Historical Cemetery #103). Today this gravel lane enters Howard Hill Road at numbers 43-43A. Once the marshy land has been traversed, it is an easy walk to the Job Place homestead, the James Phillips homestead and Moosup Valley.

101. Foster Historical Cemetery #103.

intruded. Just the quaint, narrow, stone-wall'd line of the antient road, now carpeted with soft, delicate grass and mosses and rambling in curves and twists through an incredibly exquisite variety of meadows, orchards, woods, valleys, and sleepy Georgian farmsteads. Birds sang, and the westering sun pour'd a flood of almost unreal and theatrical witchery over the graceful verdure and undulant pastures. The feeling that one walkt in a sheer vision became more and more intense as the chromatick pageantry of fresh greenery, deep-blue sky, and fleecy cumulus clouds spread more and more thoroughly within one's consciousness. The charm of the antient seats with their white-gabled houses, old-fashion'd gardens, stone walls, sloping orchards, and picturesque lines of barns and sheds became so overwhelmingly pervasive that one felt almost opprest for lack of opportunities for instant lyrical utterance. Here, indeed, was a small and glorious world of the past *completely* sever'd from the sullying tides of time; a world *exactly* the same as before the revolution, with *absolutely nothing* chang'd in the way of visual details, currents of folk-feeling, identity of families, or social and oeconomick order. Where Howards or Lyons or Phillipses or Places settled in the first half of the 18th century, there Howards and Lyons and Phillipses and Places live now—tilling the same fields in the same way, living in the same houses and thinking the same thoughts. Horse-drawn vehicles preponderate still, and the drowsy hum of summer is unvext by any discordant note of urbanism or mechanism. A gentle, elusive fragrance unknown either to towns or to ordinary countrysides pervades the whole scene, and so stimulates the imagination that even I, whose fancy is so disproportionately visual, found myself living with several senses rather than with only one. Certain appropriate lines from Milton came spontaneously into my head, and I found myself muttering:

> "As one who long in populous city pent,
>   Where houses thick, and sewers, annoy the air,
>   Forth issuing on a summer's morn, to breathe
>   Among the pleasant villages, and farms
>   Adjoin'd, from each thing met conceives delight:
>   The smell of grain, or tedded grass, or kine,

Or dairy, each rural sight, each rural sound."[102]

Verily, I told my aunt, there is no need to marvel at that circumstance noted by Horace, when he said:

"Scriptorum chorus omnis amat nemus et fugit urbes."[103]

Such, without the least difference in aspect or mood, is the agrestick realm thro' which my forefathers rov'd in the golden age of the Georges. It is beyond question that young Asaph Phillips must have strid along its length on many a sunny afternoon whilst bound for his kinsfolk's abodes in the valley beyond, and here my great-grandfather Jeremiah must often have pluckt blossoms and lain on the sward looking up at the mysterious sky and elfin clouds and fantastick treetops in the days just after 1800, when as a little boy he play'd truant from the trim white schoolhouse with its neat belfry and small-pan'd windows.[104] Today either young Asaph or little Jerry and his brothers and sisters—Benoni, Betsey, Waity Ann, James, Whipple, Anna and Esther[105]—cou'd roam thro' these selfsame meads and lanes and groves without finding anything amiss or thinking that anything had happen'd to their small, simple, Arcadian world in the interim. For after all, the antient New-England of the Magnalia,[106] the Pilgrim's Progress,[107] the

---

102. From Milton's *Paradise Lost* 9.445–51.

103. From Horace's *Epistles* 2.2.77: "Each writer hates the town and loves the country."

104. HPL certainly paints an idealized view of life, even child life, in the Foster of 1800. For a more realistic description of rural life at this period, see *Jones*.

105. The children of Asaph and Esther (Whipple) Phillips were Benoni Phillips (1788–1850) (m. Lucy Fry); Betsey Phillips (1789–1848) (m. Daniel Howard, Jr.); Waite Phillips (1791–1883) (m. Richard Fry, brother of Benoni's wife); James Phillips (1794–1878) (m.1 Susanna Paine, m.2 Mary Ann Phillips, m.3 Annie M. Davidson); Whipple Phillips (1797–1856) (m. Eliza W. Gardner); Jeremiah Phillips (1800–1848) (m. Roby Rathbone); Anne Phillips (1804–1845) (m. Gardner Lyon); and Esther Phillips (1807–1881) (m. Israel Cole). For the children of Asaph and Esther (Whipple) Phillips, see *Faig-2* 7–30.

106. *Magnalia Christi Americana* by Cotton Mather (1663–1728) was originally published in London in 1702. HPL owned a family copy of the first edition, inherited from his uncle Dr. Franklin Chase Clark (1847–1915). After HPL's death, Robert H. Barlow (1918–1951), as directed by the "Instructions in Case of De-

Bible,[108] the Farmer's Almanack,[109] the New-England Primer,[110]

---

cease" left behind by the author, sent HPL's copy of the first edition to James Ferdinand Morton, Jr. (1870–1941).

107. This famous work by John Bunyan (1628–1688) was first published in 1678. HPL owned an 1817 edition of this work (*Joshi-2* 39 [item 134]).

108. HPL owned a 1795 Edinburgh edition of the Bible (*Joshi-2* 31 [item 85]). Mary Spink also catalogued an otherwise unspecified copy of the Bible (*Joshi-2* 31 [item 86]) in his library. He also owned an 1890 New York edition of the New Testament Apocrypha (*Joshi-2* 31 [item 84]). Generally speaking, HPL did not own many religious or genealogical works. (He did, however, appreciate the beautiful prose of the King James Bible, writing to his correspondent Elizabeth Toldridge on 24 April 1930: "Dumas & Walter Scott bore me, but Dunsany, the Bible, Grimm's *Fairy Tales* & the *Arabian Nights* delight me" [*SL* 3.147].) We may presume that Mrs. Gamwell, who was more conventionally religious than her nephew and had a strong interest in family and local history, owned most of the household's books in these domains. Mrs. Gamwell worked for a time as librarian of Col. George Shepley's private library of Rhode Island history. For example, HPL owned none of the genealogical works written by John Osborne Austin (1849–1918) (e.g., *Austin*), but did own three of his works of fiction (*Joshi-2* 26 [items 53, 54, 55]). HPL's copy of Austin's *The Journal of William Jefferay, Gentleman: A Diary That Might Have Been* (Providence, RI: E. L. Freeman, 1899) (*Joshi-2* [item 53]) was auctioned by California Book Auction Galleries on 4 May 1985 (*Science Fiction & Fantasy with Manuscripts & Original Art* [sale 218], item 584, realized price $37.50). The auction catalogue noted: "This copy presented by the author to HPL's uncle, F. C. Clark, with presentation letter inserted before title; with HPL's signature & address on front free endpaper, his bookplate on front pastedown." (The book is misdated to 1909 in the auction catalog.) HPL's uncle Franklin C. Clark was a friend of Rhode Island family historian James N. Arnold (1844–1927). HPL may possibly have met Arnold and other experts in the field of Rhode Island local and family history like Austin and Sidney S. Rider (1833–1917) through his uncle.

109. HPL's main collecting interest was *The [Old] Farmer's Almanack*, begun by Robert B. Thomas in 1792. ("Old" was added to the title in 1832, to distinguish the publication from competitors like *The Farmer's Almanack*, first published in 1818 from Morristown, N.J., by Jacob Mann with David Young as editor.) *The Old Farmer's Almanack* was acquired by Robb Sagendorph of Yankee, Inc. in 1939 and continues to be published today. HPL owned a fine collection, which Robert H. Barlow sent to the author's friend W. Paul Cook following HPL's death, in accordance with his "Instructions in Case of Decease." HPL discussed his holdings of *The Old Farmer's Almanack* in his letter to Walter J. Coates of 13 October 1927 (*SL* 2.175).

and the elder poets *is not dead*. It hath meerly *retreated from visi-bility* and from oeconomick predominance—from the dirty fringe of foreignised cities and the squalid length of cement state roads with their billboards, roadhouses, tourist cabins, and hot-dawg stands. Quietly, in the tranquil and lovely by-roads where vulgar wealth and aimless progress never intrude, it still lives on in its own old way—with narrow winding roads, smiling rock-and-turf slopes, gnarl'd, brooding apple-trees, and massive, smoke-wreath'd farmhouse chimneys. There is no paradox or deception in the statement that the old Foster scene enshrin'd in my ancestral memories is likewise a reality of the 20th century, and that the pil'd-up squares and rectangles on my genealogical charts repre-sent not a dynasty and milieu that are extinct, but a breed and life which exist today as truly as they existed in those glamourous 1700's and early 1800's. The only difference is in *the relative place which these people and this life occupy in the nation and world as a whole*—and as you may easily imagine, this difference is trifling indeed to an old gentleman who repudiates *in toto* both the entire machine culture of the present, and the personality-stunted Bab-bitt-warren[111] of North-American commercialism, size-worship, and time-table servitude to which that accursed bastard-culture hath now reduc'd these once-glorious colonies. God Save the King! I am happy to say that the peril of Finnish immigration, which was an active threat to Foster when I wrote my travelogue three years ago, is waning rather than increasing. The intruding Finns were mainly summer pests who spent their winters in di-vers labours around the wharves of New-York, and as time goes on, they seem to gravitate more toward New-York than toward Foster. It was their old Finland peasant heritage which made them seek the soil upon first reaching America; but as they become as-similated into the mongrel proletariat of the usurping machine civilisation of this continent, they gradually adopt its rat-like ur-banism. Many farms, Finn-own'd a decade ago, have lately return'd

---

110. The *New-England Primer* was first published in 1687–90 by Benjamin Harris from Boston. The earliest surviving edition dates from 1727. There is no copy of this work in S. T. Joshi's catalogue of HPL's library (*Joshi-2*).

111. HPL refers to the protagonist of *Babbitt* (1922) by Sinclair Lewis (1885–1951).

to Anglo-Saxon hands. Howard Hill never had other than its old colonial stock, and now the whole South Foster region seems assur'd of an indefinite English future. The Italian wave from Providence stops ten miles east of this terrain, with a great reservoir system and barren belt as a buffer. Most of the home-keeping old folk have never seen a foreigner save from the few intruding Finns, and are inclin'd to call all foreigners "Finns"—just as you Manhattanites find all alienism summed up in the ratty Mongoloid Jew. If any ingulphment ever comes, it will probably be from the towns of Connecticut across the state line rather than from Providence—but even that menace is obviously far remote. At present, Foster is an all-Yankee colonial town carrying on the original New-England tradition of agricultural simplicity. There is less danger of change now than in the middle 19th century, when everyone flockt to the cities and dreaded the notion of being thought countrify'd. The good Foster families send their sons to Providence schools and Brown University, and sometimes (as in the case of Mr. Henry aforemention'd) engage in business of professional occupations in town; but their anchorage always remains on their paternal soil—they are on their old farms all summer, and chuse (as the lower terrace of the Phillips burying-ground attests) to be laid to rest in the end beneath the calm skies and waving grasses of the meadows their fathers knew and lov'd. For two hundred years these people and these lands have always been the same—and I hope they will always be. The sort of stock they produce is well display'd by typical sons who have caught some notice from the world—Pres. James Burrill Angell[112] of the U. of Mich., who sate next my grandmother at the Smithville Seminary;[113] U.S. Senator

---

112. James Burrill Angell (1829–1916) served as President of the University of Michigan from 1871 to 1909.

113. Smithville Seminary was established in North Scituate, R.I., in 1839. It became the Lapham Institute in 1863 and survived until 1876. Thereafter, a series of religious and vocational schools and summer camps—including the Pentecostal Collegiate Institute in 1902–19, the Watchman Institute in 1923–38, and the Watchman Summer Camp in 1938–74—occupied the premises until 1974, when the building was converted to private apartments. See *Jordy* 266–67. The village of Smithville or North Scituate is located at the intersection of Danielson Pike (R.I. Route 6) and West Greenville Road. The village historic district was en-

Nelson Wilmarth Aldrich;[114] Chief-Justice Clark Howard Johnson[115] of the R.I. Supreme Court (distant cousin and close friend of

---

rolled in the National Register of Historic Places in 1979. HPL's maternal grandmother Robie Alzada (Place) Phillips (1827–1896) was a student at the Smithville Seminary in the 1840s.

114. Nelson Wilmarth Aldrich (1841–1915) served as one of Rhode Island's U.S. senators from 1881 to 1911.

115. Clark[e] Howard Johnson (1851–1930) was a close friend and business associate of HPL's grandfather Whipple V. Phillips (1833–1904). Johnson served as Chief Justice of the Rhode Island Supreme Court in 1913–17. The editor has not found a common ancestor for Clarke Howard Johnson and Whipple V. Phillips, although he believes one likely exists. Clarke Howard(6) Johnson was born in Foster on 18 November 1851, the son of Elisha(5) Johnson [George(4) Job(3) Elisha(2) John(2) Elkanah(1)] and Matilda (Howard) Johnson. His father, Elisha Johnson (1814–1874), was born in Foster on 15 June 1814, the son of George Johnson (1790–1877) and Zilpha (Reed) Johnson (1790–1838), both buried in the Harrington Lot in Foster. His mother, Matilda Howard (1815–1894), was born in Foster on 10 May 1815, the daughter of Clarke(3) Howard (1782–1857) [Daniel(2) Isaac(1)] and Amey (Cranston) Howard (d. 1867). Clarke Howard Johnson's parents Elisha Johnson and Matilda Howard were married in Kllingly, Conn., on 3 February 1840 by Rev. Russell Whitman and named their son Clarke Howard Johnson in honor of his maternal grandfather. The given name Clarke remembers Dorothy Clarke (1758–1843), the wife of Daniel(2) Howard (1752–1827). Clarke's great-grandfather Job(3) Johnson (1754?–1832), a Revlutionary War soldier, married Martha(4) Harrington [Rufus(3) Jonathan(2) John(1)]. His great-great-grandfather Elisha(2) Johnson (1701?–1774) married (1) c. 1722–23 Mary Greene and (2) 1750 his cousin Deborah Johnson Yeates, widow of Jonathan, daughter of Elisha Johnson. John Johnson (1752?–1822) of Foster, who married Freelove Burlingame (1752–1833), was the brother of Clarke's great-great-grandfather Job(3) Johnson (1754?–1832). Note that both of Elisha(5) Johnson's grandmothers were Harringtons. George(4) Johnson's wife Zilpha (Reed) Johnson was the daughter of Reuben Reed (1751–1791) (a Revolutionary War soldier) and Zilpha(4) Harrington (1753–1796) [Josiah(3) Josiah(2) John(1)]. John(2) Johnson (1699?–1782) married Sarah Phillips, the daughter of John Phillips of Jamestown, R.I., in 1721. (Could this marriage be the origin of Whipple Phillips's claim of cousinship with Clarke Howard Johnson?) Elkanah(1) Johnson (1673–1748) married Mary — and is buried in Coventry, R.I. In her work *Blanchards of Rhode Island* (1942), Adelaide Blanchard Crandall identified John Johnson, banished from Wollaston, Mass., to Quidnick, R.I., in 1638, of Newport, R.I., in 1675, as the father of Elkanah(1) Johnson, based on information provided by Bertha Battey Harrington. However, Anthony Tarbox Briggs (d. 1917), in his manuscript Johnson family

my grandfather—executor of his will); Pres. Gilbert Anthony Phillips[116] of the Prov. Bank (my grandfather's 3d cousin); and so on. I am sorry that my direct personal line did not stay on the antient soil; for as it is, my affection and loyalty are necessarily divided betwixt these pastoral meads of ancestral memory, and the antient hill and Georgian spires and roofs of that Old Providence to which my own infant eyes were open'd. By birth urban, I am by every hereditary instinct the compleat rural squire. God Save the King!

Well—having loiter'd as long as possible along the old road, we finally came to the hilltop farm of the Lyons[117] which marks the

---

genealogy owned by the Rhode Island Historical Society, doubted this identification of Elkanah(1) Johnson's father. In her letter to the editor dated 30 December 1992, Violet E. Kettelle stated that she had been unable to prove Elkanah(1) Johnson's parentage. Miss Kettelle suspected that John Johnson, born about 1600 in Kent, England, died 29 September 1659, Roxbury, Mass., might have been an ancestor of Elkanah(1) Johnson. This John Johnson married Margery Scudder and had by her a son Isaac Johnson, admitted as a freeman of Roxbury on 4 March 1635. Isaac Johnson died 19 December 1675 in the "Narragansett Country," perhaps in the Great Swamp Fight. His son Isaac, born in Roxbury in 1642, died in Middletown, Conn., on 23 January 1719/20. Clarke Howard Johnson married Ida Susan Harrington, daughter of William O. and Eunice C. Harrington, in Providence on 21 December 1889. Daniel(3) Howard (1787–1879), the brother of Clarke(3) Howard, married for his first wife Asaph Phillips's eldest daughter Betsey Phillips (1789–1849), so there was a strong connection by marriage between the Howard and Phillips families.

116. Gilbert Anthony Phillips (born 30 June 1843, Foster; died 25 November 1908, Providence) rose to become a prominent banker in Providence. Gilbert Anthony(7) Phillips [Anthony(6) Ephraim(5) John(4) Jeremiah(3) Joseph(2) Michael(1)] was a third cousin of HPL's grandfather Whipple V.(7) Phillips [Jeremiah(6) Asaph(5) James(4) Jeremiah(3) Joseph(2) Michael(1)] through common descent from their great-great-grandfather "Great Jeremiah" Phillips (1695?–1779). Whipple V. descended from Great Jeremiah's son James(4) (d. 1807), while Gilbert A. descended from his brother John(4) (1748?–1836). Gilbert A. Phillips's grandfather Ephraim(5) Phillips (1787?–1855) was thus a first cousin of Whipple V. Phillips's grandfather Asaph(5) Phillips (1764–1829). Gilbert A. Phillips was the son of Anthony Phillips (1818?–1891) and Huldah M. (—) Phillips (1826?–1893). Gilbert A. Phillips married Emma B. Dunbar on 13 April 1870; his wife died, age 51, on 21 July 1897. In 1900, a widower with two servants, he lived at 137 Elmwood Avenue in Providence Ward 7.

117. Shown as home of George P. Lyon in *Foster Map 1895*. S. P. Lyon in *Foster*

end of its accessible part. Inquiring the way to Moosup-Valley of a kindly, antient gentlewoman, we struck out across thinly-path'd hills and dales of the greatest conceivable beauty; skirting the Lyon burying-ground[118] and traversing the pastures where the kine of Howard Hill and Moosup-Valley meet on common territory. The way became more and more difficult as we proceeded, paths being obscure and thorn-choak'd, and valleys being exceeding marshy. At one point an enormous black snake glided across our path, causing my aunt to advance with added caution. The last barrier was a brook which separated a wooded swamp from a rising meadow—and having edg'd across this on planks, we stood at the edge of Moosup-Valley, where the exquisitely beautiful James Phillips place dreams on as of old at the road's bend; nestling in the lee of its rocky hill, an looking across the elm-arcaded way at the green lower meadow, where graceful alders nod above a crystal, convoluted stream. Of this place I spoke at some length in my 1926 travelogue, telling how I visited there for two weeks in August 1896, when my grand-uncle James Phillips (my grandfather's brother—Capt. Jeremiah's eldest son) was alive, and how it is now in the hands of an agreeable couple named Bennis,[119] both collateral kinsfolk of mine. On this occasion we paus'd only for brief civilities, proceeding at once to the neighbouring Place homestead whose picture (a crayon drawing by my mother, after an oil-painting by my late great-aunt Sarah Place Vaughan[120] of East-

---

Map 1862 and Foster Map 1870. Probably same as John Lyon House (Downing 62 [#294]). The address of the Lyon farmhouse is 43–43A Howard Hill Road.

118. Foster Historical Cemetery #103. Asaph and Esther (Whipple) Phillip's daughter Anne (Phillips) Lyon (1804–1845) and her husband Gardner Lyon (1804–1849) are buried in this cemetery.

119. Either Albert John Bennis (1887–1971) and his wife Jessie Helen (Kennedy) Bennis (1889–1974) or Ellis Blake Bennis (1890–1976) and his wife Bertha Tyler (Kennedy) Bennis (1893–1974), all four of whom were HPL's fourth cousins, by common descent from Enoch(3) Place [Thomas(2) Enoch(1)].

120. Sarah Ann (Place) Vaughn [Vaughan] (1824–1901) was the older sister of HPL's grandmother Robie Alzada (Place) Phillips (1827–1896). They were both daughters of Stephen Place, Jr. (1783–1849), and his wife Sarah [Sally] (Rathbone) Place (1787–1868). They were in the sixth generation from the Place family progenitor, their ancestors being Stephen(5) Stephen(4) Enoch(3) Thomas(2)

Greenwich, R.I.) you have often seen on your grandpa's wall, and beneath whose roof my mother, my grandmother Rhoby Place, and my great-grandfather Stephen Place Jun. were born. Of the loveliness of this house, landskip, and roadside burying-ground I have spoken in the earlier travelogue; so that I need not describe in detail my pleasure at beholding the time-mellow'd gables, the climbing ivy, the stone-wall'd road, the verdant vale behind, and the downward-sloping meadows to the northwest, where the modest white belfry of the Moosup-Valley village church gleam'd thro' embowering boskage. Despite the mediocre newcomers who have inhabited the place since it left our family in 1870,[121] we on this occasion decided to inspect the interior; which I had not seen since my sixth birthday, Aug. 20, 1896, and which my aunt *had never seen in her life*—at least, with conscious eyes, since her only entrance to the house was as a toddling infant in the last days of its Place tenure.

Beholding it thus as a relative novelty, we were very much prepossess'd by the evidences of what had been—tho' the present inhabitants are rather slovenly householders with far from old-Novanglian standards of neatness and decoration. The elder Stephen Place (1736–1817)[122] who built the house toward the end of the 18th century after an older one just across the road had burn'd down, must have had something of the mediaeval-manorial in his taste;

Enoch(1). Sarah Ann Place married Russell Vaughn (or Vaughan) (1816–1911) of East Greenwich, R.I. They had children Waldo P. Vaughn (1850–1906), Joseph W. Vaughn (1853–1924), and Emma V. Vaughn (1865–1939). Emma V. Vaughn married Frederick E. Thomas (1866–1914) and had a daughter Mildred V. Thomas (1893–1932). Russell Vaughn (born in Conn. of Conn.-born parents) was a grocer and his son-in-law Frederick E. Thomas (born in Vermont of UK-born parents) a barber; both lived and worked in East Greenwich. The editor's correspondent Violet E. Kettelle (1905–2004) could recall Russell Vaughn's driving his horse-drawn grocery wagon past her girlhood home in East Greenwich. See *Faig-2* 305 for further discussion of Emma V. Vaughn and *Faig-2* 76 for discussion regarding confusion in Cooley's Rathbone family genealogy (*Cooley*) over which of Stephen Place's daughters was the bride of Whipple V. Phillips.

121. Henry Battey (1832–1919) purchased the Stephen Place, Jr., homestead after the death of Stephen, Jr.'s widow Sarah [Sally] (Rathbone) Place (1787–1868).

122. Stephen's father Enoch(3) Place (1704–1789) [Thomas(2) Enoch(1)] settled in Foster, R.I., in 1751. He married Hannah Wilcox (1710?–1802).

insomuch as he provided an enormous central room or "great hall" with fireplace, out of which many smaller rooms open'd—a design which I have never seen in any other old New-England farmhouse. The interior woodwork, though not treated as well during the last sixty years as it deserves, is still excellent; and I wou'd give much to have the carv'd white Georgian mantel in the great room to sit by of an evening with logs blazing behind colonial andirons—perhaps a pair of marching iron Hessians with bristling muskets and tall grenadier hats. The six-panell'd doors are finely wrought, and equipt with latches and hinges of a type already old-fashion'd when the house was built. Old Stephen was a man after my own heart, and I have reason to know that he fully appreciated his exquisite rural environment. It is his file of *Farmer's Almanacks* which begins my own collection, and in those numbers publisht toward the close of his life I find marginal notes in his hand, indicating timid poetick attempts bas'd upon the agrestick scene—or more, perhaps, on the conventional literature of agrestick scenes. In the 1815 issue I find the following not very original bit—

> "Hark, from the copse a tuneful sound,
>   My ears attend the cry."

which makes me regret that no more of the text is accessible. He was evidently unwilling to have any of his manuscripts survive for the edification of his posterity, since I have never seen any compleat poem of his. Incidentally—the rhetorical textbook us'd by his son Stephen Jun. (my great-grandfather) at the old Kent Academy[123] in the early 1800's (*The Reader*, by Abner Alden, A.M., Boston, 1797[124]) is the very volume out of which I first pickt up the rules of prosody myself—by coincidence, in the same year of

---

123. The East Greenwich Academy (originally named the Kent Academy) survived from 1802 to 1943. In addition to his Place great-grandfather Stephen Place, Jr. (1783–1849), HPL's grandfather Whipple V. Phillips was also educated at the East Greenwich Academy. Foster historian Margery I. (Harrington) Matthews (1923–2000), the daughter of Herman Battey Harrington and Mary (Griffiths) Harrington, was a 1941 graduate of the East Greenwich Academy.

124. HPL owned an 1802 third edition of *The Reader: Containing the Art of Delivery, Articulation, Accent, Pronunciation* [etc.] by Abner Alden (1758?–1820). *Joshi-2* 20 [item 16].

1896 wherein I visited Foster. I found it tuckt away with other Georgian reliquiae in a windowless attick room of my birth-place—454 Angell St.—and was fascinated by its long s's, well-stated precepts, and Dryden-Pope-Thomson-Addison-Johnson selections. I have it before me as I click these lines[125]—faithful guide and companion of my youth and old age alike! God bless it—a worthy preparation for the present task of revising and shaping Moe's "Doorways to Poetry"![126] Such were the influences which made old Grandpa Theobald what he is! How I lapt this up in '96 and '97—and how little Stevie Place Jun. must have lapt this same material up at the academy a century and a quarter ago! Same stuff—same book—same spirit—and here was your grandpa in the same house on a glorious August afternoon; the house where little Stevie was born, where he grew up, and where he dy'd full of placid rural memories in 1849—the year after his brother-in-law Jeremiah Phillips was kill'd in the old mill down the Moosup-Valley Road. Old days—old days—and old ways! Here I sit a century later with Steve's old book before me, a score of his other books on my shelves,[127] his file of *Farmer's Almanacks* (following his father's) in my lower table drawer, his blood in my veins, and

---

125. HPL uncharacteristically typed both the 1929 travelogue and the 1926 travelogue; perhaps he made carbon copies for his files. The 1929 travelogue also exists as a holograph letter to Maurice W. Moe held in the Lovecraft Collection in the John Hay Library at Brown University; the 1929 letter to Moe was published in part in *Selected Letters* 3. The 1926 and 1929 typescript letters to Frank Belknap Long are used herein for the text.

126. HPL worked extensively on this book-length manuscript written by his friend Maurice Winter Moe. It was never published.

127. A few books from HPL's library bearing the signature of Stephen Place, Jr., have been offered in the rare book trade. Chris Perridas (www.chrisperridas.blogspot.com) identifies one such title (and reproduces images from its eBay offering) in his post dated 4 February 2007: *The Analogy of Religion, Natural and Revealed, to the Constitution and Course of Nature* by Joseph Butler (1692–1752) (*Joshi-2* 40 [142]). HPL owned an 1822 New Haven edition of this work, originally published in 1736. This book contains ownership signatures of Stephen Place (Foster, R.I., 1833), HPL and Annie E. Phillips Gamwell (7 July 1924). (Perhaps HPL gave the book to his aunt following his relocation to New York City in March 1924.) Unfortunately, it does not seem possible to identify with certainty which score of HPL's books were originally owned by his great-great-grandfather Stephen Place, Jr.

the glowing memory of his house and native landskip in my mind
and fancy. God Save the King! Who says the Georgian past is
gone? Bring on your damn'd years—a helluva lot they can mod-
ernise this tough old Georgian bird!

> Nor can decadent change unchalleng'd thrive
> While Foster and Old Theobald both survive![128]

Well—we broke away from the hallow'd spot at last, and
walkt amongst lengthening shadows in the golden light down the
old road, the narrow, stone-wall'd road, the bending, mead-flankt
road, thro' vary'd rustick vistas to the huddle of old gables and
chimneys, barns and byres, elms and orchards, that is antient
Mount-Vernon on the Plainfield Pike. There, as twilight stole
upon us, we took the Providence stage-coach; thereafter rumbling
back thro' the fine old villages of Clayville and North-Scituate,
and finally entering the mongrel chaos of the urban penumbra.
Jangling, bustling down-town was a sad anticlimax after Foster—
but balm came when I turn'd toward the antient hill and saw the
Great Square of Pegasus[129] shimmering over the shadowy Georgian roofs and steeples on the wooded crest. Old Providence!
Here, too, the antient colonial life and spirit survive amongst the
hillside lanes where double flights of steps rise from mellow brick
sidewalks, and the early lights of evening gleam soft and yellow
from arching fanlights and small-pan'd windows.[130] God Save the
King! If one must dwell in a town, then surely there's no place
like Old Providence, round which all the memories of my youth
are cluster'd. Thank Heav'n I reside in a quiet byway[131] on the

---

128. Could these be surviving lines from the apparently non-extant poem "Moosup
Valley: An Eclogue," which HPL mentions in his 1926 Foster travelogue?

129. Pegasus is a north sky constellation first listed by Ptolemy in the second century C.E. Alpha, Beta, and Gamma of Pegasus plus the Andromedae form the
"great square."

130. Refer to *Cannon* for further discussion of this type of imagery in HPL's work.

131. Between 1926 and 1933 HPL resided at 10 Barnes Street. His aunt Lillian
Delora (Phillips) Clark (1856–1932) (widow of Franklin Chase Clark, M.D.) also
lived at this address. In 1933, HPL and his younger aunt Annie Emeline (Phillips)
Gamwell (1866–1941) combined households in a second-floor apartment at 66
College Street, just west of Brown University's John Hay Library, which today

crest of the hill; where all is as it used to be, and no sight or sound suggests anything that one might not find in a placid New-England village of 2000 or 3000 souls!

My next pilgrimage will cover the *earlier* Phillips region south of Howard Hill—on the *old* Plainfield Pike;[132] a section cut off from offensive traffick when the highway was relocated to banish a bend. Here I hope to find living and discursive a very distant cousin nam'd Frank Phillips,[133] who I am told can shew me where my great-great-great-grandfather James (Jun.—d. 1807) (Asaph's father) is bury'd—in the old God's-acre which may possibly harbour *his* father (d. 1746)[134] as well. This elder James's father Michael (1642–1686)[135] rests at antient Newport, whereof he was

---

houses HPL's papers.

132. See note 78.

133. Frank Darius(8) Phillips [Darius Olney(7) Matthew Colvin(6) Joseph(5) David(4) John(3) Richard(2) Michael(1)] was born 27 September 1872, the son of Darius Olney Phillips (1832–1916) and Malina Stone (Colvin) Phillips (1834–1896). He married Gertrude Elizabeth Howard (1872–1949), the daughter of Whipple Howard (1834–1910), on 1 November 1891. Frank Darius Phillips and his family made their home on the Old Plainfield Pike in Scituate, R.I., in the village of Potterville, centering on the intersection of the Old Plainfield Pike and Carpenter Road. Frank's usual occupation was streetcar motorman, but he was working as a foreman for the Providence Water Works when the 1935 Rhode Island census was enumerated (his census card is dated 3 January 1936). His wife Gertrude Elizabeth (Howard) Phillips and his son Alcott Howard Phillips were the other members of his household in 1935. Long-lived like his father Darius Olney Phillips, Frank Darius Phillips died on 5 April 1958. Through common descent from Michael(1) Phillips, HPL was a sixth cousin at one remove of Frank Darius Phillips. It is not known whether HPL ever had the opportunity to meet Frank Darius Phillips. *Scituate Map 1964* shows many old cemeteries in the vicinity of Potterville.

134. Pardon Tillinghast Howard (1839–1925) gave the ancestry of Asaph(5) Phillips as James(4) Jeremiah(3) Joseph(2) Michael(1). Joseph(2) Phillips died in 1719.

135. Michael(1) Phillips was already referred to as deceased in a letter written by Francis Brinley of Newport, R.I., to John Whipple of Providence dated 13 August 1676 (*Early Records of the Town of Providence*, 15.151). Family historian Dean Crawford Smith believes that Michael may have died shortly after he became a freeman of Newport on 28 October 1668, since all his children are believed to have been born between 1651 and 1667 (*Smith* 368). *Austin* 152 shows Michael Phillips's year of death as 1689 or earlier. See *Faig-2a* (xvii) for more discussion of the date of death of Michael(1) Phillips.

made a freeman in 1668; and I still hope to find his mortal remains amidst the populous slate acreage of the Farewell St. burying-ground.[136] Mike was a townsman—I'm asham'd of him!—for
Newport was a great and cultivated seaport in his day. His father
Rev. George[137] (prais'd in Cotton Mather's *Magnalia*) dy'd in 1644,
and is bury'd where he preach'd in Watertown, in ye Massachusetts Bay—a place I have never seen, but which I have all my life
been meaning to visit. On with the epitaph chase! . . . . tho' back
of Rev. George it will lead me far, since his father, Christopher
Phillips, Gent.[138]—and *all* the still earlier fathers—Tudor and
Plantagenet gentlemen of *Old England*—sleep on holier soil—
beneath the ivy'd and crumbling parish church of Rainham St.
Martin's in Norfolk. They never saw New-England—and with
lov'd, blest *Old England* stretching delectably about them they

---

136. The Newport Common Burial Ground is located on Farewell Street. Established in 1665, it contains over 7500 burials in its 500- by 500-foot area. No stone
or marker for Michael(1) Phillips (1630?–before 13 August 1676) is known to
survive.

137. Rev. George Phillips, originally of Rainham St. Martin's in Norfolk, died in
Watertown, Mass., in 1644. There does not seem to be any support for HPL's
assertion that his ancestor Michael(1) Phillips (1630?–before 13 August 1676) of
Newport was a son of Rev. George Phillips. Albert M. Phillips's 1885 Phillips
family genealogy (*Phillips*) devotes many of its pages to the descendants of Rev.
George Phillips; perhaps HPL decided that he wanted claim this illustrious cleric
as an ancestor.

138. Christopher Phillips was buried 3 February 1620/21 in Rainham St. Martins,
near Rougham in the hundred of Gallow in Norfolk, England. *Savage* (3.409–10)
makes the assertion that Christopher was the father of Rev. George Phillips
(1593–1644), whom he states to have been born in the same parish in which his
father died. Few facts concerning Christopher Phillips other then his burial
place and date of burial seem to be undisputed. The Internet site
www.geni.com/people/Christopher-Phillips/6000000003430021127, managed by
Cindy Enzenauer, last updated 12 November 2012, viewed 23 February 2013, asserts
that Christopher Phillips was a carpenter, born 17 June 1565 in Stokeinteignhead,
Devon, the son of John Phillips and Johann Watters. The site further asserts that
Christopher Phillips married Agnes Abram, daughter of Thomas Abram and Rachel Foote, on 26 October 1587 at Saint Peter Great, Chichester, Sussex, England.
Another Internet site asserts that Christopher Phillips was born c. 1570 in Rainham
St. Martins, Norfolk, and married Elizabeth Lightfoot. This site makes him the son
of William Phillips (born c. 1550 London) and Johane (Houghton) Phillips.

never needed to! The main line—by primogeniture—of these Norfolk Phillipses now sports a baronetcy, as I found during my Talman-born[139] researches of 1927; the present baronet being Sir Lionel Phillips of Boxford,[140] unless he was kill'd in the war or somehow return'd to dust since the publication of the book I found him in. And so it goes! Now back to cursed revision—but with hopes of another and more early-Georgian ramble thro' Foster's pastoral meads before the chill of winter sets in. It's a great sport, really. Had you been wise, you wou'd have made your recent Connecticut stopping place New-Haven instead of some colourless beach—for 'tis there I believe you can find the Doty and Mansfield epitaphs[141] which you really need in order to establish a perfectly harmonious terrestrial orientation!

Well—be a good young man! Here are some cuttings and oddments which may amuse you. Please return Moe's transcript of the Sirenica[142] extract. Isn't that prose a thing to marvel at and revere?

Yr obt. GRANDPA

---

139. HPL refers to his friend Wilfred B. Talman, an avid genealogist.

140. Sir Lionel Phillips (1855–1936), created 1st Baronet in 1912, spent most of his life in the mining business in South Africa. He was succeeded in baronetcy by his grandson Sir Lionel Francis Phillips, 2nd Baronet. It seems likely that these Phillipses are very distant relatives of HPL, if they are related at all.

141. The parents of Frank Belknap Long, Jr. (1901–1994), were Frank Belknap Long (b. 18 October 1870, New York, d. 28 February 1940, New York) [the son of Charles C. Long (1845?–1904) and Julia A. Long (1845?–1914)] and May Mansfield Doty (b. 13 October 1870, New York, d. 22 September 1951, New York) [the daughter of Charles Edmund Doty and Emma Augusta Mansfield]. Long's maternal grandparents were both born in 1846 and married in New Haven on 15 September 1869. Long's father was a New York City dentist; he and his wife frequently entertained the members of the Kalem Club in their home. "Doc" Long's Essex automobile enabled his son to stop to visit HPL on several family vacation trips to Cape Cod and other New England tourist destinations. The Longs sometimes took HPL along for part of their journeys.

142. HPL probably refers to Sirenica (John Lane, 1913) by W. Compton Leith [pseudonym of Ormonde Maddick Dalton (1866-1945)]. Mark Valentine and Douglas Anderson have some useful information on this work and its author on the Wormwoodiana website (wormwoodiana.blogspot.com/2010/12/w-compton-leith.html). Perhaps Maurice W. Moe had made a transcription of parts of this work, available today in its entirety for reading on Google Books.

Works Cited

Austin. John Osborne Austin. *The Genealogical Dictionary of Rhode Island.* Albany, NY: Joel Munsell's Sons, 1887. Rpt. Baltimore: Genealogical Publishing Co., 1969f.

Bayles. Richard M. Bayles et al. "The Town of Foster." In *History of Providence County, Rhode Island.* New York: W. W. Preston & Co., 1891. 2.626–39.

Bucknum. Shirley E. Bucknum. *The Place Family Research Aid.* Portland OR: Published by the author, [n.d.].

Cannon. Peter H. Cannon. *"Sunset Terrace Imagery in Lovecraft" and Other Essays.* West Warwick, RI: Necronomicon Press, 1990.

Casey. Gen. Thomas Lincoln [T. L.] Casey. "Early Families of Casey in Rhode Island." *Magazine of New England History* 3:2 (April 1893).

Colwell. Heidi Colwell et al. *Foster, 1781–1981: A Bicentennial Celebration.* Foster, RI: Foster Bicentennial Committee, 1981.

Connors. Scott Connors, ed. *A Century Less A Dream: Selected Criticism on H. P. Lovecraft.* Holicong, PA: Wildside Press, 2002.

Cooley. John C. Cooley. *Rathbone Family.* Syracuse, NY: Published for the Author, 1898. A photocopy reprint of this work was published by the New England Historic Genealogical Society in 1992.

Downing. Antoinette F. Downing et al. *Foster, Rhode Island: Statewide Historical Preservation Report P-F-1.* Providence, RI: Rhode Island Historical Preservation Commission, 1982. Sometimes referred to as "the green book" because of the color of its front cover.

Eddleman and Sterling. Dr. Bill Eddleman and John E. Sterling. *Coventry Rhode Island: Historical Cemeteries.* Baltimore: Gateway Press, 1998.

Faig-1. Kenneth W. Faig, Jr., ed. *Early Historical Accounts of Foster, Rhode Island.* Glenview, IL: Moshassuck Press, 1993. Contains "Sketches of Foster" by Charles C. Beaman (1799–1883) and "Historical Reminiscences of Foster" by Casey B. Tyler (1819–1899). Sometimes referred to as "the yellow book" because of the color of its covers.

Faig-2. Kenneth W. Faig, Jr. *Some of the Descendants of Asaph Phillips and Esther Whipple of Foster, Rhode Island.* Glenview, IL: Moshassuck Press, 1993.

Faig-2a. Kenneth W. Faig, Jr. *Corrections and Additions for Some of the Descendants of Asaph Phillips and Esther Whipple of Foster, Rhode Island.* Glenview, IL: Moshassuck Press, 1994.

Folsom-1. John R. Folsom, Jr. *Place Families of Southwest Oswego, N.Y., Volume I: The Descendants of Samuel, Hazard and Dr. Simeon G. Place.* Orlando, FL: John R. and Charlotte W. Folsom, 1994.

Folsom-2. John R. Folsom, Jr. *Place Families of Southwest Oswego, N.Y., Volume II [Draft]: Other Descendants of Enoch Place of Kings Town, R.I. and Unconnected Families.* Orlando, FL: John R. Folsom, Jr., 1995.

Foster Map 1799. Isaac Davenport (with corrections and additions by Theodore Foster). *Plan of the Town of Foster, June 20, 1799.* Redrawn by Sandra J. Campbell. Foster, RI: Foster Preservation Society, 1974.

Foster Map 1862. Henry F. Walling. *Portion of Henry F. Walling Map: Providence, R.I., 1862.* Foster portion reprinted by Foster Preservation Society (Foster, RI, 1974).

Foster Map 1870. D. G. Beers and Company. *Foster, Providence Co., R.I.* Philadelphia, 1870. Reprinted by Foster Preservation Society (Foster, RI, 1974).

Foster Map 1895. Everts & Richards. *Town of Foster.* Philadelphia, 1895. Reprinted by Foster Preservation Society (Foster, RI, 1974).

Foster Map 1971. George E. Matteson. *Foster Rhode Island Directory Map.* Coventry, RI: Matteson Map Service, 1971.

Grass. Walter W. Grass. *This Finnish Episode: Recalling the Finns in Foster, Rhode Island and Its Surrounding Areas.* Foster, RI: Parable Studio, 2005. Distributed by Foster Preservation Society.

Holman. Susan Tyler Holman. *The Family of James Tyler, Descendants of John Tyler of Portsmouth, Rhode Island.* Farmington, CT: Published by the Author, 1997.

Howard. Daniel Howard. *A History of Isaac Howard of Foster, Rhode Island and His Descendants Who Have Borne the Name of Howard.* Windsor Locks, CT: Published by the Author, 1901.

Isham and Brown. Norman M. Isham and Albert F. Brown. *Early Rhode Island Houses.* Providence, RI: Preston & Rounds, 1895.

Jones. Daniel P. Jones. *The Economic and Social Transformation of Rural Rhode Island, 1770–1850.* Boston: Northeastern University Press, 1992.

Jordy. William H. Jordy. *Buildings of Rhode Island.* New York: Oxford University Press, 2004.

Joshi-1. S. T. Joshi. *I Am Providence: The Life and Times of H. P. Lovecraft.* New York: Hippocampus Press, 2010.

Joshi-2. S. T. Joshi. *Lovecraft's Library: A Catalogue.* 3rd ed. New York: Hippocampus Press, 2012.

Matthews-1. Margery I. Matthews. *By My Kin: Stories of Foster.* Foster, RI: Foster Preservation Society, 1991.

Matthews-2. Margery I. Matthews. *Chronicles of Foster.* Foster, RI: Foster Preservation Society, 1995.

Matthews-3. Margery I. Matthews, Virginia I. Benson, and Arthur E. Wilson. *Churches of Foster: A History of Religious Life in Rural Rhode Island.* Foster, RI: North Foster Baptist Church, 1978.

Matthews-4. Margery I. Matthews. *Foster and the Patriots' Dream.* Foster, RI: Foster Preservation Society, 1976.

Matthews-5. Margery I. Matthews. *Peleg's Last Word: The Story of The Foster Woolen Manufactory.* Foster, RI: Foster Preservation Society, 1987.

Matthews-6. Margery I. Matthews. *So I've Been Told: Stories of Foster.* Foster, RI: Foster Preservation Society, 1985.

Miller. William Davis Miller. *The Silversmiths of Little Rest.* 1928. Concord, MA: Joslin Hall Publishing, 1992.

Phillips. Albert M. Phillips. *Phillips Genealogies: Including the Family of George Phillips.* Auburn, MA: Privately published, 1885.

Pierce. Frederick Clifton Pierce. *Foster Genealogy.* Chicago: Published by the Author, 1899.

Savage. James Savage. *A Genealogical Dictionary of the First Settlers of New England.* 1860–62. Baltimore: Genealogical Publishing Co., 1986.

Scituate Map 1964. George E. Matteson. *Scituate, Rhode Island Directory Map.* Hope, RI: Matteson Map Service, 1964.

Sherman. Ruth Wilder Sherman, F.A.S.G. "Descendants of John Tyler of Portsmouth, RI." *American Genealogist* 52 (1976): 220–25.

Smith. Dean Crawford Smith. *The Ancestry of Emily Jane Angell, 1844–1910.* Boston: New England Historic Genealogical Society [NEHGS], 1992.

Sowa. Iona Ingram Sowa. *The Phillips and Associated Families of Early New England, 1630–1810.* Santa Clara, CA: Published by the Author, 1988. A successor volume was published, but not seen by the editor.

Wolf-1. Raymond A. Wolf. *Foster*. Charleston, SC: Arcadia Publishing. 2012.

Wolf-2. Raymond A. Wolf. *The Lost Villages of Scituate*. Charleston, SC: Arcadia Publishing, 2009.

Wolf-3. Raymond A. Wolf. *The Scituate Reservoir*. Charleston, SC: Arcadia Publishing, 2010.

Wood. Squire G. Wood. *A History of Greene and Vicinity*. Providence, RI: Privately published, 1936.

Briefly Noted

Moshassuck Press, operated by Kenneth W. Faig, Jr., continues its micro-publications of fascinating pamphlets relating to Lovecraft. Among the most recent items is Jason C. Eckhardt and Kenneth W. Faig, Jr., *The Site of Joseph Curwen's Home in H. P. Lovecraft's The Case of Charles Dexter Ward* (2013), a 57-page booklet that discusses the recent discovery by Donovan K. Loucks of the house at 6 Olney Street in Providence that served as the basis for the Joseph Curwen house in Lovecraft's 1927 novel. To order, send payment in send payment ($10 U.S., $15 elsewhere) in U.S. funds to Kenneth W. Faig, Jr., 2311 Swainwood Drive, Glenview, IL 60025-2741.

David Haden, one of the contributors to this issue of the *Lovecraft Annual*, has been doing substantial work on tracing the more obscure and neglected corners of Lovecraft's life and work. Haden has now published the fourth volume of his series *Lovecraft in Historical Context* (2013), containing thirty-five essays on a wide range of topics. Further information can be found at: http://tentaclii.wordpress.com/2013/07/01/new-book-lovecraft-in-historical-context-fourth-collection-available-now/. Some of Haden's previous volumes are also available as e-books.

Reappraising "The Haunter of the Dark"

John D. Haefele

I find it surprising that H. P. Lovecraft would write, "In actual truth, I think ['The Thing on the Doorstep'] has a sort of middle rating. It is better than my 'Haunter of the Dark'" (*Lovecraft at Last* 173); or that noted Lovecraft scholar S. T. Joshi would assess "The Haunter of the Dark" (perhaps in deference to Lovecraft's opinion) as "fair to middling Lovecraft" (*Rise and Fall* 115–17). I personally had rated "Haunter" much closer to top-notch in the canon, unquestionably superior to "The Thing on the Doorstep"; so I decided to give the story a fresh and impromptu reading. The result is not only my old opinion confirmed, but so vastly improved that I find conventional wisdom regarding the story suspect. Perhaps the most widely circulated and generally accepted "fact" regarding "The Haunter of the Dark" is how—because Lovecraft dedicated the tale to fellow writer Robert Bloch, and even named the protagonist Robert *Blake*—it is a direct sequel to Bloch's "The Shambler from the Stars." It is well known that Lovecraft gave Bloch permission to portray in this story a character whom readers might identify as Lovecraft. And if missed, untold numbers were subsequently clued in reading the oft-reprinted *Tales of the Cthulhu Mythos* (1969), where August Derleth spotlights a coup: "One other Lovecraft tale has been included; that is 'The Haunter of the Dark', which was written in reply to Robert Bloch's pastiche on Lovecraft, 'The Shambler from the Stars', and publication of which was followed by Bloch's 'The Shadow from the Steeple'; these three connected tales appear here for the first time together in chronological order" (xii).[1] But I contend we would have had some form of Lovecraft's "The

---

1. The other story by Lovecraft in this popular collection is "The Call of Cthulhu."

Haunter of the Dark" whether or not Bloch ever wrote "Shambler."

Perhaps "Shambler" was topmost in Lovecraft's mind (following publication in *Weird Tales*) when putting "Haunter" to paper in late 1935 (Joshi and Schultz, *Encyclopedia* 105), but he admits in correspondence that the real catalysts were successful "agenting activities" going on "behind Grandpa's back" that culminated with the nearly simultaneous acceptances of *At the Mountains of Madness* and "The Shadow out of Time" (*Mysteries of Time and Spirit* 365): "as I've said, such temporary incidents surely are encouraging while they are fresh. On the strength of this one I've just finished a new tale—'The Haunter of the Dark'" (368). Lovecraft received a desperately needed payment for "Shadow" (in the mail, unexpectedly) on 3 November, which prompted him to write "Haunter" between 5 and 9 November. Will Murray confirms, "'The Haunter of the Dark' was as much inspired by the dual acceptance as it was by Robert Bloch's short story 'The Shambler from the Stars,' based upon Lovecraft's explicit remark, 'This dual stroke gave me such a psychological boost that I've written a new tale—a short specimen called "The Haunter of the Dark"'" (127). To be sure, another major story accepted, $280 up front—these are why we have "The Haunter of the Dark" to read today. Moreover, if the *impetus* was to produce a sequel, one would think back to April when Lovecraft first read the manuscript and allowed a character based on him, or to August after seeing it published in the September issue of *Weird Tales*. Rather, Lovecraft reveals the story's true *inspiration* in correspondence, his own personal experiences with lightning flashes and power losses during thunderstorms: "I've met that trouble in the past. Indeed, a case of it last year gave me the main idea for my tale 'The Haunter of the Dark'" (*Lovecraft at Last* 114). Lovecraft wrote this on 24 October 1936, which means "last year" could refer to any time in 1935. What this all suggests is a likelihood that any connection to Bloch was opportunistic, Lovecraft's apparent and appropriate reaction after a reader of "Shambler" proposed in a public forum he should return Bloch's literary "compliment."[2] Lovecraft must have thought this

---

2. This suggestion appeared in the November issue of *Weird Tales*, in "The Eyrie" letter column.

an excellent idea (and worked it into his treatment of "The Haunter of the Dark"), but he fails to mention this to Bloch until forwarding in December the completed (but never submitted) story, even then revealing nothing of the story's genesis. But there is also nothing to indicate that the theme or plot had not already (if only in his head) been a long time fermenting:

> Glad you found redeeming features in the tale—which I couldn't appraise very clearly myself. Hope other readers will be equally lenient toward it. If you ever want to write a sequel to it, I'll lend you one of the carbons again. Quite a number of the allusions could be used as a starting point for fresh horrors! (*Letters to Robert Bloch* 75)

Whether or not this happened should not diminish Lovecraft's genuine and sincere gesture in dedicating the story and developing its protagonist "Blake" to manifest Bloch's "counterpart" (82). And yet, it is only the second paragraph of "Haunter" (which if excised would not change the plot) plus throw-ins (for example, recording among Blake's frenzied jottings Bloch's actual Milwaukee address) that make the "Haunter" narrative *appear* a sequel. To the contrary, internal *negative* evidence argues against this idea, the expected connections between "Haunter" and "Shambler" that do *not* exist: Lovecraft failing to portray Blake so much as fleetingly contemplating (much less comparing) the situation in this tale against the Mythos-linked horror previously experienced in "Shambler"; Lovecraft failing to explain Blake's comprehensive knowledge of Mythos books and lore in light of previously unsuccessful attempts at achieving this in Milwaukee (recall how after much wasted effort and only by sheer chance he acquired the *De Vermis Mysteriis*). We should expect *shock* where the Bloch character now discovers the entire *library* of forbidden books; instead, we are forced to accept Blake as already well-read in many of them, including the *Necronomicon*, so that in the short interim Blake has become (shades of a Derleth-styled protagonist) well-versed in "evil older than mankind and wider than the known universe" (*DH* 100).

I submit that more attention should be paid to *general* remarks that Lovecraft made about "The Haunter of the Dark," including:

"My great aim [with "Haunter"] is to break away from all cheap and conventional patterns and really express certain shadings of human mood as Blackwood and Poe and other sincere writers have done" (*SL* 5.217), and to the important themes in the story, for which Peter Cannon provides this example: "In this final self-portrait of the artist, Lovecraft adopts his most poignant pose, lost in dream in the sunset glow of the old town he loved so well" (*H. P. Lovecraft* 122). Certainly it can be surmised that Lovecraft's own opinion of "Haunter" hinged on more than its tribute aspects, which perhaps mitigates his hesitation to submit it for publication until August in the following year (81). My own reading confirms that "The Haunter of the Dark" is too carefully plotted and planned to be the result of a "whim" (*Encyclopedia* 106). The detail Lovecraft does introduce stokes several of my own theories about Lovecraft's Mythos development. In the proverbial nutshell, I propose that all Lovecraft's settings (including the dream-world) are facets of what would today be labeled the Multiverse, which could help reconcile what might otherwise seem conflicting differences between stories; that Lovecraft alternated emphasis in later stories between "interstellar" and "interdimensional" themes (though both are to some degree always present); finally, that Lovecraft often embedded sub-narratives that subvert surface plot elements and reinterpret first impressions. "The Haunter of the Dark" embodies all these elements, but especially the first; and significantly so, because it is Lovecraft's last original tale.

Bloch's first allusion to Lovecraft in "Shambler" is to a "mystic dreamer in New England" (171). Almost immediately he narrows the locale to Providence, which he names only once in the story and which helps readers make the desired association; but later he reveals the mystic dreamer grew up in "witch-haunted Arkham" (172). With either to choose from, this begs the question of why Lovecraft made Providence the initial setting of "Haunter," when Arkham with its storied history might seem the better choice. He did so because for him the multi-world theme would tie more closely to real-world Providence, where in real life he used his imagination wistfully dreaming into existence "cosmic gates of the sunset as glimpsed beyond the familiar spires & roofs & elm-boughs of the old Rhode Island country" (*ES* 288–89). The idea that there might be other realities existing beside our own, which under the right circumstances overlap or impinge our own, fascinated him because it brings forth the conditions under which imaginative experiences become real: "If one is to step off into space, one must have a starting point" (289). This is *the* theme of "Haunter," a "spectral, unreachable world beyond the curling smoke" that is Federal Hill,

> bristling with huddled roofs and steeples whose remote outlines wavered mysteriously, taking fantastic forms as the smoke of the city swirled up and enmeshed them. Blake had a curious sense that he was looking upon some unknown, ethereal world which might or might not vanish in dream if ever he tried to seek it out and enter it in person. (*DH* 94)

Lovecraft adumbrates differences between what Blake sees and *our* world; for example, "The distant church ... is a less ancient & less sinister object in real life than in the story" (*SL* 5.220). But both are in Providence, and so far these are only small differences—Robert Blake's name compared to Bloch's reinforces their small degree. But due west of Blake's version of venerable College Hill, the cosmic gates (which symbolize the other end of the rainbow) over Federal Hill have opened. Lovecraft communicates this distinction, describing a transformed "spire-crowned mound" rising from the heart of Providence's Italian quarter, so close that Blake can view it using binoculars, so that *he* uses the descriptive terms "alien," "unreal," and "intangible." The black steeple is "unique among Lovecraft's stories in that it is clearly visible to passers by, rather than lying in a remote or hidden location ... the dark church and the religion it symbolizes indicate an alternate world view that unsettles the traditional observer by its mere presence" (Martin 114–15). Indeed, Lovecraft's regular readers must recognize a landscape one notch "over," where there is Arkham, Innsmouth, and Dunwich, where the deceased mystic dreamer grew up. It is a world apart from even Blake's sleepy Providence, a landscape where the farther *in* you go, the *less* trivial (from even his Providence) the differences become. Blake has entered a confusion of worlds, where his short story "Shaggai" could be one Robert Bloch might write in *our* world (*DH* 94), but where Shaggai is also the frightening name in the family of black planets (114).

The Haunter-thing itself is what in this story holds open (once opened) the gate between different realities—its will, still feeble, crosses the unobstructed space between steeple and window and inspires even the art of the unknowing Blake, which has been growing increasingly "alien, half fabulous, and linked to the unreal, intangible marvels" (*DH* 95). Between them is unique chemistry that sets events into motion. "The rapport Blake has with worlds beyond the visible one, combined with hints of the past experiences that drove him to Providence, suggest that he is more sensitive than others to influence from the unknown" (Dziemianowicz 193); but it takes both: "In all this there is the suggestion that . . . some alien consciousness is acting upon Blake to sap his free will" (Joshi, *Decline of the West* 108). When Blake resolves—or is commanded—to visit the church, "nowhere could he find any of the objects he had seen from afar" (*DH* 96). The gates between worlds are not wide open—"twice he lost his way" even after spying the church before finally crossing over.

Federal Hill in Blake's Providence is one of Lovecraft's points of departure (every Mythos tale has one), a place on the globe where different worlds in the Multiverse touch. Trope after trope in "Haunter" lines up consistently with other Mythos assumptions gleaned from previous analyses. The great church itself is "Cyclopean" (*DH* 99), which in Lovecraft's major Mythos tales is always a descriptive denoting Mythos architecture; here again we find the record of a "witch-cult" survival, with ties to legendry but suggesting unknown science; here again deleterious powers wax during times we (because of conditioning) prosaically associate with evil (e.g., "aeon-shadowed Walpurgis time" [*DH* 96]); again, in the past, blood sacrifices were made, this time by members of the Starry Wisdom sect (*DH* 103). And there are references to secret systems of magic (e.g., the Aklo cryptogram [*DH* 106]), and (possibly parodic) allusions to conventional religions—cult members were shown visions of *heaven* and other worlds, and it is alleged that the Haunter cannot exist where there is *light* (*DH* 103; my italics). It is easy to miss in Blake's heightened state a hint as to the nature of forces at work: "And beyond all else he glimpsed an infinite gulf of darkness, where solid and semi-solid forms were known only by their windy stirrings, and cloudy patterns of force seemed to *superimpose order on chaos* and hold forth a key to all the paradoxes and arcana of the worlds we know" (*DH* 104; my italics). Mixed with these supernatural trappings are the concepts of science fiction, grounded in Lovecraft's notion of the Shining Trapezohedron.[3] "The Old Ones brought it to earth ... It was treasured by the crinoid things of Antarctica ... salvaged from their ruins by the serpent-men of Valusia (*DH* 106).[4] Donald R. Burleson calls out Lovecraft's sophisticated use of "geometric abnormality," which plays havoc with tri-dimensional space (*H. P. Lovecraft: A Critical Study* 206). Much of this subtly conveys an important understanding, that a being called "out of the air" might only *seem* to be a supernatural event.

But if by chance something about Federal Hill did manifest an adjoining *dimensional* reality, the Shining Trapezohedron is designed to open doors between worlds separated in *space*. Palantíri-like, the Trapezohedron reveals the "black worlds" to Blake and thereby attracts the Haunter's will (*DH* 102).[5] Ultimately, across vast distances in space, it draws the "monstrous and utterly alien" entity into the steeple. The Haunter enters our world *without* blood sacrifice—which confirms that the Thing is *not* Nyarlathotep, despite Starry Wisdom's presumably Egyptian origin (and keeping in mind that the Trapezohedron's history just on earth wends back much farther).

Lovecraft describes (in correspondence) what the Haunter was doing to Blake (*SL* 5.413–15): "The night-monster has secured a hold upon Blake's brain, partly penetrating it & almost effecting an

---

3. This multifaceted polyhedron and especially the encircling "colossal images," which to Blake resembled "more than anything else the cryptic carven megaliths of mysterious Easter Island" (*DH* 102), may be Lovecraft's tip of the hat to Donald Wandrei's *Dead Titans, Waken!*

4. With this, Lovecraft seems to be intimating that the [Great] Old Ones and the star-headed Antarctic race of his mythology are *not* one and the same, which would go against most interpretations of *At the Mountains of Madness*.

5. Looking for a trace of Lovecraft in J. R. R. Tolkien's "seeing stones" is not as far-fetched as it seems; at least there is this interesting apparent coincidence: Victor Gollancz published *The Haunter of the Dark and Other Tales of Horror* in London in 1951, and Tolkien made his final revisions in 1953.

exchange of personalities. . . . With a clear head something might have been done—but the Thing had already seized his brain." Blake's inability to act was thus *"specific hypnosis from outside"* (414). This hypnotic fog is to blame for much of the mystery: Blake fails to realize how he is himself the agent responsible for blocking the windows, for ridding the tower room of the telltale body. When during one episode he partially (though not fully) awakes, bizarre visions prove the Thing to be still inside his head (*DH* 110). Only slowly will Blake begin to comprehend. He remains perplexed that he can "see" the real hill and church in the pitch darkness, until it dawns on him: "I can see everything with a monstrous sense that is not sight" (*DH* 115). In the end he scribbles, "I see things I never knew before," and "Dark . . . The lightning seems dark and the darkness seems light," a telltale sign of his personality inside the monster experiencing "cognition that was not physical sight." This leads to a familiar denouement that fans of Lovecraft criticism know well: as the Thing sweeps toward Blake, a fortuitous lightning strike destroys both simultaneously— the last thing recorded ("three-lobed burning eye") is a glimpse of the Haunter. Blake's allusion to "Roderick Usher" made seconds earlier—Burleson and Joshi concur—is about the "abnormally linked trinity of entities" in Poe's "The Fall of the House of Usher" who share "one common dissolution at the same moment" (e.g., *Encyclopedia* 106). Joshi sums it up: "the entity in the church . . . described as an avatar of Nyarlathotep . . . possessed Blake's mind . . . is struck by lightning and killed, and Blake dies as well."

But the Haunter is not *the* Old One, despite what Blake was reminded of, nor even an "avatar of Nyarlathotep" (*DH* 114). As noted, Starry Wisdom–styled blood sacrifices were unnecessary to raise it, yet blood is necessary in every other Lovecraft Mythos story in which beings from higher dimensions manifest themselves on earth, whether it be Curwen's "return" in *The Case of Charles Dexter Ward* or the spawn of Yog-Sothoth (Wilbur and his twin) in "The Dunwich Horror." Nor is this the exception that will prove the rule; rather, the few details in Blake's final entries show the Haunter to be a member of one of Lovecraft's alien races. For example, there is Blake's "experience" of the Thing's "long, winging flight through the void" (*à la* Lovecraft's winged Antarctic civilization or fungi-like Outer Ones) across "horrible abysses of radiance" that fill the contiguous known universe (*DH* 115). Moreover, Blake "calls" out "Yaddith" and "sees" Yuggoth and Shaggai (making poignant the story's epigraph, "I have seen the dark universe . . . the black planets"). In "The Whisperer in Darkness," "Yuggoth is the youngest child, rolling alone in black aether at the rim" (*DH* 226), and that story's alien race's "immediate abode is a still undiscovered and almost lightless planet at the very edge of our solar system—beyond Neptune, and the ninth in distance from the sun. It is, as we have inferred, the object mystically hinted at as 'Yuggoth'" (*DH* 240). Yaddith turns up in "Through the Gates of the Silver Key," where we learn in our age it is "a dead world dominated by triumphant bholes" (*MM* 449). Lovecraft in correspondence attests (albeit indirectly) to the Haunter's mainly physical attributes (*à la* Antarctic star-headed crinoids or members of the Great Race): "the Thing could have come quite close [to Blake]—above the house, & out of the glow of the lighted windows" (*SL* 5.414).

But if not for the above evidence, there should still be the question of whether or not Nyarlathotep (as depicted in Lovecraft's other tales) could conceivably be subject to such repeated calling and banishing, afraid of flash or candle lights. Unfortunately, much of what contemporary readers know about Nyarlathotep—including the inference that the Great Old One appears as the Haunter—derives more from Bloch than from Lovecraft. The third story in the trilogy that began with "Shambler" is Bloch's "The Shadow from the Steeple," written fifteen or so years later. There, Nyarlathotep makes an unambiguous appearance in human form, but Bloch's purpose seems to be reconciling the two stories:[6]

> I believe that in the darkness you look *different*. More like the old shape. Because when the Haunter came to you, it did not kill but instead, *merged*. *You* are the Haunter of the Dark . . . ! There is no Doctor Dexter. There hasn't been any such person for many years, now. There's only the outer shell, possessed by an entity older than the world. (217)

---

6. But in the same story Bloch sows confusion, for here again is Lovecraft as a character; is he not then the Providence dreamer destroyed in "The Shambler from the Stars"? (Or was that a world over?)

Bloch's own use of the deity-entity conveys little of Lovecraft's trademark cosmicism, but among the experts it remains a given: "[Nyarlathotep] appears in the Lovecraft canon as the familiar spirit of the Shining Trapezohedron in 'The Haunter of the Dark,' in which role he is called an 'avatar of Nyarlathotep'" (Price 91). Lovecraft did early in their correspondence explain simply to Bloch, "*Nyarlathotep* is a horrible messenger of the evil gods to earth, who usually appears in human form" (11–12).[7] But Joshi deduces that Bloch "derived most of his information on Nyarlathotep from 'The Haunter of the Dark'" (*Rise and Fall* 147), after which he developed the concept in his own Mythos stories. These Lovecraft never read, but he felt confident enough to quip: "I feel sure you've done right by old Narthy" (*Letters to Robert Bloch* 70). As for Nyarlathotep in Lovecraft's own fiction and verse, in the prose-poem "Nyarlathotep" we learn that he "came out of Egypt" and "looked like a Pharaoh" (*MW* 32); in "The Rats in the Walls" he is a "mad faceless god" reputedly occupying "caverns of earth's centre" (*DH* 44); in "The Mound" we learn that he originally "came down [with Cthulhu] from the stars" (*HM* 102–3). In the dream world Nyarlathotep threatens: "Pray to all space that you may never meet me in my thousand other forms" (*MM* 403).[8] These statements stand in contrast to what we find in "Haunter," if indeed Nyarlathotep is there in any form (apart from the allusion). All the rest give rise to one reconcilable conception—and none conflict with a popular interpretation of the ending of "The Whisperer in Darkness" (where "the false Akeley is not merely one of the [sentient alien] fungi but is in fact Nyarlathotep himself" [Joshi and Schultz, *Encyclopedia* 298]).

Besides this ambiguity, we must also ask if Blake and the Haunter-thing were actually destroyed. A "momentary burned odour after the stroke" attests to this (*DH* 113), and of course there are the remains of Blake's body; but we also were given prior knowledge that the Thing "flees a little light, and [is] banished by strong light," until it is "summoned again" (*DH* 103). So is

---

7. Here Lovecraft clearly references gods that are *evil.*

8. Interestingly enough, in the dream landscape Nyarlathotep is "baffled" by a "glare that seared his formless hunting-horrors to grey dust" (MM 406).

it possible the Thing only *fled* the lightning, causing the "inexplicable *upward* rush of air which almost stripped the leaves from the trees" (*DH* 113; my italics)? Recall a similar (perhaps characteristic) "rush of air" produced as the Thing sped "meteor-like" from the church steeple, "a sudden east-blowing wind more violent than any previous blast snatched off the hats and wrenched the dripping umbrellas of the crowd." *And if the Haunter was merely banished—returned—is Blake really dead or was his mind simply taken along?* A clue to this might be, "Both *The Case of Charles Dexter Ward* and 'The Haunter of the Dark' were written in the third person, and are not claimed to be documents" (Joshi, *Four Decades* 61n8). It is only natural to wonder if Lovecraft might not have been reprising "Alienation" (sonnet XXXII of *Fungi from Yuggoth*):

> He had seen Yaddith, yet retained his mind,
> And come back safely from the Ghooric zone,
> When one still night across curved space was thrown (*AT* 93)

There are literal truths embedded in Blake's alleged ravings to decode, which will raise a penultimate question: *Was the Thing itself fleeing from something else?* Lovecraft's paragraphing of Blake's notes suggests point-of-view changes, but this creates a problem in the fourth paragraph where only Blake would be questioning "What am I afraid of?" and where "I remember Yuggoth" must be the Haunter (*DH* 114). But further down, where perspectives have definitely coalesced, we have: "I want to get out . . . must get out and unify the forces. . . . It knows where I am" (*DH* 115). This implies that Blake during his final seconds on earth with "senses transfigured" *is* the Thing, even as it breaks out of the steeple, even as he maintains "I am Robert Blake" (*DH* 115). It is *both* then who in the end (as "I") simultaneously express, "I see it—coming here . . . three-lobed burning eye."[9] This in turn calls

---

9. Here again any significance that the "burning eye" is "three-lobed" may be parodic (if not just far-fetched); for example, recalling Dante's three faces of Satan in the center of hell, or just the more common variant of the three-headed demon, or even the three-person God. It is a question to be studied in light of August Derleth's Mythos stories.

into question what is meant by that, for it could not then be a split-second description of the Haunter, but something Blake and the Haunter-thing are perceiving together, the advent of the "three-lobed burning eye"; the interspersed "hell-wind—titan blur—black wings" being their *combined* sense of the Haunter's involuntary *response* as it flees (or is again banished), drawing Blake along. Especially in light of the Poe analogy, we must ask if Blake and the Thing were not *both* calling upon Yog-Sothoth to save them *from* the lightning-burning eye. Or we might interpret the three-lobed burning eye as Yog-Sothoth appearing.[10]

Lovecraft as he so often does leaves things deliciously ambiguous. Was it just a fortuitous lightning strike that destroys Nyarlathotep or that sends a monstrous Thing back to its home world, or were the strange prayers answered? Here at last might be the best question to study: since the appeal "Yog-Sothoth save me" occurred at precisely the same instant watchers keeping vigil at the church "sent up their prayer" (*DH* 113), is what followed in any way providential? Without a doubt there is more than hitherto suspected going on in this tale. Patently the time has come to reappraise Lovecraft's "The Haunter of the Dark."

Works Cited

Bloch, Robert. "The Shadow from the Steeple." In *Tales of the Cthulhu Mythos*, ed. August Derleth. Sauk City, WI: Arkham House, 1969. 201–21.

———. "The Shambler from the Stars." In *Tales of the Cthulhu Mythos*, ed. August Derleth. Sauk City, WI: Arkham House, 1969. 170–78.

Burleson, Donald R. *H. P. Lovecraft: A Critical Study*. Westport, CT: Greenwood Press, 1983.

Cannon, Peter. *H. P. Lovecraft*. Boston: Twayne, 1989.

Derleth, August, ed. *Tales of the Cthulhu Mythos*. Sauk City, WI: Arkham House, 1969.

Dziemianowicz, Stefan. "Outsiders and Aliens: The Uses of Isolation in Lovecraft's Fiction." In *An Epicure in the Terrible: A*

---

10. It is significant that August Derleth describes Yog-Sothoth as "great globes of light" in *The Lurker at the Threshold*.

Centennial Anthology of Essays in Honor of H. P. Lovecraft, ed.
David E. Schultz and S. T. Joshi. Rev. ed. New York: Hippocampus Press, 2011. 165–95.

Foster, Robert. *The Complete Guide to Middle-Earth*. Rev. ed.
New York: Del Rey, 1978.

Joshi, S. T. *H. P. Lovecraft: The Decline of the West*. Mercer Island,
WA: Starmont House, 1990.

———. *The Rise and Fall of the Cthulhu Mythos*. Poplar Bluff,
MO: Mythos, 2008.

———. *The Weird Tale*. Austin: University of Texas Press, 1990.

Joshi, S. T., ed. *H. P. Lovecraft: Four Decades of Criticism*. Ed.
Joshi. Athens: Ohio University Press, 1980.

Joshi, S. T. and David E. Schultz. *An H. P. Lovecraft Encyclopedia*.
Westport, CT: Greenwood Press, 2001.

Lovecraft, H. P. *Letters to Robert Bloch*. Ed. David E. Schultz and
S. T. Joshi. West Warwick, RI: Necronomicon Press, 1993.

Lovecraft, H. P., and Willis Conover. *Lovecraft at Last*. Arlington,
VA: Carrollton-Clark, 1975.

Lovecraft, H. P., and August Derleth. *Essential Solitude: The Letters of H. P. Lovecraft and August Derleth*. New York: Hippocampus Press, 2008. 2 vols. [Abbreviated in the text as *ES*.]

Lovecraft, H. P., and Donald Wandrei. *Mysteries of Time and
Spirit: The Letters of H. P. Lovecraft and Donald Wandrei*. San
Francisco: Night Shade, 2002.

Martin, Sean Elliot. *H. P. Lovecraft and the Modernist Grotesque*.
Ph.D. diss.: Duquesne University, 2008. Privately published, 2011.

Murray, Will. "H. P. Lovecraft and the Pulp Magazine tradition."
In *An Epicure in the Terrible: A Centennial Anthology of Essays
in Honor of H. P. Lovecraft*, ed. David E. Schultz and S. T. Joshi.
Rev. ed. New York: Hippocampus Press, 2011. 101–35.

Price, Robert M. "Higher Criticism and the *Necronomicon*." In *Dis-
secting Cthulhu: Essays on the Cthulhu Mythos*, ed. S. T. Joshi.
Lakeland, FL: Miskatonic River Press, 2011. 88–99.

Price, Robert M., ed. *Tales of the Lovecraft Mythos* Minneapolis,
MN: Fedogan & Bremer, 1992.

Shreffler, Philip A. *The H. P. Lovecraft Companion*. Westport, CT:
Greenwood Press, 1977.

Department of Public Criticism

(July 1918)

H. P. Lovecraft

[In a letter to Anne Tillery Renshaw (24 August 1918), Lovecraft wrote: "Permit me to apologise for my harshness toward your favourite bard in the recent UNITED AMATEUR." The only passage on Browning that appears in contemporaneous issues of the *United Amateur* is one found in the "Department of Public Criticism," *United Amateur* 17, No. 6 (July 1918): 118–26 (see discussion of Renshaw's essay "Browning as an Asset" in the March *United Amateur*). This article had not previously been attributed to Lovecraft. Lovecraft (who was elected President of the United Amateur Press Association for the 1917–18 term) appointed Rheinhart Kleiner as Chairman of the Department of Public Criticism, but (as Lovecraft writes to Arthur Harris, 12 January 1918): "He [Kleiner] has done excellent work, but the recent failure of his sight forced him to abandon it for the present. Not finding any other critic available on short notice, I am doing the work myself again—though anonymously." The January, March, and May 1918 columns have been attributed to Lovecraft, but not the July column. In my judgment, based on internal evidence, the entire column is by Lovecraft.—*S. T. Joshi*.]

The Brooklynite for April eloquently testifies to the genius and ability of its newly elected editor, Mr. Rheinhart Kleiner, under whose efficient control the publication may well be expected to attain new heights of excellence. The leading article, which opens the issue, is an informal analysis of the defects of the motion picture by Stanley W. Todd, entitled "What's the Matter with the Movies?" In this somewhat thoughtful essay, Mr. Todd delves far

beneath the surface, showing a greater familiarity with the motion
picture field than is possessed by the average layman.

"To Our Brothers 'Over There'", by A. M. Adams, is a smooth
and timely piece of verse composed on the anniversary of America's entrance into the war. The sentiment is distinguished by
equal nobility and felicity, and the whole reflects very favourably
upon Mr. Adams' poetical powers.

"Blue Pencil Shavings" is the title of Mr. Kleiner's urbane and
well-informed editorial column, in which the affairs of Brooklyn
amateurdom are discussed in pleasing and ofttimes scholarly fashion. The Blue Pencil Club is fortunate in having so delightful a
chronicler and commentator.

"What's de Use?", by Alice Lovett Lewis, is a particularly at-
tractive bit of negro dialect verse, albeit what one of our critical
staff would dub a "recipe poem"; that is, a poem composed along
certain set lines, with certain standard types of expression and imagery. The recipe is in this case "optimism", and we may say truthfully that the author has blended the ingredients with rare skill
and taste.

"I Tell My Love", by Rheinhart Kleiner, is another "recipe"
poem, characteristic of the "sentimental conceit" school. Despite
his modernism of technique, as evidenced by his eschewing of
classical ornamentation, Mr. Kleiner is at heart a disciple of Waller
and the amatory bards of the early and middle seventeenth century; weaving most of his exquisite creations about the traditional
smiles, sighs, and sobs of the lover, which may or may not have
their counterpart in real life. Obviously, this limitation of field
prevents Mr. Kleiner from achieving the heights of original expression. The present poem, for instance, is an elaboration of the
idea of literary consolation which has taken various forms and aspects with various authors, among them Mr. Waller, who wrote:

> "Yet what he sung in his immortal strain,
> Though unsuccessful, was not sung in vain.
> All but the nymph that should redress his wrong,
> Attend his passion and approve his song;
> Like Phoebus thus, acquiring unsought praise,
> He caught at love, and fill'd his arms with bays."

Mr. Kleiner gives his lines a somewhat deeper emotional significance, as one might expect from a bard of his artistic seriousness, but the general classification of the poem is indisputable. We believe that an author of Mr. Kleiner's ability and technical perfection owes it to himself and his public to soar out of this commonplace region of Venus and Cupid with greater frequency; giving us further glimpses of the genuine Pierian genius which flashes forth in such occasional masterpieces as "America, I May Not Sing", in the March UNITED AMATEUR.

The Conservative for July marks the reappearance of Mr. Lovecraft's journal after a year's absence, and presents an astonishing amount of matter crowded into the small compass of eight century-size pages. Opening the issue is "Lord Kitchener", a truly beautiful sonnet by "Wilfrid Kemble"—a name, we may state in confidence, which veils one of Great Britain's most scholarly amateur poets, and litterateurs.

"Summer", by Editor Lovecraft, is a fanciful piece of verse, somewhat in the manner of Erasmus Darwin, containing a great deal of conventional imagery without achieving any particular height of expression. As a sample of the eighteenth-century style, it is accurate and natural, which is probably all its author intended it to be. But Mr. Lovecraft does not stop here, for on the next page occurs a prose justification of the old style of composition entitled "The Despised Pastoral", wherein he adduces evidence to show the need and desirableness of the ancient strains. The present critic agrees to a great extent with the contentions here exhibited, though it cannot be denied that the pastoral has largely lost its vogue.

"On Shore", by Winifred Virginia Jordan, is a characteristic bit of this author's more serious work. The sea picture is commendably vivid, and has a fidelity which proclaims it as the product of a genuine seacoast New-Englander.

In "Criticism of Amateur Journals", Prof. Philip B. McDonald presents rather a novel brief for the careless amateur author; a brief whose force cannot be denied in certain points, yet which on the whole fails to exculpate the scribbler who wilfully neglects the common forms of rhetoric. It is to be observed, that Prof.

McDonald himself never falls into the slovenliness which he so readily excuses in less gifted wielders of the quill! The article is answered at some length in the editorial column.

"Selenaio-Phantasma", by Alfred Galpin, Jr., is an exceedingly clever parody of Mr. Lovecraft's "Nemesis", which appeared in the June *Vagrant*. Mr. Galpin's grasp of the spirit of the original is surprising, and proves him beyond a doubt the possessor a singularly deep and acute intellect. In years still a boy, this young person has a style and command of thought which place him on an easy footing with the most cultivated of adults. His future career contains infinite promise.

"Time and Space", by H. P. Lovecraft, reveals the editor in his favourite pastime of interstellar speculation. While to many readers these attenuated abstractions may be of little interest, we believe that such absolute philosophy forms a field worth exploring as far as possible, if only as an antidote to the pragmatic nonsense current amongst so many superficial thinkers.

Seemingly in line with this philosophical mood is "Upon the Brink", a majestic and reflective poem in pentameter quatrains by Dr. Eugene B. Kuntz. The theme of the lines is a noble one, and its development is of equal nobility. Dr. Kuntz's employment of the heroic line is to be commended, for he here proves that his favourite Alexandrines and heptameters are not at all requisite to the production of exalted poetry.

"Merlinus Redivivus", by H. P. Lovecraft, comments upon the pitable revival of occult fallacies brought about by the stress of the war. As proof of the extent to which these shameful delusions have crept across the Atlantic, one needs only to glance at the advertising columns of the cheaper papers. Before the critic now lies the flamboyant advertisement of a California fraud, extolling the merits of a volume revealing all the secrets of Astrology, Spiritualism, Reincarnation, the After-Life, etc., etc., *ad nauseam*. We need a rough word or two to shake us out of the morbid states of mind which lay us open to the charlatanry of those who seek to profit by the hectic psychology of war-time.

"The Prodigal", by Sub-Lieut. Ernest Lionel McKeag, is a poem of much grace and genuine pathos, felicitously cast in anapaestic metre. This young bard is one whose progress is worth watching, for we believe he has the true Aonian spark. His technique is rapidly improving, and he may be expected to become one of amateurdom's leaders in a year or two.

The editorials in this issue of the *Conservative* are all of interest, especially those introducing poetical parodies. Mr. Ward Phillips treats us to a delicious anticlimax in his Kleinerian effort, whilst the anonymous "Consul Hasting" fairly staggers us with the vivid flashes of wit in his masterly burlesque of free verse. As a whole, we think the new *Conservative* a worthy successor to previous numbers, and a publication of which the United need not feel ashamed.

The Hazel Nut for May is a "Liberty Loan Issue", and is vibrant with patriotism of the active sort. Announcement is made that the paper "has enlisted with the government in the cause of America for the period of the war". While most of the contents proceed from the pens of Mr. and Mrs. A. M. Adams, the opening feature is a delightful poem by Rheinhart Kleiner, entitled "To Raymond Pratt Adams". Mr. Kleiner, addressing a newcomer to this world, is here at his best, providing an abundance of graceful sentiments, pleasing images, and felicitous expressions, in verse of impeccable metre and melody. Mr. Kleiner's faculty for verse is a rare one, and we rejoice whenever some non-amatory fragment from his muse appears to prove that versatility is also among his virtues.

The editorials and patriotic articles by the Adamses are all powerful and worthy of repeated perusal. He who would remain pro-German after reading these terse and cogent arguments, is indeed past reclamation mentally! We hope the bond-buying suggestions will be generally followed by the amateur fraternity, and are glad that the matter has been brought up so vigorously in an amateur paper. Future issues of *The Hazel Nut*, dwelling on other features of patriotic service, would be warmly welcomed by the United.

The Roamer for April introduces to the UNITED a somewhat novel thing, a publication devoted almost exclusively to the exposition of America's natural wonders as viewed in the course of travel. Mr. Louis H. Kerber, Jr., to whom we are indebted for this pleasing journal, is by profession a traveller and lecturer; which adds interest and authority to his utterances and descriptions. "Climbing Sperry Glacier", which forms the opening article, is the first of a series entitled "Little Journeys in America"; and from the sample here presented, we find ourselves anxious to peruse further instalments. Mr. Kerber's style is a pleasing and graphic one, albeit marred by occasional inaccuracies such as the false plural *"stratas"*. This word, of course, has *stratum* for its singular, and *strata* for its plural, the latter being formed in the Latin rather than in the English manner. We assume that such forms as *accessability* and *stratafied* for *accessibility* and *stratified*, are misprints. Mr. Kerber reveals in this article a very enviable fund of geological and physiographical knowledge.

"The Proposed Sand Dunes National Park", also by Mr. Kerber, describes a somewhat singular locality and calls attention to the desirability of perpetuating its unique features as a National Park.

"From the Roamer's Cabin" is the title of the editorial column, in which Mr. Kerber gives the reader some insight into his plans and amateur ideals. We wish that in the opening item he had not spelled *led* as *lead*. The spelling of the past and participle of this verb is not like that of the present, as in the case of such verbs as *read*. In the editorial "Americanism-Nationalism-Patriotism", Mr. Kerber is commendably patriotic, though like most writers on this side of the Atlantic, he fails to consider the incalculably enormous debt we owe to our Mother Country. It is for the next generation to recognise the glory of Anglo-Saxondom, and the paramountcy of the splendid British ideal in the civilisation of this and all countries which speak the Mother language and live under the liberal institutions evolved by the English mind.

The Silver Clarion for May sounds its notes with usual sweetness, beginning with a touching and meritorious poem by Jonathan E. Hoag, entitled "And We Saw Them March Away". Many times has our venerable bard 'seen them march away' during his life, and the lines gain sincerity from the true experience which lies behind them. The first stanza suffers through the almost inexcusable substitution of *violets* for *valley* in the first line.

The second part of "Tying Her Noose" reveals Mrs. S. S. Duffee as a pleasing though not profound writer of fiction. The tale is of considerable cleverness and ingenuity, coming under the general classification of "light summer literature".

"Bethel", by Julia C. B. Webb, is a Biblical poem of no small merit, revealing a style of great accuracy and power. Indentation of alternate lines would impart a more attractive appearance.

"The Banner of the Brave", by Arthur Goodenough, is a poem of that power which might be expected of its author, though bearing a somewhat annoying technical defect—the attempted rhyme of *rage* and *brave*. It should be remembered, that the final consonants of rhyming syllables must be absolutely identical. The g and v sounds can not possibly rhyme.

"Immortality", an essay by John Milton Samples, is a good illustration of orthodox theological argument. Mr. Samples' idea of the less desirable half of the future world is rather opposed to the theories of his fellow-amateur, Mr. James Larkin Pearson, but so far as the present critic knows, both may be equally correct.

"Nacido por Una Hora", by Joseph Thalheimer, Jr., brings to our notice a young poet of great promise, from whom much may be expected in the near future. Mr. Thalheimer, whilst technically a beginner, possesses the true poetic mind, and with practice and polish will develop into a bard of great power; as indeed, his more recent "Desert Dawn" proves. The prime defect of the present poem is lack of symmetry in the structure of the stanzas.

"The Silent Land", by Harry E. Rieseberg, is a very meritorious piece of poetry so for as the thought is concerned; in fact it is quite unusual. But lack of metrical accuracy nearly spoils the effect. Mr. Rieseburg should realise that his lines must contain an equal number of syllables.

"My Universe", by John Milton Samples, is an extremely smooth and well-phrased poem, whose construction is without a flaw. The sentiment is pretty, if less than Promethean in its reach.

The Column of "Comment" is this month conducted by Mrs. J. C. B. Webb, who renders her several dicta with graceful pen and charitable mind.

The March number of the UNITED AMATEUR is fully up to the usual standard, opening with Mr. Samuel Loveman's cycle of three quatrains, "Poppies", "The Forgotten Poets", and "Space". Mr.

Loveman's genius is a rare one, and has been fostered by a life of profound study and broad culture. In youth, this author was a devotee of the Elizabethans, and the effect of this apprenticeship will never leave him, even though he now works in more contemporary media. The idea in "Space" is a particularly striking one, and all the stanzas are marked by richly poetic conceptions.

In "The Battle of the Marne", Henry Clapham McGavack again exhibits his power as an essayist and historian. Few amateurs write with so perfect a command of facts, and so ample a background of information and erudition. Mr. McGavack is the antithesis of the average amateur essayist, for his themes are genuinely original, and embody solid research work, His opinions are to be accorded profound consideration, since they are not mere reflections of current thought, as is too often the case with the non-professional writer.

"America, I May Not Sing", is a poem which we will be dogmatic enough to call the best thing Rheinhart Kleiner ever wrote. In view of Mr. Kleiner's high reputation and ability, this seems an extreme statement to make, but we believe the merit of the piece will sustain the opinion. Devoid of sentimentality but replete with genuine patriotic feeling, this faultlessly constructed bit of verification stands out as the *lucida* of the Kleiner constellation. We wish our bard would more often seek similar sources of inspiration.

"Browning as an Asset", a brief essay by Anne Vyne Tillery (Renshaw), presents forcibly and gracefully the best arguments in favour of the celebrated and somewhat cryptical bard. Though the poetry lover may condemn Mr. Browning for his harshness, and the philosopher censure him for his pragmatism, none may deny that this unusual character was a thinker, and a remarkably faithful thinker. Whether or not he was mistaken in his acceptance of subjective phenomena as a basis for a creed, he was valiantly striving for the truth, and through all his obscurity and affectation shines the gleam of the genuine poet. Mrs. Renshaw is a Browning lover, and makes the most of these points. Her essay is a pattern of nobility and a model of style.

"A Gypsy Lullaby", by Litta L. Voelchert, presents images which entitle it to a high rating in the domain of lyric poetry. The trochaic metre is delightful and regular, though a scarcity of rhyme detracts a trifle from the general effect. Miss Voelchert should cultivate technique with unusual assiduousness. As an example of the wonderfully beneficial effect of technical attention on her verse we may cite the case of her lines on the Wandering Jew, written a decade ago, and invested with beauty of the most majestic sort when turned into heroic blank verse by Mr. Maurice Winter Moe.

Miss Mary H. Lehr's Triad of Verse contains some excellent specimens, though one of them loses charm through the employment of a modified form of free verse. It must, however, be remarked that Miss Lehr does not fall into the worst excesses of imagism. The normally versified poems of the triad are delightful in conception and execution.

Theodore Draper Gottlieb's lines "To John Keats" display a genius of no common order, and stamp their author as foremost of the poets who have lately become active in the Association. Mr. Gottlieb is untainted by the false notions of the present, and produces heroic couplets with all the grace, purity, and felicity of Pope and his contemporaries. The concluding couplet of the poem under consideration has haunted our memory ever since we read it first:

> "Youth's fresh, sweet, scented touch is on thy page;
>   Thou wert not born for thine, but ev'ry age!"

THE UNITED AMATEUR for May opens with one of the most delightful seasonal poems to appear in the amateur press this year, "'Tis Maytime in the Pine Tree State", by Winifred Virginia Jordan. The long, sweeping lines flow with all the freedom of a May sea-breeze, whilst the diction and images possess a corresponding felicity. Its choice for the May official organ is particularly apt. More of the vernal atmosphere is afforded by the brief sketch or study by Margaret Abraham, entitled "Spring Thoughts". Miss Abraham is one of our juvenile contingent, but in this bit of prose-poetry exhibits very encouraging signs of genius.

"Cloud Banks in the West", by Eugene B. Kuntz, is a poem of impressive power and elevation, teeming with word-pictures of the rarest skill. Dr. Kuntz has a place all his own amongst the very foremost and most original bards of the United. He is the least imitative poet, or one of the two least imitative poets, in amateurdom; being really the founder of a distinct school of verse. One might wish his lines shortened to pentameter in many cases, but the present poem wears its Alexandrine garb with perfect grace.

"My Fern Dish", by Mary Frances Robinson, is a sonnet of great merit and commendable originality of idea. It is a credential, though it has seen previous publication in the professional world.

"Natural Bridge, Kentucky", is a descriptive sketch or vignette by C. A. Shattuck, a new member. The general construction is quite smooth, and the conclusion is especially felicitous.

In "Greenwich Village", Mr. Victor Opper Schwab introduces himself to us as a friend of Washington-Square æstheticism—a friendship which we hope is more poetical than actual. The lines are bright and well constructed, but we protest violently at any attempt to "puff" the morbid denizens of Bohemia. "The clear, fervent truth of the Village" is a rather paradoxical line, since so far as we are able to judge, one finds the very antipodes of truth in the artificial excitement of *Quartier Latin* radicalism.

But after this excursion into New York folly, we are led back "Within a Quiet Town", by Miss Coralie Austin, who furnishes three stanzas of pleasant thought and musical flow.

"True Love", by Olive G. Owen, is a genuinely poetical lyric, though the present critic cannot help regretting the reliance our Literata seems to place on italics and dotted lines.

"English History and Social Customs at the Time of Jane Austen", by Anna H. Crofts, is an interesting and informative essay on the days of the Third and Fourth Georges. The period is well covered and aptly illustrated, though we cannot refrain from commenting on the lack of individual development. Miss Crofts offers an accurate transcript of facts, but fails to elaborate or interpret them with original observations. The best way to criticise this point is to contrast Miss Crofts' essay with one of the very opposite sort, such as Mr. McGavack's Marne article. Mr. McGavack, it will be noted, employs his facts as steps in an original argument to prove a point, which after all is the vital thing in essay-writing.

"A Song of Her", by John Milton Samples, is a commendable lyric clothed in a short and striking metre. The chief objection lies in the lack of fluency which characterises some of the lines. The bard should strive to select words whose accents and syllables ripple onward as gently as the current of his thoughts.

"The Little Lady", by Elizabeth Barnhart, is announced as a credential; and the announcement is needed when one considers the perfect finish and delightful quality of this child story. It might well pass as a professional effort, so perfect is the construction and so acute the character analysis. Miss Barnhart possesses narrative ability of the most marked sort; coupled with a sympathetic humour which adds life to her work. She may well be expected to duplicate the Laureateship record of her celebrated sister, who last year became the only fiction Literata in the United.

"Sunset", by Howard Phillips Lovecraft, is rather out of the ordinary channel of this writer's work; indeed, it is said to have been first published under a pseudonym. In the technique alone do we recognise the author's familiar touch. The allowable rhyme in the last stanza is rather out of accord with the spirit of the present—this being probably the reason it was perpetrated.

"The Grey North Sea", by Sub-Lieut. Ernest Lionel McKeag, is a splendid marine piece which we read and re-read with pleasure and appreciation. The long trochaic lines are absolutely fascinating, and stamp their author as one of the coming giants of amateur poetry.

"A Silent Tryst", by our honoured Laureate, Perrin Holmes Lowrey, affords a genuine treat to the lover of exquisite poetry. Atmosphere, colouring, imagery, melody, phraseology, are all above criticism, the whole blending into a delectable work of art.

No review of this splendid number of the official organ would be complete without reference to the Reading Table, whose annotations are compiled with infinite pains and skill by the Official Editor. This feature is of inestimable value to the Association, and will make bound volumes of this year's UNITED AMATEUR in great demand in the future.

The Vagrant for June is an achievement surpassing anything else of its kind within the memory of this generation of amateurs. Never since that bygone era which forms an object of reverence and reminiscence amongst the elders of this tribe, has an amateur magazine equalled in excellence and amplitude this latest product of Mr. W. Paul Cook. The case is one concerning which the critic feels at liberty to indulge in superlatives to his heart's content; confident that not even the most invidious of commentators can in any way dissent from his opinion, or accuse him of partiality. Magazines of 148 pages, with appropriate illustrations and tastefully designed covers, are, to put it mildly, somewhat uncommon occurrences in our circle of writers and publishers!

In an editorial note Mr. Cook deplores the difficulty of applying individual official criticism to the contents of volumes as bulky as those which he has recently issued; but we shall here endeavour to surmount this obstacle by following a rigidly selective principle, treating only those pieces whose authors are United members in active good standing. Even thus, the list will prove astonishingly long.

Andrew Francis Lockhart appears to advantage in his lines entitled "Give Me the Love of a Little Child". The theme is not new, but Mr. Lockhart's treatment of it is fresh and pleasing. "Where the Grape Vine Is Twinin' Still" goes far to sustain the frequently expressed parallel between his work and that of the late James Whitcomb Riley. Mr. Lockhart is inspired and felicitous in the field of homely dialect verse.

"Little Princess—Model" marks the return to amateurdom of Mrs. Flora Emory McGraw, one of the most gifted fiction writers the United has ever produced. In the present story a very smooth technique and cleverly realistic atmosphere serve to excuse, or atone for, a choice of subject and locale which may not entirely appeal to all readers. In this issue is also a poem by Mrs. Emory-McGraw, entitled "Life", which is capably conceived and gracefully phrased. The Association welcomes the reappearance of so prominent an author of the earlier days.

"Sonnets of a Bashful Man", by J. Clinton Pryor, are very clever amatory lines, though on account of their subject they can hardly lay claim to perfect originality of atmosphere. Whilst the versification is excellent, and the images well developed, we might well ask for an added urbanity or stateliness in choice of words and constructions. The following line, for example, is too frankly colloquial:

> "About us folks all shiver as they go."

However, Mr. Pryor's defects in this direction at least serve to stamp him as no servile copyist in his methods, and may after all constitute a bright prophecy for his future development in the poetic art.

"The Church and the World", by Maurice Winter Moe, is a typically pragmatical argument against the more superficial anti-religious theories of the Utopian agnostic. Practically speaking, much sound sense is here displayed; for as a matter of fact only the most idealistic and asinine of dreamers can for a moment think of mankind in the mass as governable by pure reason. Human nature is absolutely stationary, and we must base all working philosophies on the same fundamentals which characterised the beliefs of the ancients. It is important to remember this, for amidst the march of external and superficial progress we are apt to forget that the mental essentials are unchanging, and that we act from the same motives and according to the same natural laws as the Egyptians and Assyrians of old. We are in the grasp of blind forces whose power is loosened only in the case of a few thinkers, who can never constitute a majority of the population. The old superstitious appeal of religion is absolutely necessary to hold the bulk of the race in check. But Mr. Moe does agnosticism rather an injustice by ignoring its higher aspects. He assumes, for the purpose of argument, that the agnostic's only objection to religion is its effect on mankind, and that if religion be proved beneficial and necessary, the cause of agnosticism is lost. Herein he errs, for the crux of rational scepticism concerns mankind and the world not at all. The problem is one of infinite and eternal forces, amidst which the earth and all humanity are as nothing. The agnostic fails to see proof of a sentient will in the natural forces of creation, and his only objection to religion is that the theologian arbitrarily assumes the existence of such a will without adequate proof. Religion may or may not be good for the masses. With this the philosophic rationalist has no concern. What interests him is the ultimate, absolute truth about the governing forces of space and their relation to each other and to him. The average sceptic has no quarrel with the church, and is not at all disposed to belittle its achievements.

"To a Worthy Centenarian", by Jonathan E. Hoag, is a most delightful tribute to a lady on her 101st birthday, in which the author weaves in many beautiful philosophical observations. A touch of melancholy interest is added by the recent death of the person to whom these lines are addressed, a passing touchingly described by Mr. Hoag's verses toward the back of the magazine. In "The Elusive Muse", our bard displays his infinite versatility by dashing off five rollicking stanzas of light and captivating imagery on a deliciously fanciful theme. Amateurdom is to be congratulated on the possession of so felicitous a singer.

Mrs. Winifred V. Jordan, unsurpassed as a poet of the fancy, is represented in this issue by two poems. "I Have Tasted of the Waters" is in her more serious style, which contains an appealing hint of Poe. The general construction of this piece is exceedingly meritorious, though the second line of the second stanza is marred by the rendering of the word *hours* as a dissyllable. In "Adoration", Mrs. Jordan writes in a vastly lighter vein, exhibiting her usual sprightliness of fancy and skill in the creation of delicate imagery.

"The Reason", by Rheinhart Kleiner, is a sonnet of masterful technique but somewhat saccharine sentimentality. Mr. Kleiner is perhaps the most perfect technician amateurdom possesses, his lines being animated throughout by an impeccable melodiousness which bespeaks infinite care, sound scholarship, and extensive genius. We can but wish his abundant talent were directed to loftier themes, as it undoubtedly will be when maturity mellows his fancy and substitutes the reflectiveness of middle life for the amatory exuberance of the young man. In Mr. Kleiner are the beginnings of great things; he is a bard whose future progress should be watched with care, for he will reflect bright credit upon our amateur circle.

"In the Regions of the Damned", by Willis Tete Crossman, is a story of vivid plot and almost classical technique, by an author not represented among us for many years. Fiction, it is said, is a criticism of life; and in this rather sordid tragedy Mr. Crossman reveals himself as anything but a favourable critic. His estimate of human honour and human motives is deplorably severe; and if true, is one whose literary display tends toward no particularly good or useful object, either ethical or artistic. Stories of this type have, in the present critic's opinion, little *raison d'être*. Ugly in their recitals and implications, they have slight kinship with true art in its exalted sense, and must of necessity repel rather than please the reader. Mr. Crossman bases many of his tales on the fallacy that any subject is a legitimate field of art if frankly and scientifically approached; a fallacy long common amongst the French, but less prevalent up to the present in English literature. The disproof of this fallacy ought not to be difficult, for since the province of art is the exaltation of beauty, there can be but a modicum of art in anything designed to arouse the repulsion of the untainted reader. Attention is here called to a somewhat perplexing misprint. In the newspaper extract toward the conclusion of the tale, the name "Morton" should read "Howard".

"Nemesis", by H. P. Lovecraft, is another piece for which it is hard for the artistic critic to assign a *raison d'être*, though the author has the justification of illustrious precedent in American literature. The hard-headed pragmatist can descry but slight value in the Poe-like mysticism and elusive horror of these nightmarish lines, though the allegorical mind can glimpse an interpretation which may or may not be artistic. It is a moot question how much of real art or beauty may reside in this type of writing, wherein the emotions are stirred by vague hints of things beyond common experience. "The Beast in the Cave", a short story written several years ago but now published for the first time, reveals Mr. Lovecraft in a similarly dark vein, though in this case no hint of the supernatural is present. The technique of the tale is by no means bad, yet we feel that the theme lacks interest for the average modern reader. Mr. Lovecraft is a dweller in the classical past, and is unwilling to cultivate that light piquancy which our contemporaries demand. He is much less likely to succeed than Mr. Crossman.

"A-Gypsying", by Edna Hyde (formerly Edna von der Heide), is a lyric of intense feeling and skilful construction, whose somewhat intricate technical form displays the sentiment to wonderful advantage. Miss Hyde has well earned her celebrity in amateurdom. By the same author is "To Someone—Somewhere", a more sedate lyric whose theme and melody are above criticism.

"In the Sweet Long Ago", by Arthur Goodenough, is a beautiful bit of anapæstic melody, reminding one of Mr. Ames Rowley's "Laeta", in a recent *Tryout*. Mr. Goodenough's work contains a genuine inspiration, seriousness, and sincerity quite rare in amateur journalism, and has gained him a richly deserved fame. He strikes the lyre with a certain assured mastery of thought which stamps him as being almost above the limitations of technique; one feels that it is the subject, and not the literary medium, which animates him; yet his felicity of expression is in every case adequate. "The Thing Has Often Been Done Before", shows Mr. Goodenough in his favourite role of the moralist, and is a thoroughly excellent piece despite the "allowable" rhyme of *revenge* and *strange*, to which the ultra-modern technician would take exception.

In "A War-Born Dream", Rev. Eugene B. Kuntz reveals the fire and genius which are rapidly bringing him to the fore amongst amateur poets. The Alexandrine measure is well suited to the solemnity of the subject, and the whole presents an harmonious unit worthy of the highest commendation. Also by Dr. Kuntz is "The Master Musician", a poem in iambic heptameter, whose long flowing lines convey a wealth of delicate fancy and beautiful imagery. A considerable knowledge of music and musical principles lends added charm to the author's rendering of this stately theme.

"When Der Frost is on Der Turnips", by J. Morris Widdows, is a bright and clever parody containing more than a little genuine rural verisimilitude.

"Losers Weepers, Finders Keepers", by Jennie M. Kendall, is a pretty and conventional Christmas story of low life, whose plot is clever and well handled. Such a story would, we fancy, be readily salable to *The Youth's Companion* or some other magazine of that type.

"If Love of Mine", by Litta L. Voelchert, is a lyric poem whose felicity of fancy and imagery cannot be too highly praised. Words and ideas blend in rare perfection. The rhyming plan, however, is vague and inadequate, sadly contrasting with the conspicuous excellence of the other features. We should recommend that four-line stanzas of alternate rhyme be used throughout the composition. Miss Voelchert is a poet of genuine merit, whose only weakness is on the technical side.

"To Autumn", by Anna Helen Crofts, is a very pretty seasonal piece in short, quaint metre. The general effect is pleasing and polished, though the style is not precisely a matured one.

"Two Fathers", by Olive G. Owen, is an appealing and acceptable child piece, containing much genuine pathos.

"A Spirit Christlike", by Julia R. Johnson, is a brief bit of moral or didactic verse whose sentiment is adequate, and whose technique is good, save for the want of an internal rhyme in the long line of the second stanza, to correspond with that in the first. It should be impressed upon the poetical beginner, that the various stanzas of any ordinary poem should be absolutely alike in metre and rhyming plan.

"Blunders and Democracy", by Prof. Philip B. McDonald, is a terse and informing essay on a subject of great contemporary interest, in which the author exhibits much clearness of observation and soundness of opinion. Prof. McDonald's style is a commendably correct one, its freedom from ornamentation being due to his rhetorical ideal—"the elimination of the superfluous".

"The Atlantic", by John Milton Samples, is a meritorious poem by a new amateur poet, suggesting in several ways Mr. Hoag's "Ode to Old Ocean". The sentiment is noble and the treatment skilful save in one or two instances, such as the rhyme of *men* and *sin* in the third stanza, and the presence of a superfluous syllable in line 2 of the fourth stanza.

"I Thought I Loved the Country", by James Joseph Moloney, is a clever and captivating bit of light verse whose technique flows smoothly and flawlessly. Amateurdom will soon have the pleasure of becoming more fully acquainted with Mr. Moloney, through the excellent paper he is about to publish.

"From an Empty Attic" is the grossly self-libellous title of Mr. Cook's editorial column, in which *The Vagrant's* witty and capable publisher entertains the reader with a pleasing variety of comment and miscellany. The little sketch of the two Italian draftees is a charming fragment, which deserves more prominent featuring. In his critical notes on amateur literature Mr. Cook displays acute judgment and sound opinion, particularly when analysing the amorphous lump of radicalism entitled *Les Mouches Fantastiques*.

The Vagrant is more than a pleasure to read; it is a revelation. Never within recent years have the solid worth and permanent prosperity of amateur journalism been so forcibly demonstrated as in this monumental contribution to non-professional letters. Mr. Cook's devotion to the cause is a model and an inspiration for his contemporaries.

A Mountain Walked or Stumbled

Stephen Walker

Cthulhu's famous metaphoric description (or non-description) making up the title is eventually followed by the simile "like Polypheme cursing the fleeing ship of Odysseus" (*DH* 153) during the pursuit of Johansen (a Norwegian Ulysses) and his fellows.[1] Lovecraft chose the line deliberately, as an examination of the scene in the *Odyssey* persuades.

According to Samuel Butler's 1900 translation of the *Odyssey*, Polyphemus "was a horrid creature, not like a human being at all, but resembling rather some crag that stands out boldly against the sky on the top of a high mountain." This is appropriate not only as a way of establishing the size of the monster[2] but because the Cyclopes make their home in the mountains. The mountain comes up again, literally, for as a result of Ulysses' taunt Polyphemus "got more and more furious ... so he tore the top from off a high mountain, and flung it just in front of my ship so that it was within a little of hitting the end of the rudder."[3] A modern poet,

---

1. My guess is the introduction of Polyphemus is the editorial intrusion of Francis Wayland Thurston rather than Johansen. How much any narrator interprets a story in HPL's corpus could prove an intriguing subject.

2. "Odysseus stresses the creature's size, which is dreadful in itself: the word πελώριος ... connotes 'terrible', 'monstrous', as well as 'large' ... Polyphemus is weird because he is too much a part of nature; watching him walk and hearing him talk is like seeing trees walk and stones speak." Elizabeth O'Keefe, *The Cyclops in Literature from Homer to Joyce: The Evolution of an Ogre* (B.A. Research Paper. Smith College, 1972), 7–8. Cthulhu's mountainous stature is prefigured as "a gigantic thing 'miles high' which walked or lumbered about" (*DH* 130).

3. "Both the Cyclops and the Laestrygones are giants whose size is conveyed through a comparison with a mountain" (Marianne Govers Hopman, *Scylla: Myth, Metaphor, Paradox* [Cambridge: Cambridge University Press, 2012], 57). In

Robert Fagles, translated the appearance of Polyphemus as

> Here was a piece of work, by god, a monster
> built like no mortal who ever supped on bread,
> no, like a shaggy peak, I'd say—a man-mountain
> rearing head and shoulders over the world.[4]

While it is possible that he knew the Butler translation, and impossible that he read the Fagles, Lovecraft certainly was familiar with the one by Alexander Pope.[5] An edition was in his library, and he gave Pope explicit credit in his 1897 *The Young Folks' Ulysses or The Odyssey in Plain Old English Verse*, which makes the Cyclops episode prominent, giving it 16 of the poem's 88 lines that cover the post-Troy career of Ulysses. Pope also provided a mountain image for Polyphemus:

> A form enormous! far unlike the race
> Of human birth, in stature, or in face;
> As some lone mountain's monstrous growth he stood . . .

Pope uses the form "Polypheme"—presumably due to its scannability—and so, presumably, Lovecraft follows.

Besides Pope, the link from Polyphemus to Cthulhu could also be essayist Charles Lamb, whose *The Adventures of Ulysses*, written for a juvenile audience, was in Lovecraft's library.[6] Edith Hall has said that "Lamb had altered the structure of the Odyssey so as to upgrade the incident with Polyphemus the Cyclops, making it

---

another section of the poem the crew finds the wife of a Laestrygonian "to be a giantess as huge as a mountain, and they were horrified at the sight of her" (Butler).

Fans of the movie classic *The Seventh Voyage of Sinbad* will recall that the Harryhausen-animated Cyclops hurls a rock that swamps a fleeing boat and then, like Cthulhu, wades into the sea.

4. The text is available at www.scribd.com/doc/52280051/9/Book-IX. Viking first published the book in 1996.

5. Even though it resulted in poetic productions of "eighteenth-century rubbish," I reckon the influence of Pope greater on HPL than that of Poe or Dunsany.

6. See *LL* 510. Though not indicated, it is a section in *The Complete Works in Prose and Verse of Charles Lamb*. For a discussion of Lamb's *The Adventures of Ulysses* as it relates to Harper's Half-Hour Series, check the several posts (beginning 3 April 2010) by Chris Perridas in *H. P. Lovecraft and His Legacy* (chrisperridas.blogspot.com).

the centrepiece of his first chapter. Lamb seems instinctively to have recognized how appealing children would find the tale. . . . Lamb's vivid adaptation partly explains the robust cultural presence Polyphemus has enjoyed ever since."[7] It's a small leap to think that Lovecraft read it when young, thrilling to such descriptions as "The first sign of habitation which [Ulysses and his men] came to was a giant's cave rudely fashioned, but of a size which betokened the vast proportions of its owner. . . . Polyphemus, the largest and savagest of the Cyclops . . . He looked more like a mountain crag than a man." Inhospitably he grabs two men, "as if they had been no more than children . . . dashed their brains out against the earth, and (shocking to relate) tore in pieces their limbs, and devoured them, yet warm and trembling, making a lion's meal of them, lapping the blood: for the Cyclops are *man-eaters*, and esteem human flesh to be a delicacy far above goat's or kid's."

Homer's comparison of Polyphemus with a mountain makes sense in a way that doesn't for Cthulhu. The Cyclops lives in a mountainous region—symbolically the abode of gods and supernatural beings—and is a personification or extension of the landscape and its various associations of wilderness, inimicality, and unknownness. While Cthulhu, like its predecessor, represents a force of nature, the comparison with the mountain has much less artistic justification.

Yet the Cyclopes inspired Lovecraft. A favored word in his fiction, "Cyclopean" is evoked in at least a dozen tales, its most frequent association being with architecture and building. According to *The Columbia Encyclopedia*, "The Cyclopean technique involves the use of huge, irregular boulders, carefully fitted together without the use of mortar."[8] The word is also a synonym for "huge." Taken together, the two aspects of "Cyclopean" reinforce each other and add up to the concept of a "mountain."

Ironically, the comparison of Cthulhu with a mountain is demythological, a step back in mythological evolution.[9] In their

7. Edith Hall, "Modern Myths of the Cyclops," *Times Literary Supplement* (24 May 2006).

8. Retrieved 8 March 2013 from http://www.credoreference.com.cyrano.ucmo.edu:2048/ entry/columency/cyclopean

9. While I've looked at Cthulhu as Polyphemus-like, another comparison is with

book *When They Severed Earth from Sky* the Barbers examine the origins of myth.[10] To take one example from many, they argue that the story of Prometheus (that stealer of fire for mankind) was originally a first-hand witnessing of a volcanic mountain in eruption that eventually became a symbolic narrative as a way to transmit the event orally and compactly. The same process, it seems to me, is more obvious for the Polyphemus episode. The rock heaved at the crew is a bomb—a boulder—that a volcano (Polyphemus) spews. More explicitly, another myth has the Cyclopes helping Hephaestus, a god of volcanoes.[11]

In a second irony—and perhaps a window on the myth-making process—Polyphemus was involved with a story of transformation, as told by Ovid.[12] Using a rock again, this time with full effect, he killed his rival-in-love Acis, a shepherd who turns into a river. Here are two nature personifications, with a volcanic mountain become a giant and a man become a river.

Prior to "The Call of Cthulhu," there are several references to Polyphemus. In "Dagon" the title being is Cthulhu lite—"vast, Polyphemus-like, and loathsome" (*D* 18); "Under the Pyramids" features a "yawning Polyphemus-door" (*D* 241), which presumably evokes the Cyclops' stature.

---

certain monsters of fairy stories. O'Keefe observes that Virgil's "Polyphemus is very much like the one-dimensional ogre of the folk tale; he is allowed no character traits which would detract from his monstrous nature" (42). That is, a *pure* monster. When the "monster" character becomes decadent, it is tamed into a comic figure. This happened with Polyphemus in his treatment by such artists as Euripides and James Joyce. This has also happened with Cthulhu, as witness Mythos toys and the several children's books that feature it.

10. Elizabeth Wayland Barber and Paul T. Barber, *When They Severed Earth from Sky: How the Human Mind Shapes Myth* (Princeton, NJ: Princeton University Press, 2004).

11. In the *Aeneid* the poet Virgil describes eruptions of a volcano "which are said to be caused by the restless movements of a giant imprisoned within it for his revolt against Jupiter. This wild, terrible region is a fitting home for the Cyclopes, who resemble the volcano in size and in their destructive natures" (O'Keefe 41). Cf. the lines from Horace: "Vulcan feeds / The fires that heat the Cyclops' busy home."

12. In the *Metamorphoses*, Book 14, the sailor survivor Achaemenides gives a blood-curdling account of the encounter with Polyphemus. O'Keefe calls it a "cheap, penny dreadful style, steeped in gore" (46).

Mountainous size is not the only shared attribute between the things. Both have a man-killing ability; fatally "three men were swept up by the flabby claws" (*DH* 152) of Cthulhu, and (thanks to Lamb) the reader is vividly acquainted with the Cyclops' sanguinary appetite (in another poetry translation, "His bloody hand / Snatched two unhappy of my martial band").[13] The Greeks are cowed by Polyphemus, though not to the depth of pure fright.

It is possible to think of Polyphemus in moral terms—arrogance and impiety—but what morality has Lovecraft's monster?[14] In a sense Cthulhu is Polyphemus without an Odysseus, who represents the triumph of cunning or rationality over the brute and irrational, over "a universe in chaos"; whereas Lovecraft's tale has reversed this.[15] But though he might invade your dreams, Cthulhu still has a way to go to rival Polyphemus "the best known ogre in literature."[16] However, I wander away from the theme of simile and mountain.

This subject could be expanded. In what various ways did the Cyclops episode resonate through and fashion Lovecraft's imagination? How did Lovecraft represent the mountain in his works? In what way did he use other similes? How does Polyphemus/Cthulhu tie into the running appearance of Cyclopean buildings? Did illustrations of Polyphemus have any affect on his imagination? Perhaps the future will bequeath us a book such as *Classical Allusions in H. P. Lovecraft*, currently a jerry-built nothing à la the *Necronomicon* that could join my similarly nonexistent *The Annotated Lovecraft*—which I playfully "cited" a decade or so ago—in some bibliographical never land.[17]

---

13. Quoted in Anna Letitia Barbauld, "Reflections on the Pleasures of Distress and Terror," *New England Review* (Summer 2001): 183.

14. See Shirley Clay Scott, "Man, Mind, and Monster: Polyphemus from Homer Through Joyce," *Classical and Modern Literature* (Fall 1995): 19–75 (esp. 49–50). The article traces Polyphemus' literary lineage.

15. O'Keefe 44. She also writes, "Polyphemus' defeat was a reassurance that man could exercise control over superior strength by the use of his intelligence" (26).

16. O'Keefe [i].

17. I would be less than puckish if I omitted observing that the tale's exhortative final line—"see that it [the manuscript] meets no other eye" (*DH* 154)—recalls the blinding of the Cyclops.

Excised Passages from "The Thing on the Doorstep"

S. T. Joshi

In my proposed multi-volume edition of *The Variorum Lovecraft*, which could begin publication as early as next year, I hope to present all the relevant textual variants for all the stories that Lovecraft wrote over his short literary career. One phase of that project may include the printing of passages from handwritten or typed manuscripts (chiefly the former) that were excised as Lovecraft was writing the story or as he performed a subsequent revision of it. One very interesting example, because of the number and relative significance of such excised passages, is "The Thing on the Doorstep."

This tale was written frenetically in a matter of four days (21–24 August 1933, as indicated at the end of the autograph manuscript) in a scribbled pencil draft that was so illegible that, when Lovecraft (unwisely) passed the manuscript on to a "delinquent [revision] client" (*SL* 4.310) for typing, he or she missed some of Lovecraft's section divisions, typing the story in only five sections when it contained seven. Naturally, the typist did not transcribe the excised passages, which were clearly crossed out in pencil. They are printed here for the first time, and they shed interesting light on the development of the story as Lovecraft was writing it.

The first excised passage of any consequence occurs in the middle of the first section of the story, which supplies a potted biography of Edward Derby from his childhood to the time he met Asenath Waite. At the end of the paragraph discussing Derby's "self-reliance and practical affairs" (*DH* 278), we find the following:

> By the time he was 25 Derby was a fairly well-known minor poet and fantaisiste, though his lack of contacts & experience had

slowed down his literary growth by making his products deriva-
tive & over-bookish. I was perhaps his closest friend, seeing him

The passage breaks off in the manuscript, and Lovecraft resumes
with a new paragraph, "Derby's parents . . ." (*DH* 278). The above
passage was in fact transferred to a paragraph three paragraphs
later, although there Lovecraft adds that Derby was "a prodigiously learned man and a fairly well-known poet and fantaisiste"
(*DH* 279). Clearly, Lovecraft wished to add additional biographical
detail about Derby, especially in terms of his relations to the narrator, Daniel Upton; it is in the intervening paragraphs that he
supplies the key detail that Derby would come to Upton's house
and either knock or ring the doorbell in a characteristic manner—
"three brisk strokes followed by two more after a pause" (*DH*
278), a detail that plays a crucial role at the end of the story. Lovecraft also adds information about Derby's attendance of Miskatonic University and also about his reading of occult books (the
usual litany of the *Necronomicon,* the *Book of Eibon,* and others
follows [*DH* 279]); it is no doubt for this reason that he added the
detail that Derby was "prodigiously learned," which was missing in
the first draft of the passage.

   In the middle of Section II occurs another excision. By now
Derby has met Asenath and fallen under her sway. In a paragraph
in which Upton describes how Derby brought Asenath to his
house for a call, the text states that Upton "perceived that their
intimacy was beyond entangling" (*DH* 282). There follows this excised passage:

> This rather disturbed me, for the Derbys are old Essex County
> stock & I did not wish to see any incongruous element enter in.
> Not only did my daughter's recollections influence me, but I had
> hear from others that Asenath was in every way an "uninhibited
> young modern" of the sort that good old families cannot well as-
> similate.

Not much need be made of this excision, aside from the fact that
it reflects Lovecraft's customary disapproval of "mixed" marriages,
going well beyond his horror of interracial unions (or "miscegenation") to disapproval of marital unions even of members of differ-

ent social classes. Lovecraft may have considered the passage re-dundant, because Asenath's portrayal as an "uninhibited young modern" may have seemed unduly repetitive of an earlier passage in which she is described as a member of the "intelligentsia" (*DH* 281) at Miskatonic.

The next excised passage is of considerably greater significance. It occurs at the very end of Section II, which discusses the new household that Edward and Asenath have established in Arkham, although she has brought along three servants from her home in Innsmouth. At the end of the section Lovecraft writes:

> My first call at Derby's new home was by no means unpleas-ant. The servants—especially the flat-nosed wench who opened the door—distinctly repelled me; & my wife, who was with me, thought Asenath's expression was vaguely sardonic. Of the con-versation I recall only a queer outburst from our hostess, who re-peated vehemently that wish to be a man which had so impressed my daughter at school. This was fixed in my mind because of an even queerer & surprisingly tasteless rejoinder of Edward's—a re-joinder which had the aspect of a sly "dig", & which was cut off by a crushing glance from Asenath. He had murmured 'that some people would give a good deal to be wholly human'—no doubt referring to the anile whispers of grandams about Innsmouth folk.

There is much in this passage that Lovecraft would have found objectionable in the overall context of the story. First, the passage needlessly duplicates an earlier passage in which Upton's daugh-ter—presented as a classmate of Asenath's at the Hall School (*DH* 280), presumably a private secondary school—notes that Asenath's "crowning rage . . . was that she was not a man" (*DH* 281). (Lovecraft has revised that earlier passage so that it is the daughter of a friend, rather than Upton's own daughter, who makes the observation.) More significantly, Lovecraft probably decided that Edward's "rejoinder" would at this stage be uncharac-teristic of him, since he had only a few paragraphs earlier empha-sised "Edward's weak will" and Asenath's "strong will" (*DH* 282). Moreover, the suggestion that Asenath was not "fully human" would have telegraphed some phases of the climax. Lovecraft was certainly wise in omitting this passage.

At the end of the first paragraph of Section III, a lengthy excision was made. Lovecraft is passing quickly over the next two years of Asenath and Edward's life, recounting that "Occasionally the Derby's would go on long trips—ostensibly to Europe, though Edward sometimes hinted at obscurer destinations" (*DH* 284). At this point, several lines have been erased; then we find the following:

> ... which professional ethics ought to have held back. He had been summoned one Candlemas to the lonely Crowninshield place; & could not feel easy after what he had seen. Fortunately, it was dead. He had known monstrous births before—but when monstrosity takes certain directions, there are questions one has to ask oneself ... questions about people, & about the universe itself. Candlemas is nine months after the Witches' Sabbat, & country legend has much to say about it. Were not Innsmouth folk said to keep the Sabbat? Where were the Derbys last May-Eve? Dr. Hathorne allowed that if he were Edward Derby he would leave Asenath while the leaving was good. He was never quite specific, though, until that night at the last when the horror came to my doorstep. Now he will back me up in trying to do what must be done.

The passage appears to discuss a character—Dr. Hathorne, presumably the Derbys' family physician—who has been entirely removed from the narrative. (The name seems to be a clear allusion to John Hathorne, one of the judges in the Salem witch trials; he is mentioned in passing in *The Case of Charles Dexter Ward* [see *MM* 150] and "The Dreams in the Witch House" [*MM* 263].) It appears that we are to understand that Asenath has given birth to a stillborn "monstrosity." Lovecraft must have determined (rightly) that this development was too sudden in its evocation of weirdness than what the story's narrative pace required at this time. It would have constituted too explicit a turn to horror, so Lovecraft removed it.

Toward the end of Section III another excised passage occurs. Here Lovecraft is discussing how Derby is becoming increasingly alarmed about the strange travels that Asenath compels him to make, and the bizarre "objects" brought back from those expeditions. At the end of a paragraph in which Derby expresses doubt about whether old Ephraim Waite is really dead ("in a spiritual as well as corporal sense" [*DH* 286]), we find the following, after some erasures:

> upstairs—but sometimes she couldn't hold on, & he would find himself suddenly in his own body again in some far off, horrible, & perhaps unknown place. Sometimes she would get hold of him again & sometimes she couldn't. Often he had to find his way home from frightful distances, getting somebody to drive the car after he found it. The worst thing was that she was holding on to him longer & longer at a time. She wanted to be a man—to be fully human—that's why she got hold of him. Some day she would crowd him out & disappear with his body—disappear to become a great magician like her father & leave him stranded in that female shell that wasn't even quite human. Yes, he knew about the Innsmouth blood now. There had been traffick with things from the sea—it was horrible. . . .

Once again, Lovecraft has determined that this passage telegraphs matters in an unsatisfying way. He went on to write a passage about Derby being stranded in Chesuncook, Maine, and having to call Upton to fetch him, since he could not drive his own car. It is only as Upton is driving him back that the above passage— somewhat expanded—becomes incorporated into the narrative (*DH* 288). This leads one to wonder whether Lovecraft, in the course of composing the story, decided to add the Chesuncook passage as a more vivid way of suggesting Asenath's increasing control of Edward's body, rather than having it simply stated bluntly by Edward.

Toward the end of this episode—when Asenath has mentally taken over Edward's body, ousted Upton from the driver's seat (a tricky maneuver at best, one would imagine), and begun to reassure Upton that nothing is really amiss, especially in regard to the relationship between Edward and Asenath—a fascinating excision occurs. Asenath (in Edward's body) tells Upton: "I shall take a rest from now on—you probably won't see me for some time, and you needn't blame Asenath for it" (*DH* 291). Then:

> "Don't be frightened on her account, either—in case I've been unloading any savage nonsense. *She is better protected than you can*

realise. I'd be a fool to harm her, for it would all come back on me sooner or later. And of course I don't wish to harm her. Those spells of mine are just overwrought nerves.["]

What could the "protection" referred to by Asenath be? Is this an anticipation of the climax, where Asenath reveals the power to cast her mind out of her own (dead) body and into that of Edward? If so, Lovecraft again must have concluded that it was too clear a telegraphing of the conclusion, so he removed the passage.

In the early portion of Section V, a final excision occurs. Here Lovecraft is discussing the increasing rumours that the sounds of Asenath sobbing have been heard at the Derbys' house. After the sentence "And then someone complicated matters by whispering that the sobs had once or twice been in a man's voice" (*DH* 293), we find this:

> The tragic culmination came in mid-October. It was Thursday, the night when the three Derby servants went out—always together, & always heading for the same unknown haven in their native Innsmouth. I was waked about three in the morning by a frantic ringing & pounding of the knocker at the front door, & when I slipped on a dressing gown & went down I found Edward [erasure]. It was Edward, & I saw in a flash that his personality was the old one which I had not encountered since the day of his ravings on that terrible ride from Chesuncook. His face was distorted by a mixture of wild emotions in which fright & triumph seemed incongruously to have dominance. I could see

This passage was in part revised into the paragraph that follows, but it seems as if the excised passage was actually meant to initiate the climax of the story. It is possible that Lovecraft was initially planning to have Derby admit at this point that he had killed Asenath (not merely that she had "gone on a long research trip" [*DH* 293]). But Lovecraft must have felt that this would have rushed the conclusion of the story, so he had the "final nightmare" come four months later, just "before Candlemas" (*DH* 298).

The various excised passages in the manuscript of "The Thing on the Doorstep" suggest that Lovecraft, even if he had had a synopsis of the story drawn up (or, indeed, two synopses—one detail-

ing events in order of occurrence, the other in order of narration—as he advises writers to prepare [CE 2.176]), realised that
changes must be made in the course of a narrative as it is being
written. As he states in "Notes on Writing Weird Fiction" (1933),
written probably just before he began work on "The Thing on the
Doorstep":

> Change incidents and plot whenever the developing process
> seems to suggest such change, never being bound by any previous
> design. If the development suddenly reveals new opportunities for
> dramatic effect or vivid storytelling, add whatever is thought ad-
> vantageous—going back and reconciling the early parts to the new
> plan. Insert and delete whole sections if necessary or desirable,
> trying different beginnings and endings until the best arrangement
> is found. But be sure that all references throughout the story are
> thoroughly reconciled with the final design. Remove all possible
> superfluities—words, sentences, paragraphs, or whole episodes or
> elements—observing the usual precautions about the reconciling
> of all references. (CE 2.176–77)

"The Thing on the Doorstep" is far from being one of Lovecraft's stellar tales, but the very difficulties Lovecraft experienced
in its composition, as testified by the numerous passages he excised and reworked, are an exemplification of the fluid and organic manner in which he fashioned a tale so that it would achieve
maximum impact.

Additions and Corrections for "Lovecraft's 1937 Diary"

David Haden

Kenneth W. Faig, Jr.'s very useful research article on the H. P. Lovecraft address book and 1937 diary appeared in the 2012 *Lovecraft Annual.*[1] Faig suggested some candidates for a number of elusive correspondents of Lovecraft, and he followed his article by giving the full 1937 address book along with his own copious annotations. Inspired by Faig's work, in spring 2013 I undertook a series of intensive online investigations into the lost or uncertain names and addresses. The full details of my discoveries will appear as illustrated essays in my book, *Lovecraft in Historical Context: The Fourth Collection of Essays and Notes* (July 2013). But for readers of the *Lovecraft Annual* I present here a short outline of my discoveries. I hope that, given the elusiveness of these correspondents and erratic coverage offered by online materials, Lovecraftian scholars will excuse my inevitable gaps in knowledge. It is to be hoped that others, especially those who have access to commercial databases of old newspapers and genealogical matter, or to fannish archives, may be able to develop and deepen or even disprove my lines of enquiry.

---

1. Kenneth W. Faig, Jr., "Lovecraft's 1937 Diary," *Lovecraft Annual* No. 6 (2012): 153–78.

Frederick A. Wesley, 6 Hammond Street, Providence

Frederick A. Wesley (1885[2]–1948[3])

I have discovered a "Wesley, Fred A." listed in the *Rhode Island School of Design Year Book* 1903, taking a foundational course "I" (one) there.[4] Faig has already usefully established a likely October 1885 birth date for Wesley (162). It follows that in 1903 this Wesley would have been of the right age to have been an eighteen-year-old student at the Rhode Island School of Design (RISD). One of Wesley's key teachers at RISD would have then been the artist Stacy Tolman of Providence (1860–1935), head of the RISD Department of Drawing and Painting from 1889 to 1905.[5] Tolman is known to have made an ink drawing[6] of Wesley, presumably a portrait, which is still extant, though it seems the picture has not yet been inspected by Lovecraft scholars:

> Rhode Island Historical Society–Graphics Dept.:
> ACCESS RESTRICTED. APPOINTMENT REQUIRED
> 1. Ink drawing, "Frederick Allen Wesley" (call# Graphics XXB Painting T652 1)

---

2. The parents of Wesley are noted in Faig's article. I have found that the book *The Life and Times of Samuel Gorton* (1904) has a genealogic entry noting that a Martha A. Allen (b. 1861) married a Warren B. Wesley, and had a "son Fred'k." My finding confirms Faig's details of Allen's parents. I calculate that Frederick's father, Warren B. Wesley, was probably born c. 1854.

3. There is a record of a burial of a Frederick Allen Wesley at the Grace Church Cemetery, Providence (Elmwood Ave. at Broad St.), but no dates or transcription of the stone are online, if any is available. Faig suggests a death date of 20 April 1948 for Wesley.

4. *Rhode Island School of Design Year Book* 25–28 (1903): 69.

5. There are three works on Tolman: Ralph Davol, "An Appreciation of Stacey Tolman," *Brush and Pencil* 7 (December 1900): 163–72; John I. H. Baur, "A Painter of Painters: Stacy Tolman," *American Art Journal* (January 1979): 37–48 (14 illustrations); and *Memorial Exhibition of Paintings, Drawings and Etchings by Stacy Tolman*, 1935 (a catalogue, 77 works listed).

6. Listed in: Elinor L. Nacheman, *Unveiled: A Directory and Guide to 19th Century Born Artists Active in Rhode Island, and Where to Find Their Work in Publicly Accessible Rhode Island Collections* (self-published, 2007). My list item on Wesley's ink drawing is from Nacheman via an art dealer, who gave Nacheman's full list of Tolman's works online in the hope of selling a picture.

Tolman was a key figure in the Providence art world of the 1880s–1920s, and from 1895 onward he had his studio with other artists in the Fleur de Lys building in Providence. One wonders if the Wesley who is shown in the ink drawing might have become Tolman's private student or a studio assistant.[7] Wesley's name does not show up in the further editions of the RSID *Year Book* that I have been able to inspect, but Tolman dramatically reduced his teaching load in 1905 and he is also known to have taken private pupils.

It is interesting to note that the last "A. W." initials of the Henry Anthony Wilcox artist character in "The Call of Cthulhu" are the same as the A. W. of Frederick A. Wesley.

Geo. FitzPatrick, Box 3413 R, G.P.O. Sydney, NSW, Australia
George William Sydney Fitzpatrick (1884–1 Aug 1948)
George William Sydney Fitzpatrick was a book collector and *the* pioneering public-relations man[8] of Australia the 1920s and '30s. In the 1920s Fitzpatrick collected bookplates, and at the end of his life he had a collection of 840 plates.[9] In May 1929 Fitzpatrick placed notices in the American press, in search of new literary bookplates for his collection.[10] Lovecraft scholars will remember that Lovecraft had his own notable personal bookplate designed in late summer 1927, and he was very proud of it. My guess would be that he sent Fitzpatrick some of his new bookplates and thus sparked a correspondence. Fitzpatrick was a director of the *Sunday Times* newspaper in Sydney, and of its associated sports paper *Referee*, until 1929 and possibly thereafter. In 1920 he was also

---

7. He seems unlikely to have been the 'other' Fred A. Wesley (b. 1888) of Rhode Island, found by Faig, who was recorded as a streetcar conductor in 1910 and later as a steamfitter's helper in 1917.

8. Damian John Gleeson, "George William Sydney Fitzpatrick (1884–1948): An Australian Public Relations 'Pioneer,'" *Asia Pacific Public Relations Journal* 13, No. 2 (2013).

9. Presented to the State Library of New South Wales by Mrs G. Fitzpatrick, 1949, where his collection is held today. The collection is titled "Australian bookplates, pre-1949," but given George Fitzpatrick's calls to American authors it is likely to also contain many from outside Australia.

10. "Book Plates Wanted," *Milwaukee Journal* (18 May 1929): 6. I also found his notices in *Time* magazine and *Plain Talk*, both from 1929.

noted as being a director of the *Freemason Magazine* in Australia.[11] My research into his business connections indicates that 'director' does not mean that he was actually the 'editor' of these publications, so he may not have been in a position to place Lovecraft's poetry or fiction. He may, however, have told Lovecraft of a suitable outlet for his fiction, the notorious *Smith's Weekly* (1919–1950) of Sydney,[12] but that is just my speculation. Fitzpatrick corresponded at least once with the William Quan Judge Theosophical Club of Lomaland, sending them a letter on the weird curiosities of the Australian topography and flora, a letter later reprinted in the theosophist *Lucifer* magazine in 1930.[13]

C. L. Stuart of 17 Brockett St, E Milton, Mass.

Charles Leonard Stuart (1860–?)
I suggest this address should have been read as "Brackett St.," not Brockett. This then gives a location four miles south of the center of Boston, in what Google Street View shows as a very pleasant village-like atmosphere among trees and quite near the coast. I have been unable to pin this address to anyone, but it looks like a suitable retirement spot for the East Coast author and popular encyclopedia editor Charles Leonard Stuart (also publishing under the name of Leonard Stuart). A "Charles Leonard Stuart" has a 1922 copyright registry entry for his book *The Age of Understanding; or, Americanism and the Standard of World Nationalism: A True Outline of History and Science* (Boston, R. G. Badger, 1922). This cranky racialist book is freely available online, and it has a very useful biography page for Stuart, including the core: "settled in New York City in 1897 [. . .] since has been continuously associated with international encyclopedic and educational book publishing work."

This biography goes on to show that in the early 1920s Stuart

---

11. "From Messenger to Director: A Successful Australian," *Evening Post* (24 December 1920): 2.

12. It appears that there is no index for the stories published in *Smith's Weekly*, which was not averse to printing short tales of horror and the weird in the mid-1930s.

13. "A Letter from Australia," *Lucifer: The Light-Bringer* 1, No. 3 (May–June 1930): 174–75.

had an interest in Lyonesse, the Cornish/Arthurian folk story of the lost land under the sea, and that he had 'published' *A Roamer in Lyonesse* (1922).[14] He had key Cornish ancestors, which may have coincided with Lovecraft's own genealogical researches. The biography also states that he had written and published a 35-page pamphlet or monograph titled *The Great God Pan*.[15] It further states that he then had in hand, in manuscript, an esoteric-sounding book *The Eon or The Quest of the Lotus* (alternatively heralded as *The Eonic Quest* on the book's title page). Any one of these three items might have been suitable revision work for Lovecraft. I can find no trace of any likely book on Lyonesse published around that time, nor an '*Eon*' work under that or any variant title. A linking of the terms Eon, Eonic, and Lotus appears to imply Buddhism,[16] but I suppose they might also imply theosophy. After 1922 Stuart vanishes from the online record, and I have been unable to find any death date or record in the open online sources.

Bell—15 Pine Ave., Old Orchard, Ne. c/o E. Dixon, Box 292
Edith Bell (1914–2002)

The address should have read: "Old Orchard Be[ach]" or Old Orchard, Me.[17] Old Orchard Beach is located some 60 miles north along the coast from Providence. There was an Edith Bell (b. 19 July 1914) who died in 2002, age eighty-eight, at Old Orchard Beach. There is a record of her living there at 22 Pine Ave. In the 1940 census there is an Edwin E. Dixon living at 15 Pine Ave., Old Orchard Beach. Edwin died 13 January 1964, at Old Orchard Beach, age 75. Given these facts, one might then surmise that Edwin E. Dixon passed Lovecraft's letters to Edith Bell at 22 Pine Ave. Since Bell was under twenty-one until c. 1935, my guess would be that

---

14. My searches suggest that this never actually appeared, at least not under his own name.

15. Leonard Stuart, *The Great God Pan: An All-Time Story*, New York: Tudor Society, 1913.

16. I have found an indicative online reference on an online discussion forum of "the eonic character of the Lotus Sermon" in regard to Buddhism.

17. ME meaning Maine. As a Briton my understanding of American geography is somewhat hazy, and so I am indebted to Kenneth W. Faig, Jr., for the latter suggestion.

her parents did not approve of her interest in weird literature. Hence the need to pass letters via the fictitious (?) "Box 292" of near neighbor E. Dixon. An absolute need for discreetness would also suggest why Lovecraft listed her simply as "Bell," rather than giving her full name in his 1937 address list. I can find no other online record of Edith Bell, and I assume she was perhaps a young fan who had written to Lovecraft. I find no further trace of an Edwin E. Dixon.

Curtis F. Myers, 70 Clifton Ave, Clifton NJ
Curtis F. Myers (1897–1985)
There is a Clifton Blv around the corner from Clifton Ave., which raises the possibility of another transcription error for the 1937 Diary, from "Blv" to "Ave". The 70 Clifton Boulevard address housed a small startup firm, Electronic Mechanics, Inc., from 1935 until around 1945/6. The address is one mile from the 31 Harrison Place, Clifton NJ, home of the Myers candidate found by Faig in the 1930 census, a man then working as a machinist in a woolen mill. Electronic Mechanics, Inc. was creating new types of ceramic radio and radar insulators from mica and glass.[18] The skills needed for working with mineral and glass fibers are apparently similar to those needed for working with wool, and so I suggest Faig's candidate Myers may have taken a machinist's job with Electronic Mechanics, Inc. The owner of this firm, the magnificently named Delbert E. Replogle, is known to have permitted staff members to receive mail at the firm's address while living elsewhere.[19] There is no online trace of this Myers as any kind of author or fan writer. If I am correct in my placing of him, then my guess is that he may have been a blue-collar fan who had written fan letters to Lovecraft.

---

18. Delbert E. Replogle's firm was prosecuted for back taxes after the war, and the history and purposes of the firm were minutely detailed in the government's legal paperwork. See Electronic Mechanics, Inc. v. Commissioner 15 T.C. 489 (1950), freely available online.

19. The *American Institute of Electrical Engineers Yearbook* of 1944 has one "Shima, Rindgh" giving the "70 Clifton Blvd" address as his address "for mail" while he lived at an address elsewhere.

Fred Anger, 2700 Webster St Berkley Calif

William Frederick Anger (probably b. 15 Sept 1920[20]–possibly d. 1997)

Louis C. Smith, 1908 98th Ave, Oakland Calif

Louis C. Smith (1900?–1980s?)

Correspondent Fred Anger was a young Lovecraft fan and letter writer to the pulps. His *Lovecraft Encyclopedia* entry[21] states he planned an index to *Weird Tales* and an edition of Lovecraft's *Fungi from Yuggoth*, both with Louis C. Smith, though neither of these volumes appeared. The online Locategrave.org usefully gives the location of a grave for a likely Anger:

> William F Anger, died 09/02/1997 buried at Bath National Cemetery in Bath, NY.[22]

This has enabled me to find a picture of the relevant gravestone at Bath National Cemetery (Plot: R, 0, 53), the inscription of which shows that this Anger served in the U.S. Navy during the Second World War. "YN3" on the gravestone indicates a "Petty officer third class" in the Navy. If Lovecraft's Anger re-entered civilian life on the East Coast, and lived there c. 1947–97, then he has left no trace in the current open online record under his own name.

Anger's partner-in-bibliography Louis C. Smith is now far easier to track, having left a fragmented but clear record scattered across the online fannish histories and bibliographies, and in the catalogues of book dealers. In the late 1920s Smith was a member of early SF fan clubs in San Francisco, and thereafter published many articles in SF and fantasy fanzines and wrote letters to the pulps, including five letters published in *Weird Tales* between 1933 and 1936.[23] Smith published his own fanzine *Tellus*, now held at the Special Collections Department at the University of Iowa: "*Tellus* Nos. 1, 2

---

20. *An H. P. Lovecraft Encyclopaedia* gives 1921, but this is corrected to 1920 in S. T. Joshi's *I Am Providence*.

21. S. T. Joshi and David E. Schultz, *An H. P. Lovecraft Encyclopaedia* (2001; New York: Hippocampus Press, 2004).

22. www.locategrave.org/l/3983399/William-F-Anger-NY

23. *The FictionMags Index*, online.

(1941), 3 (1942), 4 (1943), 5 (1944), 6 (1945)." This fanzine run might be usefully inspected for articles on Lovecraft or his circle. It might also give biographical details for Smith's friend Fred Anger and details of their post-1945 plans. Smith was hosting weekly meetings for SF fans at his home in 1942.[24] His last fannish publication was probably *Unknown Index* (n.d., 1944 or 1946), a bibliographic index to the pulp *Unknown* and *Unknown Worlds*.[25] In the mid-1940s he appears to vanish from fandom and the online record.

Decades later a Louis C. Smith appears just once in the online record, giving a paper at the first Popular Culture Association National Conference (1971). Yet my searches show that he does not appear to have published other papers and books in the 1960s and 70s, as a regular senior academic might have done. If this is indeed Lovecraft's Smith, then my guess would be that he had become an academic librarian, since the bibliographic urge was obviously strong in him. If there is a printed program extant for the first PCA national conference, if might be investigated for a possible Smith biography.

Horatio L. Smith, 36 Dodd St, Montclair NJ
Horatio Elwin Smith (1886–1946)
I suspect "Horatio L. Smith" is another mistranscription from the 1937 Diary. Montclair is a leafy suburb some 15 miles from the Columbia University campus. A likely candidate is then Horatio Elwin Smith (1886–1946), a lecturer at Columbia University c. 1934–46. Regrettably, I have been unable to pin him or his wife to 36 Dodd St. or any other home address around Columbia. But Smith is a likely candidate for several reasons other than the name and location. He published the scholarly article "Poe's Extension of His Theory of the Tale" in the August 1918 edition of *Modern Philology*, and he was head of the Romance Languages Department at Brown University[26] from 1925[27] to c. 1934.[28] As a keen specialist in con-

---

24. *Astounding Science Fiction* 28, No. 6 (1942): 110.

25. The description of contents from a book record at the WorldCat book database.

26. In 1926 the *Smith Alumnae Quarterly* gave the address of his wife Ernestine (née Failing) as "168 Irving Av., Providence, R.I.," which was about a mile east of Brown University. In 1934 there was a "new address" given for Ernestine of

temporary European fiction, one wonders if Smith could have told Lovecraft of the new developments in French and Spanish literary surrealism. Some may think it unlikely that Lovecraft was known, to any great degree, by an important faculty member at Brown University. Yet Lovecraft was apparently known by sight[29] to Robert Kenny (1902–1983)[30] of the English Literature Department at Brown. One wonders if Kenny mentioned Lovecraft to Smith in either 1925/6, or between 1928 and c. 1934. Smith's papers and correspondence, if still held in the archives at Columbia or elsewhere, might be usefully investigated for possible Lovecraft materials.

"89 University Av., Providence, R.I." just a block north from the old address.

27. Martha Mitchell's *Encyclopedia Brunoniana* history article on "Modern Languages" at Brown states: "Horatio E. Smith came to head the Romance Languages Department in 1925." *Encyclopedia Brunoniana* does not give a departure date for him.

28. A good short biography of Smith is given in the uncredited official "A Brief History of the Romance Languages at Amherst College" (online at www.amherst.edu). The Amherst article is unable to supply any exact date for Smith's move from Brown to Columbia, nor can the *Encyclopedia Brunoniana*. Through tracing notes on Smith's wife in her alumni magazines, and by noting Smith's affiliation details in the *College Entrance Examination Board* report of 1933, I have been able to establish that Smith's move to Columbia occurred in or just after 1934.

29. Kenny was the one who notably remembered spotting HPL working in a ticket booth in a downtown Providence movie house, the sighting being probably c. spring 1930.

30. Robert Webb "Pat" Kenny (1902–1983). Kenneth W. Faig, Jr., stated in a comment on my blog www.tentaclii.wordpress.com that Kenny was "an instructor in the English Department [at Brown] in 1925–26, received his M.A. in 1926 [then taught at Brown] 1928–71." Kenny was a specialist in eighteenth-century literature, according to Martha Mitchell's *Encyclopedia Brunoniana* history article on "English" at Brown. This fact might establish why he knew of HPL, who was of course an expert on eighteenth-century literature and also on the architecture of the period. I know of no essay exploring the extent of HPL's links with Kenny, and Kenny does not appear in the index of S. T. Joshi's definitive Lovecraft bibliography. Kenny is not in the contents list of *Lovecraft Remembered* and has no entry in *Lovecraft Encyclopaedia*.

Lovecraft, Reality, and the Real: A Žižekian Approach

Juan Luis Pérez de Luque

1. Lovecraft and Žižek's Real

Slavoj Žižek's analysis and expansion of the Lacanian concept of the Real provides a powerful tool for approaching H. P. Lovecraft's ideas of reality beyond reality. When, in his tales, the protagonist apprehends a dark past in which the Earth was occupied by evil and terrifying creatures, or understands that there are also other planes of existence for alien gods and creatures, or even that these creatures are sharing our own planet, he is apprehending a new reality that can be read in terms of the difference between Real and reality proposed by the French psychiatrist.

For Lacan, the Real is a concept closely linked to the Symbolic and the Imaginary, since its own definition and nature are described in relation with the other two elements: the Real is what is not imaginary and cannot be symbolized. In his *Seminar I: Freud's Papers on Technique*, Lacan says that "the real, or what is perceived as such, is what resists symbolisation absolutely" (66). According to Evans, "[the real] is impossible to imagine, impossible to integrate into the symbolic order, and impossible to attain in any way. It is this character of impossibility and of resistance to symbolisation which lends the real its essentially traumatic quality" (187).

The Real is something that escapes from language, that cannot be apprehended because its own irrepresentability, and has to be distinguished from reality, which is the result of the different representations produced by symbolic and imaginary articulations.

Žižek goes a step further in the analysis made by Lacan, and he divides the Real into three different categories, which coincide with the imaginary/real/symbolic division:

> There are thus THREE modalities of the Real, i.e. the triad IRS
> reflects itself within the order of the Real, so that we have the
> "real Real" (the horrifying Thing, the primordial object, [. . .]), the
> "symbolic Real" (the signifier reduced to a senseless formula, like
> the quantum physics formulae which can no longer be translated
> back into –or related to– the everyday experience of our life-
> world), AND the "imaginary Real" (the mysterious je ne sais quoi,
> the unfathomable "something" that introduces a self-division into
> an ordinary object, so that the sublime dimension shines through
> it). (*On Belief* 82)

From this subdivision of the real made by Slavoj Žižek, the three
categories are of interest for my analysis, as I will discuss below.
When reading H. P. Lovecraft one of the key points of his universe is the existence of a hidden truth, like one of his most famous creations, Cthulhu and the sunken city of R'lyeh. The
revelation of this new reality beyond reality is a shock for the
character who, in general terms, cannot even symbolize with
words the monster he is trying to depict. I will exemplify this aspect with two particular moments in Lovecraft's narrative, where
the narrator witnesses something horrible—a demonic landscape
in the first one and an evil creature in the second text.

In "The Music of Erich Zann," the main character looks
through a window where he was expecting to get a panoramic
view of the city. Instead, what he gets is:

> [. . .] only the blackness of space illimitable; unimagined space
> alive with motion and music, and having no semblance to any-
> thing on earth. And as I stood there looking in terror, the wind
> blew out both the candles in that ancient peaked garret, leaving
> me in savage and impenetrable darkness with chaos and pande-
> monium before me, and the daemon madness of that night-baying
> viol behind me. (*DH* 90)

On the other hand, *At the Mountains of Madness* offers the following description of a shoggoth: "It was a terrible, indescribable thing
vaster than any subway train—a shapeless congeries of protoplas-
mic bubbles, faintly self-luminious, and with myriads of tempo-

rary eyes forming and unforming as pustules of greenish light" (*MM* 101).

I would like to anticipate a lexical aspect in Lovecraft's descriptions that I will explore later. The use of adjectives such as "indescribable," "unnamable," "shapeless," "impenetrable" permeate all the descriptions of the monsters with a clear sense of something that cannot be represented, explained, or symbolized. Lovecraft's monsters are the symbolization of the Lacanian Real; they are something impossible to describe, which escapes language because its own frightening unknown nature. During the epiphanic moment in which the character contemplates the truth, he is having a glimpse of the Real, and there is no way he can explain it. According to Žižek, the Real is the starting point and precedes the symbolic order, and at the same time it is the leftover of this process of symbolization (*Sublime Object* 191).

Moving forward to the division of the Real made by Žižek, it is challenging to explore if Lovecraft's monstrous creations would fit into the realm of the imaginary Real, the real Real, or the symbolic Real. Žižek raises this triad of the Real in relation to religion, and he gives the example (*On Belief* 82–83) of God the Father as real Real, as the primordial Thing, God the Son as the imaginary Real, and the Holy Ghost as the symbolic Real.

From the three different categories, the symbolic Real is the most cryptic. It is the futile attempt to symbolize the Real into reality, and the result is a "senseless formula." Would it be possible to link the symbolic Real to Lovecraft's monstrous creations? I suggest that a linguistic analysis of the descriptions made by Lovecraft results in this version of the Real. It is a metalinguistic Real that is reached from the lexical analysis of the text. When trying to figure out what is the nature of a particular creature of the Mythos, what the reader gets is just a linguistic barrier. The obscurity of the language used by Lovecraft is much more noticeable in his descriptions of monsters. The abuse in the use of adjectives, archaisms, and the semantic field related to things that cannot be described or named give an overall impression of confusion and chaos. It is very difficult to recreate a mental image of how Nyarlathotep or a shoggoth look like, because the narrator that Lovecraft offers to the reader is unable to symbolize the Thing, and the result is a poor and dark description that is not reliable in its accuracy.[1]

For my analysis and interpretation of the symbolic Real, I will follow Graham Harman's theory of the existence of two different gaps between language and reality in the texts of H. P. Lovecraft:

> And here we have the two major axes of Lovecraft's literary style: the "vertical" gap between unknowable objects and their tangible qualities, and the "horizontal" or "cubist" gap between an accessible object and its gratuitous amassing of numerous palpable surfaces. . . . Any time we run across a passage in Lovecraft that is *literally* impossible to visualize we are dealing with this first kind of tension between a real object and its sensual qualities, so reminiscent of Heidegger's tool-analysis. At other times, there is the "cubist" tension between sensual or non-hidden objects and their sensual qualities that pile up in disturbing profusion. (31, 34)

The "vertical" gap corresponds with the accumulation of "unknowable"-like words and expressions. The abundance of vocabulary filling paragraphs, resulting in an unintelligible and void description, configures the "vertical" gap. The "horizontal" gap, on the other side, is produced when there is an abuse of meaningful adjectives and lexical constructions that try to reproduce all the features and characteristics of the object-monster. When doing so, Lovecraft provokes a fracture in language, since the overembellishment of the narrative through excessive use of adjectives does not allow the recreation of a proper image of the object. So the symbolic Real may be present as a "vertical" gap or as the cubist "horizontal" gap.

The following passage exemplifies the "vertical" gap. It is an excerpt from "The Unnamable," in which the impossibility to represent the Monster is discussed:

> Manton remained thoughtful as I said this, but gradually reverted to his analytical mood. He granted for the sake of argument that some unnatural monster had really existed, but reminded me that even the most morbid perversion of Nature need not be unnam-

---

1. Notice that the topos of the indescribable is not exclusive to Lovecraft. In fact, it is inherited from the Romantic tradition and Poe, and it can be traced in modernist works such as Conrad's *The Heart of Darkness*.

able or scientifically indescribable [. . .] if the psychic emanations of human creatures be grotesque distortions, what coherent representation could express or portray so gibbous and infamous a nebulosity as the spectre of a malign, chaotic perversion, itself a morbid blasphemy against Nature? Moulded by the dead brain of a hybrid nightmare, would not such a vaporous terror constitute in all loathsome truth the exquisitely, the shriekingly *unnamable*? (*D* 205)

The "cubist" gap is appreciated, for instance, in the fragmentary descriptions of Cthulhu given in "The Call of Cthulhu." The most accurate ones are based on sculptures of the monster, one of them having "yielded simultaneous pictures of an octopus, a dragon, and a human caricature" (*DH* 127).

So the symbolic Real is physical, tangible, always terrifying and impossible to describe in its fullness. It is equivalent to the alien in Ridley Scott's 1979 film *Alien*, described by Žižek:

> The 'alien,' the eight, supplementary passenger, is an object which, being nothing at all in itself, must none the less be added, annexed as an anamorphic surplus. It is the Real at its purest: a semblance, something which on a strictly symbolic level does not exist at all but at the same time the only thing in the whole film which actually exists, the thing against which the whole reality is utterly defenceless. (*Sublime Object* 86)[2]

The imaginary Real, on the other hand, is a change in reality that modifies it. According to Žižek, it "forever distorts our perception of reality, introducing anamorphic stains in it, or the pure Schein (appearing) of Nothing that only "shines through" reality" (*On Belief* 81). The imaginary Real can be read as a trace of the Real itself, as a clue of the existence of something beyond reality. It is the uncanny feeling, the mysterious noise, the subtle evil glance, the small detail that drives to the Real.

In terms of literary language, the imaginary Real equals the

---

2. Notice that Žižek did not develop his Real triad until 2001. In 1989 he just talked about the Real as a whole, and from this exemplification of what the Real is, it can be said that his idea of the Real at this time matches the real Real that he will stipulate later.

moments of the narration in which the reader gets the impression that there is something weird undergoing the succession of events of the plot. The drops of blood falling from the ceiling in "The Picture in the House," which reveal that the kind old man hides a terrible truth, are part of this imaginary Real.

The third element of the triad, the real Real, is the embodiment of the truth beyond reality, what the hero in Lovecraft's narration discovers. My hypothesis is that Lovecraft's literary production hides a real Real that is overdetermined with semes of the writer's own ideology. Both the symbolic and the imaginary Real are representations of the anxieties the author is presenting in his texts. The Real in his narrative is the set of social and cultural situations and problems Lovecraft is not able to understand and rationalize. Topics related with the past in general and the origins of humankind in particular—racial issues, New Englandness, immigration—are in the background of many of Lovecraft texts. Lovecraft, as his own characters, cannot cope with the truth he finds in his world and tries to project it into the realm of the symbolic and the imaginary.

Through the interaction of the symbolic Real with the imaginary Real, the real Real is re-symbolized in the literary proposal of the writer, in an attempt to assimilate and reproduce it. The Real changes its shapes in those of the different elements appearing in Lovecraft's stories.

At this point, I would like to formulate and recapitulate the correspondences between the triad of the Real and Lovecraft's literary discourse:

1. The symbolic Real is a lexical construction. It is the result of the irrepresentability of the Real itself when in contact with language. When the Lovecraftian hero unfruitfully tries to depict the horror he is watching, the resulting failed symbolization, shaped as an obscure passage of text, full of adjectives, archaisms, and imprecisions, is what constitutes the symbolic Real. There are two main ways in which the symbolic Real is present in Lovecraft's literary production:

    a. The overuse of words from the semantic field of the unmentionable, defined by Harman as the "vertical" gap. Language fails in its basic communicative task, since the Real cannot be named or mentioned.

    b.   The overwriting of the passages in which the Real is being depicted. The accumulation of adjectives trying to describe it creates what Harman defines as a "cubist" gap, which has the effect of blurring the object. The reader is unable to grasp the sensual qualities of the image because the saturation of the narration.

2.   The imaginary Real is a narratological resource. The tricks used by Lovecraft in order to slide the uncanny Real into the realm of reality are of a different nature, but they are normally present in the tradition of the genre. Like clues for Doyle's Sherlock Holmes or Poe's Auguste Dupin, Lovecraft spreads details that reveal the existence of the Real both to his hero and the reader.

3.   Finally, the real Real transcends the narration. It is the result of the ideological background of the author in the text, which is represented by the other two elements of the triad.

2. A Case Study: "The Shadow over Innsmouth"

"The Shadow over Innsmouth," to a certain extent, turns around the importance of time from a very Gothic point of view. The Gothic influence comes from the fact that the presence of a cursed lineage is the central axis of the plot, and the main character finally discovers that he is part of that family.[3] In words of Lovett-Graff: "The narrator of 'Shadow,' in his trip from fictitious Newburyport to the mythical Arkham, is caught up in a quest for answers far more intimately linked to his past than either he or the reader at first suspects" (180). Far from being an Usher-like family, which ends up with its own destruction in Poe's tale, Lovecraft's House of Marsh is not a menace for themselves, but for human beings as a whole.

Before Robert Olmstead reaches Innsmouth, everything related to the town has a halo of mystery and superstition. All the refer-

---

3. As Botting points out in his analysis of Radcliffe's *The Mysteries of Udolfo*, "ghosts of past family transgressions become the major source of awful emotion" (1996:69). The transgressions committed in the past by the Marsh family affect the narrator and main character of "The Shadow over Innsmouth".

ences the narrator finds about the seaport are obscure; inhabitants of the neighboring villages evade it and its people; "people don't like it" (DH 305), "Animals hate 'em" (DH 308),[4] and whenever the protagonist finds somebody who is not reluctant to talk about Innsmouth, the information given does not unravel the mystery but embroils it even more. The seaport is modeled upon the principles of the symbolic Real and, especially, the imaginary Real. The reader soon gets the impression that something strange is happening in the town, when in the first lines of the tale Lovecraft narrates how the government and the police took some special actions in the seaport, blowing up many buildings and arresting several citizens. The presence of the uncanny, the imaginary Real that warns the reader about the presence of a hidden truth in the plot, is evident because no clear explanation of what the government was doing in Innsmouth is given. Harman remarks the difference between this situation—the governmental interference into the Mythos—and the typical Lovecraftian tale:

> In most of Lovecraft's stories, the terrible truth is known only to a small number of people, and is either purposely shielded from the public for their own good, or offered to the public and met with disbelief. [. . .] In the case of Innsmouth things work in reverse: the authorities already know too much, and prefer that the public should continue to know very little. (174–75)

As the story continues, the atmosphere around Innsmouth thickens, and it is described as an "ill-rumoured and evilly shadowed seaport of death and blasphemous abnormality" (DH 305). When the protagonist visits the museum to examine the tiara, he discovers an object he "can hardly describe" (DH 311). The tiara, as

---

4. Notice the mythic image of animals being afraid of the Innsmouth people, as happened with the dogs in At the Mountains of Madness. According to Lovett-Graff, "This moral 'sixth' sense capable of distinguishing good from evil thus becomes a dramatic device to accentuate the difference between socially constructed appearances and biological (read 'natural') realities" (180–81). Animals afraid of monsters and uncanny creatures are a classical image from the gothic and horror tradition, and it helps to reinforce the imaginary Real in the tale. It triggers the reader's imagination and makes him think that there is something strange happening in Innsmouth.

will be known later in the tale, is an artifact taken from the Deep Ones, belonging to the realm of the Real, engraved with patterns that "all hinted of remote secrets and unimaginable abysses in time and space" (*DH* 311). This sentence joins together the imaginary Real and the symbolic Real. On the one hand, the remote secrets giving the impression that there is something obscure and latent in the origins of the tiara will spoil the reader's imagination to think that strange events underlie the general plot, becoming a reference to the imaginary Real; it is a clear hint that uncanny things are to come. On the other hand, the unimaginable abysses are the example of the narrator's incapacity to recreate the reality he is contemplating. He is not able fully and accurately to describe the bas-reliefs and engravings of the tiara, because language is not sufficient for this task; the appearance of an object that belongs to the Real into the domestic world of the narrator is reflected on the adjective "unimaginable." The symbolic Real is present at the very moment this word—lexically related to the incapacity to reproduce reality—is used by Lovecraft in the description, creating a "vertical" gap in language.

The narrator is both fascinated and disturbed when observing the item, and in spite of giving a more or less comprehensible description of it, Lovecraft introduces the presence of the symbolic Real when his character mentions how indescribable the tiara is, but also when he points out that he is unable to attribute the workmanship that produced the piece of jewelry to any "known racial or national stream" (*DH* 311). The lack of a clear origin for the tiara, as well as its manufacturing, which seems "that of another planet" (*DH* 311), put the object beyond our daily reality. In words of Harman:

> We encounter objects that are utterly startling in their novelty, yet which are nonetheless recognizable as belonging to a distinct and otherworldly style. Our attention is thereby shifted from the surface content of such objects to whatever barely detectable regularities in its structure alert us that they belong to a settled tradition. (178)

So even before the narrator arrives at Innsmouth, the text is already hinting at the existence of the Real, by means of the incapacity to reproduce the qualities of the tiara—the symbolic Real—and the elements which make the reader (not the protagonist) think that something uncanny is happening in the seaport.

The first encounter with the bus driver provokes in the narrator a "wave of spontaneous aversion which could be neither checked nor explained" (*DH* 313). Before introducing any kind of physical description, Lovecraft notes the abnormal and indescribable repulsion this character causes: once again, the symbolic Real and the imaginary Real come together.

Following this first wave of aversion, the physical description reinforces the sense of monstrosity derived from the man. He is presented as a figure with "deep creases in the side of his neck," with "narrow head, bulging, watery blue eyes," "long, thick lip and coarse-pored, greyish cheeks," and whose "hands were large and heavily veined, and had a very unusual greyish-blue tinge." To complete the portrait, his "inordinately immense" feet produced a "peculiarly shambling gait" (*DH* 314). The narrator tries to find a scientific explanation for such a deformed being, and the arguments he weighs to himself have some interesting racial connotations: "Just what foreign blood was in him I could not even guess. His oddities certainly did not look Asiatic, Polynesian, Levantine, or negroid, yet I could see why the people found him alien. I myself would have thought of biological degeneration rather than alienage" (*DH* 314).[5] The main character cannot associate the strange physical characteristics of the bus driver to any known race because the physical degradation he has makes it impossible. Harman states that "Sargent would appear to belong to a known earthly race in a state of inbred genetic decline" (183). The whole description of Joe Sargent is representative of the "cubist" gap postulated by Harman. The accumulation of adjectives and description of features of the man are an obstacle, in the end, when trying to imagine the physical appearance of the driver.

The feelings resulting from the first look at the inhabitants of the place are not much different from those expressed when the narrator observed the bus driver. He asserts that he "instinctively

---

5. Notice that, according to the protagonist, the Esoteric Order of Dagon is probably something "imported from the East" (*DH* 312).

disliked [certain peculiarities of face and motions] without being able to define or comprehend them" (*DH* 317). Again, the instinctive dislike toward Innsmouth folk is related to the imaginary Real, and the feeling of strangeness emanating from the inhabitants of the town warns the reader. At the same time, the narrator expresses his own incapacity to describe or understand this rejection, making the symbolic Real present at this moment as well.

The encounter with Zadok, and his long speech about the secrets of Innsmouth, results in the narrator rationalizing the whole story. According to him, everything is the product of Zadok's insanity. The implications of what is happening in the seaport have a strong scientific and ideological background. In short, the Deep Ones, alien marine creatures, are intermingling with human beings.

Lovett-Graff asserts that Lovecraft was a belated eugenics supporter. By writing "The Shadow over Innsmouth" in 1931, seven years after the passing of the Immigration Restriction Act of 1924,[6] the writer was still giving his support to a social movement that was already "losing members as the Great Depression swept up citizens with more pressing issues" (176). According to Lovett-Graff, the association between Deep Ones and immigrants is too obvious to be avoided in this tale of biological horror. The references made in the tale to the trips of Obed Marsh to "Africa, Asia the South Sea, and everywhere else" (*DH* 307) overtly point to several groups of immigrants, since "there must be something like that back of the Innsmouth people" (*DH* 307). Zadok explains that the Deep Ones live in underwater nests all around the globe, but the allusions to Africa and Asia are clearly expressed, and the two continents are the source of the "Innsmouth look." The intercourse between the monsters and human beings is the beginning of the process of blood degradation and degeneration.

This comparison between the monster and the foreigner has been well noticed and remarked by Maurice Lévy:

> For Lovecraft [. . .] the displaying of these execrable mutants seems perhaps, in an obscure and confusing way, a testimonial to

---

6. This federal law limited the amount of immigrants that could be admitted in the United States to 2% of each foreign-born group living in the country in 1890.

the failure of America's politics of racial assimilation, a deliberate rejection of the notion of the "melting pot," which forms so integral a part of the American dream. In this man, ever faithful to the ideologies of the past, any infringement of the strictest segregation ends in disastrous, in monstrous ˌ consequences. [. . .] Thus the monsters, fruit of repugnant matings of humans with "outsiders," represent the ultimate level of degeneracy that lies in wait for American civilization if it continues to encourage, or simply to tolerate, the mixture of bloods and races, hybridism, crossbreeding are at the source of the monstrous. (61–62)

Lévy also highlights the concept of invasion, which is the ultimate risk that has to be avoided for Lovecraft. The monster has the ability to corrupt, and "is revolting not only because it escapes logic and constitutes a disturbance for the reason, but also because it is propagated and, little by little, corrupts the individuals of a healthy race" (57).

For Lévy, the formula "Deep One equals immigrant" is clear, as it is for Lovett-Graff. The inherent racism of Lovecraft[7] is reflected in his writing, and the Puritan New England tradition triggers it, playing the same role "as medieval myth did in the Gothic novels" (119). The process of progressive invasion and degeneration carried out by the Deep Ones over the community of Innsmouth is analyzed under the scope of the Lovecraftian fantastic by Lévy: "The bizarre does not fall from space to terrify or confound, but to corrupt. It is a type of gangrene that gnaws, wears away, and finally rots the familiar world through and through" (38). The organic metaphor of gangrene used by Lévy is perfectly suitable for the events happening in the seaport. Reality, in a Lacanian sense, is under the menace of the gangrene of the Real: the New England that Lovecraft knew and loved was under the siege of immigrants.

The description of the grotesque parade of Deep Ones the narrator peeks from the bushes (DH 360–61) is done with an emphasis on the most physical aspects of the creatures. The accumulation of adjectives to provide an overelaborated portrait of the sounds, movements, colors, and shapes that the narrator is witnessing follows Harman's idea of the cubist description, with a

---

7. See Lévy (27f.) for a detailed explanation of this matter.

profusion of "sensual qualities that pile up in disturbing profusion" (34). This I have assimilated as symbolic Real, because of the disruption and interference it produces in language, similar to that produced by the use of unspeakable-like adjectives. The description is so excessive that it obstructs the representation of the object.

The group is defined as a malignant saraband. According to the *Encyclopaedia Britannica*, the saraband or sarabande is a dance, probably originating in Central America in the sixteenth century, which was derived from a Spanish-Arab dance. It was forbidden in Spain because of its obscenity.[8] The noun used to define the group of creatures condensates two decadent aspects for Lovecraft: eroticism and non-Aryan races—Hispanic and Arab. Lovett-Graff proposes that the sexual connotations of the whole tale are closely related to Lovecraft's prejudices against the supposedly vigorous and more active sexual activity immigrants had, which would lead to the complete corruption of the pure blood and race he belonged to (186–89).

During the time he lived in New York, Lovecraft had the opportunity to observe the masses of immigrants overcrowding the underground, and he felt repulsion against them, as he states in a letter written on 21 March 1924. In that letter, the writer says that immigrants could not be called human but "monstrous and nebulous adumbrations of the pithecanthropoid and amoebal" (*SL* 1.333). Lovett-Graff develops this analysis further (182–83), comparing the description of the Deep Ones with that made of the immigrants by Lovecraft in the quoted letter. Apart from the resemblances in the use of decadent and repulsive adjectives, he also pays attention to the sounds produced by the monstrous speech, concluding that "In spite of the fantastic form he gives 'Shadow,' Lovecraft's personal disgust with immigrant speech is barely contained by the 'babel' of sound that threatens to overwhelm the pure English of his Nordic America" (183). The croaking, baying voices they produce are, for Lovett-Graff, no more than a transposition of the different languages spoken by the immigrants living in the United States.

---

8. Probably the most famous sarabande was the one composed by Georg Friedrich Handel for his *Keyboard Suite in D minor* (c. 1703–06; HWD 437).

It is at the end of "The Shadow over Innsmouth" that the reader knows that Olmstead is corrupted by the blood of the Deep Ones. In terms of ideology, he is the result of immigrant miscegenation. He is the offspring of foreigners coming from distant places, and when he discovers that, he decides to come back to the sea, the place his ancestors came from, to spread their degenerated blood in Lovecraft's New England. "The Shadow over Innsmouth" has, in my opinion, two different meanings, which are related to the real Real hidden behind the story.

The first point of view is the triumph of immigration. The narrator, a scientific mind, a curious young person with intellectual and cultural interests, is also corrupted by the blood of the monster. In the context of the horror tale, that would be one of Lovecraft's more hideous nightmares. In one of his letters to Frank Belknap Long, in 1927, after digging in his family tree back to the time of George III, he admits that his great-great-grandmother was a "Welsh gentlewoman of unmixed Celtick blood!" (SL 2.181), and his great-great-great-grandmother was a "full-blooded Celt" (SL 2.183). But, probably half-serious, half-joking, he asserts that "the Celtick taint hath not reached my rural Saxon heart!" (SL 2.182). The idea of not having a clear and clean lineage obviously obsessed the writer, and making his protagonist fall into the decadent spiral depicted in Innsmouth can be read as the ultimate failure of America in its immigration control policies (Lévy 61). It is true that when Lovecraft wrote "The Shadow over Innsmouth," during the Depression years, the number of immigrants reaching the United States was almost insignificant in comparison with previous years (1,200,000 in 1914 and 23.000 in 1933, according to the U.S. Department of Homeland Security[9]). However, they were already in the country and it was something disturbing for him.

My second reading of Olmstead's assimilation of his origins is related to a possible underground proposal exposed by Lovecraft: the solution to avoid the degeneration of the American nation is

---

9. Complete statistics of persons obtaining legal permanent resident status from 1820 to 2011 can be found at http://www.dhs.gov/yearbook-immigration-statistics-2011-1 (last accessed 6/5/2013).

to expel the immigrants, forcing them to return with their fellow beings in their native countries. Robert Olmstead escapes and moves back to his origins, with his fellow alien creatures, and that would be, for Lovecraft, a way of restoring the social equilibrium. In words of S. T. Joshi:

> What Lovecraft wanted was simply familiarity—the familiarity of the milieu in a racially and culturally homogeneous Providence that he had experienced in youth. In stating that even art must satisfy our "homesickness ... for the things we have known" ("Heritage or Modernism"), Lovecraft is testifying to the home-sickness he himself felt when, as an "unassimilated alien" in New York or even in latter-day Providence, he witnessed the increasing urbanization and racial heterogeneity of his region and his country. (*H. P. Lovecraft: A Life* 591)

At this point, I have already analyzed the presence of the symbolic Real and the imaginary Real throughout "The Shadow over Innsmouth." As has been said, the presence of elements that subtly suggest the existence of uncanny events is linked to the representation of the imaginary Real. On the other hand, the moments in which language is fractured or obstructed, via the incapacity for describing reality or the overexaggerated descriptions, are the ways in which the symbolic Real invades textual reality. The previous discussion about the ideological background behind the tale tries to elucidate the real Real hidden in the decadent Innsmouth. The imaginary Real points to the processes of miscegenation and immigration observed by Lovecraft in his reality, and it matches the intermingling between monsters and humans. The symbolic Real, the unnamable creature, points to the immigrant. The real Real underlying "The Shadow over Innsmouth" is the social alien whom Lovecraft observed in his daily life, the immigrants whom he mentioned in New York and their slow but steady process of establishment in the New England of his time. According to Morgan, "such writers much project and objectify their suffocating biological anxiety in order to survive" (101).

3. Conclusion

"The Shadow over Innsmouth" depicts some of the most noticeable obsessions Lovecraft had in terms of social ideology. There is a fear of the immigrant and the decline of the purity of races as a result of miscegenation underlying the story, and science is used as a way to convey this anxiety. The writer is applying his knowledge of sciences to portray the reality he is observing and experiencing in the New England of the 1920s and 1930s New England, following, according to Lovett-Graff, the principles of eugenics.

The constant presence of the symbolic Real and the imaginary Real, together with the general decadent and degenerated tone of the narration, are the means by which Lovecraft exposes his ideology in the text, his way to rationalize the fragments of the Real he has discovered and cannot cope with. In words of Joshi, "we can relate this decline to Lovecraft's belief that miscegenation can lead to the collapse of civilization" ("Alien Civilisations" 122).

Works Cited

Botting, Fred. *Gothic*. London: Routledge, 1996.

Evans, Dylan. An Introductory Dictionary of Lacanian Psychoanalysis. London: Routledge, 1996.

Harman, Graham. *Weird Realism: Lovecraft and Philosophy*. Winchester: Zero Books, 2012.

Joshi, S. T. *H. P. Lovecraft: A Life*. West Warwick, Necronomicon Press, 1996.

————. "Lovecraft's Alien Civilizations: A Political Interpretation." In Joshi's *Primal Sources: Essays on H. P. Lovecraft*. New York: Hippocampus Press, 2003.

Lacan, Jacques. *The Seminar: Book I. Freud's Papers on Technique, 1953–54.* Cambridge: Cambridge University Press, 1988.

Lévy, Maurice. *Lovecraft: A Study in the Fantastic*. Trans. S. T. Joshi. Detroit: Wayne State University Press, 1988.

Lovett-Graff, Bennett. "Shadows over Lovecraft: Reactionary Fantasy and Immigrant Eugenics." *Extrapolation* 38 (Fall 1997): 175–92.

Morgan, Jack. *The Biology of Horror. Gothic Literature and Film*. Carbondale: Southern Illinois University Press, 2002.

Noys, Benjamin. "The Horror of the Real: Žižek's Modern Gothic."
    International Journal of Žižek Studies 4, No. 4 (2010). (online
    publication). http://zizekstudies.org/index.php/ijzs/article/
    view/274/372 (last accessed: 26/05/2013).
Žižek, Slavoj. *On Belief.* New York: Routledge, 2001.
————. *The Sublime Object of Ideology.* London: Verso, 1989.

Reviews

H. P. LOVECRAFT. *The Classic Horror Stories.* Edited by Roger Luckhurst. Oxford: Oxford University Press, 2013. xxxvi, 487 pp. Reviewed by S. T. Joshi.

The book under review was compiled by Roger Luckhurst, a professor of modern literature at Birkbeck College in the University of London. He has no obvious qualifications for assembling the book, since to my knowledge he has not written a single book, article, or review about Lovecraft. Instead, he has written a book on mummies and edited some Victorian works of the supernatural for Oxford University Press. But one must not condemn a book merely because its compiler may be a relative newcomer to the field; after all, we are all newcomers once.

There are at least three ways to assess this volume: 1) its selection of material; 2) its preparation of the texts; and 3) its notes and commentary. In all these ways, but especially in the second and third, this book fails lamentably.

As for the selection of stories: it is unexceptionable—except for the inclusion of "The Horror at Red Hook" (1925), a shoddy and contrived story that nearly every Lovecraft scholar regards as one of his worst tales. The choice of this story is particularly anomalous because Luckhurst avows that his selections "primarily focus on Lovecraft's work after his return from his traumatic years in New York in 1926." Why the exception for "Red Hook"? Evidently it embodies "Lovecraft's engagement with the actual city of New York." If this formulation makes any sense, it would surely have been better to have included the poignant story "He" ("My coming to New York was a mistake . . .") or the compact and satisfying horror tale "Cool Air." And if Luckhurst had already decided to violate his general rule of printing stories from the 1926–31 period (which he in any case has violated in the other direction by printing "The Dreams in the Witch House" [1932] and "The Shadow out of Time" [1934–35]), he could have done so by printing "The Outsider" (1921), one of Lovecraft's signature stories, or "The Rats in the Walls" (1923), a nearly perfect example of short story construction.

In regard to his preparation of the texts, Luckhurst has made the regrettable decision to return (more or less) to the original pulp magazine editions of the stories. At this late date, when my corrected editions of Lovecraft's stories have been available for nearly three decades, the logic of this decision can seriously be questioned. What is to be gained by this procedure? Was Luckhurst or his publisher unwilling to pay the modest fee I might (or might not) have charged for the use of my texts? If push came to shove, I would have provided the texts gratis. Did they not know how to contact me? I hear from people around the world every day and usually reply in minutes. I could have provided Luckhurst with the corrected texts with one click of a mouse, as I have recently done to Leslie S. Klinger for his forthcoming *Annotated H. P. Lovecraft* (W. W. Norton).

Or, if Luckhurst didn't wish to rely on my editions, he could have done the job himself. For every one of the stories in his book (with the exception of "The Colour out of Space"), a fairly clean typescript exists in the John Hay Library of Brown University. He need not even have made the tedious (but no doubt pleasant) trip to Providence to consult the texts; the library would probably have sent him copies at his request. In these particular instances (with the possible exclusion of *At the Mountains of Madness*), the preparation of the texts from the typescripts would not qualify as rocket science. He could probably have delegated the job to a graduate student or even an eager undergraduate.

How does Luckhurst defend this return to corrupt texts? Well, in reality he doesn't. He states: "The texts have been checked against the first publication of the stories, nearly all in pulp magazines, with obvious mistakes silently corrected." There is a considerable ambiguity in this utterance. Let us consider the text of "The Call of Cthulhu." Luckhurst has in fact *not* followed the *Weird Tales* (February 1928) text in certain particulars, especially as regards Lovecraft's British spellings, which appear in his text but do *not* appear in the *Weird Tales* text. Surely he cannot claim that the (proper) restoration of the British spellings constitutes a "correction" of "obvious mistakes"; what is more, not *all* of Lovecraft's British spellings have been restored, as Luckhurst has not printed "connexion" (found in Lovecraft's typescript) where *Weird Tales* (and all previous texts prior to mine) print the American "connection." Luckhurst does follow *Weird Tales* in (erroneously) printing "Eskimos" where Lovecraft wrote "Esquimaux." He follows *Weird Tales* in some paragraphing errors as well. Then he prints "This data," whereas *Weird Tales* and earlier Arkham House editions printed "These data." The fact is that "This data" is a grammatical error found in Lovecraft's typescript, and I printed it in my text. *Weird Tales* was actually correct in printing "These data." But I need not go on. The end result is a textual mishmash more worthy of some fly-by-night publisher rather than of one of the world's great academic presses.

The most unfortunate decision was to use the *Astounding Stories* appearances of *At the Mountains of Madness* and "The Shadow out of Time." Even Luckhurst appears dimly aware that the former, in its butchered appearance in *Astounding*, is so corrupt as to be unusable; so he has essentially used the version that August Derleth prepared in 1939 (reprinted, with further errors, in 1964), based on Lovecraft's corrected copies of *Astounding*, where at least the paragraphing has been repaired and the omissions of text (especially toward the end) mostly filled in. But the result is still a text that contains about 1500 divergences from the typescript. In the case of "The Shadow out of Time," the decision is also regrettable. Consider this passage in *Astounding:*

> I was born and raised in Haverhill [. . .] and did not go to Arkham till I entered Miskatonic University as instructor of political economy in 1895.

The actual text reads:

> I was born and reared in Haverhill [. . .] and did not go to Arkham till I entered Miskatonic University at the age of eighteen. That was in 1889. After my graduation I studied economics at Harvard, and came back to Miskatonic as Instructor of Political Economy in 1895.

Luckhurst actually supplies the above passage in a footnote; but the degree of his ignorance of Lovecraft textual scholarship is betrayed by his comment: "*Astounding* simplified this sentence from HPL's original . . ." What actually happened, in all probability, was that R. H. Barlow, in preparing the typescript of the story for Lovecraft, skipped a line or two of text (probably because his eye saw "Miskatonic" twice and largely skipped from the first usage to the second), causing the omission.

Luckhurst tries to justify his use of the *Astounding* texts by declaring that he wants to "retain some of the pulp energy that *Astounding Stories* wanted to inject into Lovecraft's tales." This is, I humbly submit, blithering idiocy. The only reason *Astounding* chopped up the long paragraphs in both stories is that, in the two-column format of the magazine, the paragraphs would seem even longer than on an ordinary printed page, and therefore would presumably be intimidating to the brainless sods who would be reading the stories. And if Luckhurst really wanted to give present-day readers a taste of "how they [the stories] were first encountered by their audience in the Golden Age of science fiction," he should have printed the *Astounding* version of *At the Mountains of Madness* intact, without Derleth's restoration of the paragraphing and of the passages omitted toward the end.

Let us consider Luckhurst's annotations. For a text of 447 pages, he has about 40 pages of notes. For the same stories, I have 74 pages of annotations in my various Penguin editions. But quantity isn't everything, I suppose. Perhaps Luckhurst has found some nuggets of information that I overlooked? It doesn't appear so. In his notes to "The Horror at Red Hook," he largely copies my own notes, but entirely fails to indicate that Lovecraft had provided his own (often erroneous) definitions of the words in the Hebrew/Greek incantation in the story; I quote them in full in my notes. Where he doesn't copy my notes, Luckhurst gets things wrong. He claims that, in "The Call of Cthulhu," Lovecraft's use of the terms *tornasuk* and *angekok* may have been taken from E. B. Tylor's article on "Demonology" in the *Encyclopaedia Britannica;* in fact, they were taken from Tylor's article on "Eskimos." In his notes to *At the Mountains of Madness*, Luckhurst states that Poe's *Arthur Gordon Pym* was "serialized in 1837 and 1838." In fact, only the first few chapters were serialised in the January and February 1837 issues of the *Southern Literary Messenger;* it was published in book form in 1838.

As for Luckhurst's introduction, it is routine at best. It presents a fairly straightforward, if highly condensed, chronicle of Lovecraft's life and work, although he fails to mention Lovecraft's reading of Poe at the age of eight, the single most significant influence on his weird writing. Luckhurst also dwells far too long on Lovecraft's racism, which is only a relatively small aspect of his philosophy and only enters into a few of his major tales. The introduction is also full of annoying little errors, such as the misspelling (twice) of Gustave (not "Gustav") Doré's name; the implication that Clark Ashton Smith and Robert E. Howard were part of the amateur journalism movement (Smith was only tangentially, Howard not at all); the idea that "Dagon" (1917) was influenced by Lord Dunsany, whom Lovecraft would not read until 1919; the omission of the macron for Dunsany's first book, *The Gods of Pegāna;* the statement that Lovecraft published in *Astounding Science Fiction* (the magazine was called *Astounding Stories* at the time it published Lovecraft's two stories in 1936); the notion that Lovecraft "mov[ed] back to amateur circulation" for his stories after 1931 (he published no fiction in the amateur press after 1925); that Lovecraft was 47 when he died (he was 46 and a half); the dating of Colin Wilson's *The Strength to Dream* to 1962 (it came out in the UK in 1961); the misspelling of the name of Jason Colavito (as "Cavolito"), author of *The Cult of Alien Gods;* the mistitling of Lovecraft's essay "Notes on Writing Weird Fiction" as "Notes on Weird Literature"; the mistitling of Jeff and Ann VanderMeer's collection *The Weird* as *Weird Compendium* (and the misspelling of the editors' names to boot); and so on and so forth.

Luckhurst's "Select Bibliography" of primary and secondary sources is, to be frank, a disgrace. I suppose it was to be expected that he would not list either the two *Annotated H. P. Lovecraft* volumes (1997, 1999) or my three Penguin editions (1999, 2001, 2004), as they are all direct competitors to his own book (he does cite one of the Penguins in a footnote in his introduction). But the omission has apparently led at least one naïve and uninformed re-

viewer—one Jess Nevins, in the *Los Angeles Times Book Review*
and Salon.com—to say of Luckhurst's book: "One might argue
that it is past time for a short form, one-volume critical edition" of
Lovecraft. (Let it pass that this is not a "critical edition," since it
does not formally record textual variants.) For Lovecraft's essays,
Luckhurst lists *Miscellaneous Writings* (1995), which has been out
of print for years and has been totally superseded by *Collected Essays* (2004–06), of which he appears to be unaware. He cites no
edition of Lovecraft's poetry—not *Collected Poems* (1963), not *A
Winter Wish* (1977), not *The Ancient Track* (2001). For letters, he
of course cites *Selected Letters* (1965–76), but cites none of the
many other editions of letters that have appeared since the 1990s.

   In his list of biographical and critical studies, Luckhurst stum-
bles immediately out of the gate by citing Lin Carter's *Look Behind the "Cthulhu Mythos"* (1972). I suppose it was too much to
expect him to know of my *Rise and Fall of the Cthulhu Mythos*
(2008); given that ignorance, it would probably have been better
to have passed over Carter's flatulent popular tract in merciful si-
lence. He does cite the three versions of my biography (1996,
2001, 2010) and—rather to my surprise—does not cite de Camp's
biography. He lists Shreffler's *H. P. Lovecraft Companion* (1977)
but does not list the Joshi-Schultz *H. P. Lovecraft Encyclopedia*
(2001). And imagine citing John Taylor Gatto's *The Major Works
of H. P. Lovecraft* (Monarch Notes, 1977)! For those of you unfa-
miliar with the Monarch Notes series, it can be charitably described as Cliff Notes for the poor. Gatto, it will be recalled, was
the one who put forth the novel theory that "The Whisperer in
Darkness" was subtly pornographic, and who printed an erroneous
death date for Lovecraft by taking it from a book review in *Time*
magazine.

   It is nice that Luckhurst cites Peter Cannon's *H. P. Lovecraft*
(Twayne, 1989)—but not so nice that he dates it to 1982. His
omission of Cannon's *Lovecraft Remembered* (1998), a definitive
anthology of memoirs of Lovecraft, is cavernous. He cites my
H. P. Lovecraft: The Decline of the West (1990), but not Timo
Airaksinen's *The Philosophy of H. P. Lovecraft* (1999). Also missing
are such seminal works as Scott Connors's exemplary critical anthology *A Century Less a Dream* (2002) and Robert H. Waugh's

two scintillating collections of essays (2006, 2011). No Lovecraft bibliography is listed—not Wetzel (1955), not Chalker (1962), not Owings-Chalker (1973), nor either of mine (1981, 2009). Luckhurst seems never to have heard of *Lovecraft Studies* or the *Lovecraft Annual*. In his notes he cites no articles on any of the stories he prints, even though there is a superabundance of very perspicacious criticism on all these tales.

And for someone who puts himself forth as an authority on weird and Gothic fiction, Luckhurst's list of works on that subject is peculiar to the point of idiosyncrasy. He lists not one, not two, but three short articles by China Miéville, one of which is exactly one page long—but does not list David Punter's *The Literature of Terror* (1980, 1996), the last incarnation of which is *two volumes*. And it was written by an Englishman, to boot! Important treatises on weird fiction or the Gothic by Les Daniels, Julia Briggs, Jack Sullivan, Terry Heller, and many others are missing. I will be charitable in assuming that my *Unutterable Horror: A History of Supernatural Fiction* (2012) came out too late for Luckhurst to cite; I am less charitable in pointing out the omission of my *Weird Tale* (1990), *Modern Weird Tale* (2001), and *Evolution of the Weird Tale* (2004).

In *At the Mountains of Madness*, Lovecraft states, in regard to the protagonists' first view of the shoggoth: "It was the utter, objective embodiment of the fantastic novelist's 'thing that should not be.'" This volume is, prototypically, the Book That Should Not Be. It has no reason for existence, aside from putting a few pennies in the pockets of its editor and publisher. The decision to use pulp magazine texts—especially those from *Astounding*—borders on the moronic; the selection is flawed, the introduction is windy and contentless, the notes disappointingly skimpy when they are not ripped off from my own work. The paper and typography are nice, and the dust jacket presents a curious and rather spooky illustration of a sea creature (*Ascidia*) from an old book by Ernst Haeckel (whose *Riddle of the Universe* [English translation 1900] is, incidentally, misdated to 1903). But that's about all the good that can be said about this *rudis indigestaque moles*.

I guess the lesson one has to draw from this book is: Don't entrust an amateur to do a professional's job.

ROBERT H. WAUGH, ed. *Lovecraft and Influence: His Predecessors and Successors.* Lanham, MD: Scarecrow Press, 2013. xi, 195 pp. Reviewed by Scott Connors.

Editor Waugh reminds us from the start that every author lives within a web of texts, and that "We call this experience 'influence.'" Calling influence a "web" is a particularly appropriate metonym, for it is something in which many writers feel themselves entangled. H. P. Lovecraft was certainly no exception, as witnessed by his plaintive cry "There are my 'Poe' pieces & my 'Dunsany' pieces—but alas—where are any *Lovecraft* pieces?" Peter Penzoldt, in his landmark study *The Supernatural in Fiction,* went further, suggesting that Lovecraft was "too well read," that his exhaustive reading in the field had somehow subsumed his own voice.

Conversely, it is not viewed with favor by many in the fantasy and horror community for a contemporary writer to show that the tentacular touch of Grandpa Cthulhu has left its mark. As one of the most prominent workers in the Lovecraftian vineyard today, W. H. Pugmire has commented: "Writing such fiction seems to be a phase that young horror writers pass through on their way to individual voice and vision."[1] To show that a writer has absorbed the lessons of the masters who have preceded him is to cast into doubt his originality. Like the jaded Roman mob at the arena, the would-be literary Caesars of today demand the appearance of originality, which in practice means any influence shown reflects those canonical writers then in favor.

This concern reflects what Harold Bloom calls "the anxiety of influence." Borrowing from Freud and Nietzsche, Bloom has the strong poet living in the shadow of the older poet, who is a domineering father-figure standing between the poet and the fulfillment of his vision. The strong poet enters into the work of his predecessor, changing it from within until he has recast the elder poet's work in his own image. What the authors in the first part of this collection are examining is whether or not Lovecraft is a strong writer, who transmutes the themes and memes he ab-

---

1. Theric Jepson, "Latter-Day Saint, Latter-Day Lovecraft: An Interview with W. H. Pugmire." http://www.motleyvision.org/2010/pugmire-interview/

sorbed from Poe, Dunsany, and so many others. In the second part, the authors examine whether Lovecraft's shadow, like the tall trees in a rain forest, has stunted the growth of the writers following him.

Robert M. Price, a noted authority on both Lovecraft and the Bible, opens the first half with an examination of the inspiration that the former derived from the latter. Despite his well-known religious skepticism, Lovecraft was a child of New England, and the shadow of Puritanism weighed heavily upon him. Much of what Dr. Price discusses is familiar to those familiar with his mock-serious "sermons" at the "Cthulhu Prayer Breakfasts" conducted at various venues. His discussion of how Lovecraft might have found inspiration in the various millennialist movements that sprang up in the nineteenth century, however, is so self-evidentiary that the current writer, who grew up near the home of one such movement, the Harmonites of Western Pennsylvania, is smacking his forehead for allowing this to escape his notice. Regardless of whether or not one believes in the existence of God, this essay is a strong exhibit for the case that knowledge of scripture, as with Homer, Dante, and Shakespeare, is an essential part of the Western Canon.

J. D. Worthington's "Queen Anne Is [Not] Dead: Lovecraft and the Augustans" traces the influence of Dr. Johnson, Dean Swift, Pope, Dryden, et al. from his discovery of eighteenth-century books in his grandfather's attic while still a child through his championship of its metrical forms. For instance, it is from Swift, he argues, that Lovecraft formed his "sardonic view of human presumption," while from Dr. Johnson he learned how to combine the techniques of prose poetry to the classic essay form, especially the use of a philosophical thesis to open a story. Bierce and Poe may be due some of the credit for Lovecraft's sardonicism and his waxing philosophically at the start of a story, but as Worthington argues, he saw them here first. Most important, it was from the essays published by Addison and Steele in the *Spectator* that he learned to think of himself as "a sort of floating, disembodied eye which sees all manner of marvelous phenomena without being greatly affected by them." Worthington's contribution may only be scratching the surface of the extent of Lovecraft's debt to the writers of the late seventeenth and eighteenth centuries whose work he idolized not a whit less than that of Poe.

James Goho looks for Lovecraft's roots in the American Gothic canon. Unlike the European Gothic, the American variety deals with a recognition of the "hidden blackness of the human soul and human society," as Leslie Fiedler put it so well. Goho sees Lovecraft's primary influences in this arena as Cotton Mather, Charles Brockden Brown, and Ambrose Bierce, with Robert W. Chambers and others. Goho provides examples aplenty of ideas and techniques used by these and other writers that later found echoes in Lovecraft's work. His discussion of the use Lovecraft made from his ancestral copy of Mather's *Magnalia Christi Americana* is illuminating, as are the parallels between what Lovecraft called the "malignly supernatural" tales of Bierce and Lovecraft's own aesthetic of "a malign and particular suspension of those fixed laws of Nature which are our only safeguard against the assaults of chaos and the daemons of unplumbed space." Not all the sources cited by Goho are necessarily germane to Lovecraft; for instance, his discussion of slavery as one of the evils casting its shadow over American letters. While this is certainly the case, it is not developed as regards Lovecraft. This is a pity, since a case can certainly be made that the revolt of the shoggoths in *At the Mountains of Madness* was inspired by Edgar Allan Poe's pathological fear of "servile insurrection." Mr. Goho also has a tendency to ask questions instead of statements, for example, in writing of Mather's *Magnalia:* "Is it possible that book was the inspiration for Lovecraft's imaginary diabolical text, the *Necronomicon?*" Or, in discussing Brown's *Arthur Mervyn,* "Could this have influenced the mirror scene in Lovecraft's 'The Outsider'?" I make no judgment regarding the validity of this rhetorical device, but I do find it personally irritating.

Two of the contributions present an interesting case study in the progress Lovecraft studies has made in the last thirty-five years. Donald R. Burleson's piece examining the influence on Lovecraft of another New England master, Nathaniel Hawthorne, covers the same ground as an earlier essay on the same subject by

Peter Cannon.[2] While both essays present strong cases demonstrating the impact of Hawthorne on Lovecraft, Burleson's is the more detailed, documenting the impact of Hawthorne's *A Wonder Book* and *Tanglewood Tales* made upon the young Lovecraft, leading him both to an appreciation of Greco-Roman beauty and, ultimately, a skepticism regarding the validity of religion and the impetus to his creation of a personal myth-cycle. Burleson also illustrates that Lovecraft's use of Hawthorne's notebooks may be more profound than previously suspected. Similarly, Darrell Schweitzer, in "Lovecraft's Debt to Dunsany," risks comparison with his 1976 work "Lovecraft and Lord Dunsany."[3] Where the earlier work discusses how Lovecraft discovered the Irish peer and specific instances of Lovecraft's use of plot devices from Dunsany's fantasies, the current essay deals with narrative technique and traces how Lovecraft's voice evolved through each of his Dunsanian pastiches. He also chronicles how Lovecraft found Dunsany's increasing use of irony not to be to his taste, as well as his failure to master the use of metaphor that perhaps is Dunsany's most distinguishing stylistic characteristic.

Alex Houstoun wisely limits his discussion of Lovecraft and Poe to an illuminating examination of how both writers used the dramatic monologue. Poe's characters, he suggests, are attempting to create a bond with the listener as a means of defeating the sense of alienation that engulfs them. Lovecraft's characters, on the other hand, in attempting to grasp the knowledge that has exploded their sense of security in the universe, *share this knowledge* with their auditors, thereby infecting them with the same sense of cosmic unease with which they are afflicted.

The late Sam Moskowitz documented the extent of the young Lovecraft's readership of the Munsey pulps, but it falls to Gavin Callaghan to point out the specific tropes in his work that may be traced back to the stories by Edgar Rice Burroughs, George Allan England, and other writers whose commercialism he would later

---

2. In S. T. Joshi's *H. P. Lovecraft: Four Decades of Criticism* (Athens: Ohio University Press, 1980), 161–65.
3. In Schweitzer's *Discovering H. P. Lovecraft*, 2nd ed. (Mercer Island, WA: Starmont House, 1987), 91–112.

come to disdain. Significantly, though, Lovecraft would transmute these ideas in the light of his own social and political ideas, whose aristocratic and reactionary leanings were often in opposition to the egalitarian and populist ideas of the writers in Munsey's stable.

Fictional accounts of invasion were a staple of British popular fiction, from 1871's *The Battle of Dorking* (an account of a German invasion of the British Isles) onward. These cautionary tales warn of how we might find ourselves strangers in our own homeland. As T. R. Livesey notes in "Green Storm Rising: Lovecraft's Roots in Invasion Literature," it is not known if Lovecraft had read any of the works he discusses, with the exception of H. G. Wells's *The War of the Worlds*, so it remains unclear how much of stories such as "The Shadow over Innsmouth" were inspired by what he found in this genre, and how much originated within his own anxieties regarding his deteriorating social position and the resentment he felt toward the foreign interlopers who prospered where he could not.

The second part of *Lovecraft and Influence* examines his successors, and thankfully the essays herein are for the most part free of the listings of the gods, grimoires, and imaginary towns that for so many years dominated what passed for criticism in this area. Here we find accounts of how the writers discussed absorbed the lessons Lovecraft had to teach them and made them their own. One exception to this is John Langan's "Nature's Other, Ghastly Face," which deals with how Stephen King has come to terms with Lovecraft's shadow. To his credit, Langan does not concentrate on the handful of overtly Lovecraftian stories to be found in King's work, but on parallels between King's early story "Graveyard Shift" and "The Rats in the Walls." This story does not come off well in comparison with Lovecraft's, being bombastic where Lovecraft was sublime, loud and vulgar where Lovecraft was (comparatively) restrained, at least until the climax. Ultimately, "Graveyard Shift" is one of King's freshman efforts, and one yearns for an examination of whether King has escaped the penumbra of Grandpa Theobald in his mature works.

Frank Belknap Long was the first of Lovecraft's disciples, and, as T. E. D. Klein brilliantly depicted in "Black Man with a Horn," he never escaped being regarded as such. As its title suggests, "What Stays in Lovecraft's Sieve Once Frank Belknap Long Is

Strained Through It" is an examination, by Norm Gayford, of one of Long's later, ostensibly non-Lovecraftian novels, *Journey into Darkness* (1967). Unfortunately, this is a fairly obscure work with which even the present writer, an avowed admirer of Long's who was well acquainted with him during the 1970s, is not familiar, and his textual reading is predicated upon such a familiarity; without it, the argument of the essay is simply not comprehensible.

Editor Robert H. Waugh and novelist Michael Cisco look at writers who are not commonly thought of as having been influenced by Lovecraft: in Waugh's case, science fiction writers Arthur C. Clarke and Philip K. Dick (along with Fritz Leiber, who had long acknowledged his debt to Lovecraft), and in Cisco's case, William S. Burroughs. The 1950s, which was roughly the period where Clarke and Dick began coming into their own, are often regarded as the nadir of Lovecraft's acceptance by the science fiction community: this was the period when his work was attacked by writers such as John Brunner, Damon Knight, and later Avram Davidson and Brian Aldiss. Waugh chronicles not only the admiration Clarke, Leiber, and Dick had for Lovecraft's work, but also specific instances where they had borrowed, and often changed almost beyond recognition, concepts and ideas from his stories. To read that Clarke's octopoid aliens may have been an attempt to rehabilitate these creatures in the post-Lovecraft world proved particularly satisfying. Cisco, on the other hand, does not argue that Lovecraft was an influence upon Burroughs, despite his sometimes startling awareness of Lovecraft's writings, and discusses them "in terms of differences and similarities in development from similar genealogical points of difference."

As mentioned at the beginning of this review, the strong writer masters the lessons of his predecessors and remakes them in his own image. Ramsey Campbell and Thomas Ligotti are two writers who have simultaneously embraced and transcended Lovecraft's influence. S. T. Joshi, who is perhaps Campbell's strongest (but by no means only) champion, examines his early Lovecraftian pastiches, then Campbell's experimental stories written in reaction against Lovecraft, and then his later tales in which he simultaneously makes his peace with Lovecraft and goes beyond him, combining both the cosmic with the personal and creating a tragic fusion of the two. Ligotti, argues Mariconda, is not so much a writer influenced by Lovecraft as a writer who worked in the same tradition as the Old Gentleman from Providence, finding in their mutual antipathy toward logic and reason a common ground in the tradition of the Symbolists, Surrealists, etc., as they trace their paths toward cosmic disorder and chaos.

One area where Lovecraft's influence may be felt is among writers who deliberately set out to reject what they perceived as that influence. One example of this is John W. Campbell, Jr., whose story "Who Goes There?" is a reworking of *At the Mountains of Madness* free of "phony atmosphere . . . the kind of stuff Lovecraft doted on." During the 1950s members of the Southern California writers group called simply The Group (Ray Bradbury, Charles Beaumont, Richard Matheson, William F. Nolan) wrote stories that would seem to be the very antithesis of Lovecraft. However, as poststructuralist literary theory suggests, whenever something is erased a trace always remains, and one wonders what a close examination of the stories by these writers might reveal. Nolan acknowledges admiring Lovecraft's stories, and one wonders just where Matheson conceived of the tentacular horror in his story "Born of Man and Woman." Dennis Etchison, a writer who consciously tried to avoid being influenced by Lovecraft, conceded in a panel discussion at MythosCon in 2010 that perhaps he was not as successful in evading him as he once thought.

In "Tradition and the Individual Talent," T. S. Eliot theorized that a writer must reflect the whole of European literature (we might argue world literature today) and his contemporary environment, creating a fusion of past and present that he described as a "simultaneous order." In this collection, editor Waugh and his contributors have, for the most part, put Lovecraft and his successors into the tradition of the weird tale, the Gothic, whatever label we may wish to pin on this genre. The writing is, for the most part, rigorous without being pedantic, and the influences cited are not the superficial type familiar to us from decades of fan criticism. *Lovecraft and Influence* is another milestone in the development of the study of H. P. Lovecraft and is well worth the attention of students of his work.

www.ingramcontent.com/pod-product-compliance
Lightning Source LLC
Chambersburg PA
CBHW051824090426
42736CB00011B/1639